EEC DIRECTIVES ON COMPANY LAW
AND FINANCIAL MARKETS

EEC Directives on Company Law and Financial Markets

EDITED BY
D. D. PRENTICE

CLARENDON PRESS · OXFORD
1991

Oxford University Press, Walton Street, Oxford OX2 6DP

Oxford New York Toronto
Delhi Bombay Calcutta Madras Karachi
Petaling Jaya Singapore Hong Kong Tokyo
Nairobi Dar es Salaam Cape Town
Melbourne Auckland
and associated companies in
Berlin Ibadan

Oxford is a trade mark of Oxford University Press

Published in the United States
by Oxford University Press, New York

British Library Cataloguing in Publication Data
data available

Library of Congress Cataloging-in-Publication Data
EEC directives on company law and financial markets/edited by D. D. Prentice.
1. Corporation law—European Economic Community countries.
2. Financial services industry—Law and legislation—European Economic Community
countries. I. Prentice, Daniel D. (Daniel David)
KJE2448.A42 1991 346.4'066—dc20 [344.0666] 91-7166
ISBN 0-19-825259-5

Typeset by Rowland Phototypesetting Ltd
Bury St Edmunds, Suffolk
Printed in Great Britain by
Biddles Ltd, Guildford & King's Lynn

Acknowledgements

The text of directives is taken from the *Official Journal of the European Communities* (OJ).

I would like to thank Mrs Jane Welch, Securities Investment Board, Mrs Judith Freedman, Institute of Advanced Legal Studies, University of London, and Mr Derrick Wyatt, St Edmund Hall, Oxford, for their assistance.

Contents

A

Introduction

Introduction

The aim of this collection of material is very modest—it is simply to make conveniently available (primarily for students) the 'legislation' of the European Community relating to company law and the legal regulation of certain aspects of the financial markets. As regards the material on financial markets, a number of areas, for example, insurance, banking, and the capital market directives, have been excluded.[1] The justification for this is that the collection is intended for use by those taking a basic course in company law, or in the regulation of the financial markets, and normally the excluded matters do not feature as part of these courses. No draft directives have been included. There are two good reasons for this. First, draft directives change considerably during their legislative journey, the end result often bearing very little resemblance to its progenitor. Second, many draft directives remain in this state for an inordinate length of time, if not in perpetuity. Relevant articles of the Treaty of the European Community have also been included plus one or two other miscellaneous matters.

The Nature of Community Legislation: Directives and Regulations

The harmonization programme of the European Community both in the field of company law and in the regulation of the financial markets[2] is implemented primarily by means of either directives or regulations.[3] It is proposed to examine the nature of these different types of legislation in turn.

Directives. A directive is defined by Article 189 of the Treaty of The European Community as having the following effect: 'A directive shall be binding, as to the result to be achieved, upon each Member State to which it

---

[1] See Blair, 'Europe 1922 and the Harmonisation of Standards for The Regulation of Financial Institutions' (1990) 16 *CBLJ* 97, for a survey of some of the initiatives in the field of banking and, in particular, a very lucid explanation of the techniques of harmonization in this area.

[2] It is not proposed to discuss the justification of this programme, particularly that relating to the harmonization of company law, which is not free from controversy. For an excellent discussion see R. M. Buxbaum and K. J. Hopt, *Legal Harmonization and the Business Enterprise* (Berlin and New York, 1988). An interesting comparison with United States developments is Kitch, 'Regulation and the American Common Market', in A. D. Tarlock (ed.), *Regulation, Federalism, and Interstate Commerce*.

[3] See Wyatt, 'Enforcing EEC Social Rights in the United Kingdom' (1989) 18 *Ind L. Jrl* 197, which examines the way in which social rights provided by Community law are implemented.

is addressed, but shall leave to the national authorities the choice of form and methods.' For reasons which will be explained below in the section entitled 'Legal Basis of European Legislation' it is primarily by means of directives that the Community implements its programmes in the fields of company law and financial markets law.

An issue of critical importance is the legal effect of a directive on the laws of the member states once it has been adopted by the Community. Obviously a member state to which a directive applies will have to take appropriate steps to introduce measures to achieve the 'effect' of the directive.[4] However, even where a member state fails to implement the directive, or implements it in a manner that is defective, it can give rise to legal consequences; the potential of directives as a source of law is 'quite considerable'.[5] This is because in certain circumstances a directive can be 'directly effective' which entails that it can be invoked in the courts of a member state against the state itself or against a public body charged with the responsibility for implementing the directive. To be capable of having direct effect, a Community provision must be clear and unambiguous, be unconditional, and its operation must not be dependent on further action being taken by national or Community authorities.[6] Obviously these criteria are not self-executing and inevitably in some situations their application will be problematical. It is not proposed to deal with these difficulties here.[7] One point does, however, need to be expanded. The concept of public body is not confined to direct emanations of the state and will include bodies carrying out public regulatory functions even though they may take the form of a private body. For example, although the Securities Investment Board (SIB) is a company limited by guarantee there can be little doubt that it would be seen as a public body for the purposes of the doctrine of the direct effect of directives.[8] The same would apply, it is submitted, to the International Stock Exchange and the Panel on Takeovers and Mergers,[9] in so far as they are carrying out

[4] See Art. 5 of the Treaty Establishing the European Economic Community 1957.

[5] D. Lasok and J. W. Bridge, *An Introduction to the Law and Institutions of the European Communities* (4th edn., London, 1987), p. 126.

[6] Dashwood, 'The Principle of Direct Effect in European Community Law' (1977) 16 *JCMS* 229 at 231. This is often referred to as 'vertical direct effect' to denote the relationship between a citizen and the state. See also Steiner, 'Direct Applicability in EEC Law: A Chameleon Concept' (1982) 98 *LQR* 229; Steiner, 'Coming to Terms with EEC Directives' (1990) 106 *LQR* 144.

[7] There is considerable literature on this. As well as the material in n. 6 see also T. C. Hartley, *Foundations of European Community Law* (2nd edn., Oxford, 1988), ch. 7.

[8] See e.g. *The Financial Services Act 1986 (Delegation) Order 1987* (SI 1987 No 942) delegating pursuant to s. 114 of the Financial Services Act 1986 certain functions to be carried out by the Secretary of State to the SIB.

[9] See e.g. s. 142 (6) which makes the Council of the Stock Exchange the competent authority for Part IV of the Act which in part implements the 'listing' directives: see Green, 'Directives, Equity and the Protection of Individual Rights' [1984] *ELJ* 295 at 311–13; Hartley, *Foundations*, pp. 210–11. If a body is subject to judicial review under English law then a strong

functions associated with the implementation of a directive or relating to a matter covered by a directive.[10]

A directive does not have, however, what is referred to as horizontal direct effect, that is, it cannot be invoked by one citizen against another. Because the binding nature of a directive under Article 189 exists only in relation to 'each member state to which it is addressed', it has been held that a directive may 'not of itself impose obligations on an individual and that a provision of a directive may not be relied upon as against such a person'.[11]

Although a directive does not affect the relationship between individuals directly, it can do so indirectly. First, and most importantly, as a matter of domestic law, if a directive has been implemented by United Kingdom legislation the House of Lords has held that the courts should look to the directive when interpreting such legislation implementing it and the latter should be given a purposive interpretation so as to ensure as far as possible that it complies with the directive. As was stated by Lord Oliver in *Litster* v. *Forth Dry Dock & Engineering Co. Ltd. (in Receivership)*:[12]

> The approach to the construction of primary and subordinate legislation enacted to give effect to the United Kingdom's obligations under the E.E.C. Treaty have been the subject matter of recent authority in this House . . . and is not in doubt. If the legislation can reasonably be construed so as to conform with those obligations—obligations which are to be ascertained not only from the wording of the relevant Directive but from the interpretation placed upon it by the European Court of Justice at Luxembourg—such purposive construction will be applied even though, perhaps, it may invovle some departure from the strict and literal application of the words which the legislature has elected to use.

The effect of this is that indirectly a directive could affect the legal relationship between private citizens.[13]

The second way in which a dircctive may affect the relationships between

argument can be made that it would be a public body for the operation of the direct vertical effect of directives. As regards judicial review, see Beatson, 'The Courts and the Regulators' (1987) *Professional Negligence* 121.

[10] See also *Rolls Royce plc* v. *Doughty* [1987] IRLR 447 (EAT); *Foster* v. *British Gas plc* [1988] 2 CMLR 697 (CA); [1991] 1Q.B. 405 (EC5); The Times, 19 April 1991. In the latter case the European Court of Justice held that since British Gas plc had been made responsible by the state for providing a public service it was a body against which a directive could have direct effect.

[11] *Marshall* v. *Southampton and South West Hampshire Area Health Authority (Teaching)* [1986] QB 401 at 422 (European Court of Justice).

[12] [1989] 2 WLR 634 at 641; see L. Collins, *European Community Law in the United Kingdom* (4th edn., London, 1990), 117–22.

[13] See e.g. *International Sales and Agencies Ltd.* v. *Marcus* [1982] 2 CMLR 46; [1982] 3 All ER 551.

individuals is illustrated by the cases of *Van Colson and Harz*.[14] In that case the court held that as a matter of Community law it follows from the obligation imposed on member states by Article 5 of the Treaty that 'in applying national law and in particular the provisions of national law introduced in order to implement [a directive] . . . national courts are required to interpret its national law in the light of the wording and the purpose of the directive in order to achieve the result referred to in the third paragraph of Article 189'.[15] However, for this principle to operate there must have been some attempt to introduce the directive in question since this rule of construction simply could not operate in the abstract.[16]

Regulations. The other principal method by which harmonization measures can be introduced is by means of a regulation. As regards this type of instrument, Article 189 provides that '[A] regulation shall have general application. It shall be binding in its entirety and directly applicable in all Member States'. A regulation can thus supplant or supplement national law in a way that a directive cannot. Although a regulation is given direct effect, its terms may nevertheless contemplate that certain matters have to be done by the member states before it becomes fully operative. For example, Article 35(2) of the regulation establishing the European Economic Interest Grouping (EEIG) provides that the 'liquidation of a grouping and the conclusion of its liquidation shall be governed by national law'. This obviously contemplates that member states will introduce legislation to deal with this issue[17] since it is difficult to see how it could be given direct effect.

A number of general points can be made with respect to the use of directives and regulations in effecting a harmonization of law.

First, it is inevitable that directives will be more loosely structured than regulations as member states have a discretion as to how the effect of the directive is to be achieved and therefore the *ipsissima verba* is of less importance.[18]

Second, the extent to which these directives and regulations produce

---

[14] Cases 14/83, 79/83, [1984] ECR 1891, 1921. This argument is taken from Steiner, 'Coming to Terms with EEC Directives' (1990) 106 LQR 144 which is a most helpful discussion of the issue.

[15] [1984] ECR 1891, at 1909.

[16] Cf. Steiner, 'Coming to Terms with EEC Directives', p. 158. The point has been made that: 'It seems anomalous that if a Member State chooses to rely on pre-existing legislation it is thereby excused the duty to take Community law into account when construing it, in the event of a potential conflict': Wyatt, 'Enforcing EEC Social Rights', p. 211. See also *Organon Laboratories Ltd.* v. *DHSS* [1990] 2 C.M.L.R. 49.

[17] See *The European Economic Interest Grouping Regulations 1989* (SI 1989, No. 638), para. 8.

[18] See also Buxbaum and Hopt, *Legal Harmonization*, p. 233, who stress the fact that directives have the effect of protecting to some extent the sovereignty of member states.

anything like a harmonized system as between member states, is often problematical. This is so for a number of reasons. There is the point already made that in the case of directives the implementation of these measures depends on national law and this inevitably gives scope for divergence; member states may simply place different interpretations on the directive, or it may not be easy (if at all possible) to graft the directive onto national law. For example, as regards the latter point, it is difficult to implement the First Directive (68/151/EEC)[19] into United Kingdom law since it uses the concept of corporate 'organ',[20] a concept with which the United Kingdom company law is not familiar. Second, harmonization relies either explicitly or implicitly on general principles of law in order to fill in the inevitable gaps[21] in a directive or regulation and there is no necessary guarantee that these general principles will be uniform. For example, Article 24 of the regulation on the EEIG provides that its members shall have 'unlimited joint and several liability' for its debts. There is no definition of what constitutes 'joint and several' liability but, if this crucial provision for the operation of the grouping is to produce anything like a uniform result throughout the member states, the underlying assumption must be that the concept enjoys a somewhat uniform meaning in the different member states. Another example which illustrates the extent to which a directive permits national variation with the consequence that harmonization may not be achieved is the Prospectus Directive (EC/89/298). Article 1 of that directive provides that it 'shall apply to transferable securities offered to the public'. As the DTI stated in a consultative document which it issued on the directive:[22]

Although the Prospectus Directive requires a prospectus to be published when non-listed transferable securities are first offered to the public, the Directive contains no definition of what constitutes an 'offer to the public'—which is in part a reflection of differences in practice among Member States. Accordingly, individual Member States have considerable latitude in defining the boundary between those offers they wish to regard as offers to the public—requiring compliance with the terms of the Directive—and those which they consider inappropriate for such treatment.

Third, and somewhat related to the previous point, the directives and regulations often for their operation rely heavily on the *company law* of member states. For example, the Third Directive (78/855/EEC) on mergers of public limited liability companies relies to such an extent on the domestic

---

[19] This was passed before the United Kingdom became a member of the European Community.

[20] See Art. 9.

[21] These gaps may of course be deliberate as the member states may have failed to reach agreement on a particular matter.

[22] *Listing Particulars and Public Offer Prospectuses: Implementation Of Part V Of The Financial Services Act 1986 and Related Directives* (July 1990), at 27.

laws of the member states for its operation that the extent to which it will produce anything like a harmonized system is problematical.

Fourth, it is not uncommon for European legislation to accord a range of options to the member states; for example it is claimed that the Fourth Directive (78/660/EEC) leaves 'no less than 41 options open to the Member States in addition to the 35 options left to the members themselves'.[23] Inevitably, the greater the range of options the lesser the chances of a harmonized result.

Lastly, there are certain critical areas of company law where the absence of harmonization in other areas makes it difficult to produce anything like a harmonized result because of the extent to which they pervade company law. Thus, for example, the absence of a uniform system on insolvency reduces significantly the likelihood of achieving a harmonized company law.[24] It was because of the absence of a harmonized insolvency law that the winding up of the EEIG was left to be dealt with by the laws of the various member states.[25]

An important feature of the directives is that they often are restricted to public limited liability companies. The reason for this is presumably that it is only companies that are public limited companies that are believed to have sufficient market impact to justify regulation. The validity of this assumption is far from self-evident as there are a number of private companies which possess a substantial commercial presence; there are, however, obvious reasons of expediency for restricting the application of community legislation to public limited companies.

A consequence of community involvement in regulating company law and financial markets is that, once the community has occupied the field, it makes change very difficult. There are a number of reasons for this. First, there does not appear to be any programme whereby European legislation is kept under review to assess whether or not it continues to serve any beneficial purpose. Directives and regulations often provide for the establishment of a contact committee[26] composed of representatives of the member states which can be convened to discuss matters pertaining to the application of the directive or the regulation. There is no evidence to suggest that these committees meet with any great frequency. Second, if a directive or regulation is seen as being necessary in order to develop the common market then there will be a strong a priori reason for assuming that the need

---

[23] Buxbaum and Hopt, *Legal Harmonization*, p. 235.

[24] See the 'Draft Convention on Bankruptcy, Winding-up, Arrangements, Compositions and Similar Proceedings' (Commission of the European Communities, *Bulletin of the European Communities*, Supp. 2/82). Other areas where the absence of harmonization on specific topics affects the overall harmonization programme are taxation and groups. On the latter see the consultative document issued by the DTI in February 1985: *European Communities Draft Ninth Company Law Directive on the Conduct of Groups Containing a Public Limited Company as a Subsidiary*.

[25] Art. 36.   [26] See e.g. art. 52 of the Fourth Directive (78/660/EEC).

for such legislation will be virtually permanent; since the legislation relates to the structure of the market, the assumption can be made that these structural characteristics will need to endure. Third, there are considerable political difficulties in enacting directives and regulations and these will inhibit proposals for change. The net effect of this is to produce at community level a commercial law which is virtually immutable. Or, to put it slightly differently, 'each time the Community legislates the relevant national competence in that field disappears down a one way street'.[27]

Legal Basis of Community Legislation

There are a number of provisions in the Treaty under which the Community can enact legislation.

Article 54 (3) (g).   Article 54 required the Council, before the end of the first stage (long since passed), to draw up a general programme for the abolition of existing restrictions on freedom of establishment. To this end, Article 54 (3) (g) empowers the Council on the Commission's initiative to issue directives for the purpose of 'coordinating to the necessary extent the safeguards which, for the protection of the interests of members and others, are required by Member States of companies or firms within the meaning of the second paragraph of Art. 58 with a view to making such safeguards equivalent throughout the Community'. It is under this provision that earlier directives were introduced. It is important to note that under this provision a directive must be justified in terms of eliminating restrictions on the freedom of establishment. However, the safeguards that the directive can introduce relate not only to the interests of 'members' but also to 'others'. This obviously includes 'creditors' and there is no reason why in appropriate cases employees should not be considered creditors for this purpose. It is on this basis that the directive providing for employee participation in the affairs of the European Company could be justified.[28]

Article 100A.   Article 8A of the Treaty of the European Economic Community, which was introduced by the Single European Act 1986, provides that the Community shall adopt measures for the creation of the 'internal market'. The internal market is defined as an area 'without internal frontiers

---

[27] Close, 'Harmonisation of Laws: Use or Abuse of the Powers under the EEC Treaty?' (1978) *EL Rev.* 461, at 481.

[28] See 'Statute for a European Community' (*Bulletin of the European Communities*, Supp. 5/89). This proposes a regulation under Art. 100A to deal with the company law aspects of the Societas Europa and a complementary directive under Art. 54 (3) (g) to deal with the issue of employee participation.

in which the free movement of goods, persons, services and capital is ensured in accordance with the provisions of this Treaty'.[29] To achieve this goal of establishing the internal market, Article 100A[30] empowers the Council acting on proposals from the Commission to 'adopt measures' by qualified majority vote. This legislative power, however, does not apply, *inter alia*, to fiscal matters or to matters involving the rights and interests of employed persons.[31] Article 100A is not confined, as is Article 54, to directives connected with the right of establishment and, given the definition of the internal market, it accords extremely broad legislative powers to the Community. In addition, the measures that can be adopted under Article 100A are not confined to directives and regulations can also be adopted under it; for example, it is proposed that the European Company should be set up by a regulation introduced under this provision.[32]

Article 235. This is a catch-all provision. It provides that if the Community lacks the necessary powers to attain one of the objectives of the Community or the Treaty, it may through the Council acting unanimously take appropriate measures to achieve the objective. Resort to this provision is not permitted where the power to carry out the act in question is given by another provision of the Treaty.[33]

---

[29] Article 8A of the Treaty of the European Community.

[30] This also was introduced by the Single European Act 1986.

[31] Article 100A (2).

[32] See n. 28.

[33] Buxbaum and Hopt, *Legal Harmonization*, p. 211. Also of slight relevance is Article 220 of the Treaty which enables *inter alia* conventions between the member states to be entered into. It was under this provision that it was proposed that the bankruptcy convention should be introduced: see footnote 24.

B

Community Laws:
Treaty Provisions

Treaty Establishing the European Economic Community as Amended

[EXTRACTS]*

Part Two. Foundations of the Community

TITLE III. FREE MOVEMENT OF PERSONS, SERVICES AND CAPITAL

CHAPTER 2. RIGHT OF ESTABLISHMENT

Article 52. Within the framework of the provisions set out below, restrictions on the freedom of establishment of nationals of a Member State in the territory of another Member State shall be abolished by progressive stages in the course of the transitional period. Such progressive abolition shall also apply to restrictions on the setting up of agencies, branches, or subsidiaries by nationals of any Member State established in the territory of any Member State.

Freedom of establishment shall include the right to take up and pursue activities as self-employed persons and to set up and manage undertakings, in particular companies or firms within the meaning of the second paragraph of Art. 58, under the conditions laid down for its own nationals by the law of the country where such establishment is effected, subject to the provisions of the Chapter relating to capital.

Article 53. Member States shall not introduce any new restrictions on the right of establishment in their territories of nationals of other Member States, save as otherwise provided in this Treaty.

Article 54. 1. Before the end of the first stage, the Council shall, acting unanimously on a proposal from the Commission and after consulting the Economic and Social Committee and the Assembly, draw up a general programme for the abolition of existing restrictions on freedom of establishment within the Community. The Commission shall submit its proposal to the Council during the first two years of the first stage.

---

* Treaty provisions are taken from *Basic Community Laws*, ed. B. Rudden and D. Wyatt (2nd edn., Oxford, 1986).

The programme shall set out the general conditions under which freedom of establishment is to be attained in the case of each type of activity and in particular the stages by which it is to be attained.

2. In order to implement this general programme or, in the absence of such programme, in order to achieve a stage in attaining freedom of establishment as regards a particular activity, the Council shall, acting on a proposal from the Commission, in co-operation with the European Parliament and after consulting the Economic and Social Committee, issue directives, acting unanimously until the end of the first stage and by a qualified majority thereafter.

3. The Council and the Commission shall carry out the duties developing upon them under the preceding provisions, in particular:

(a) by according, as a general rule, priority treatment to activities where freedom of establishment makes a particularly valuable contribution to the development of production and trade;

(b) by ensuring close cooperation between the competent authorities in the Member States in order to ascertain the particular situation within the Community of the various activities concerned;

(c) by abolishing those administrative procedures and practices, whether resulting from national legislation or from agreements previously concluded between Member States, the maintenance of which would form an obstacle to freedom of establishment;

(d) by ensuring that workers of one Member State employed in the territory of another Member State may remain in that territory for the purpose of taking up activities therein as self-employed persons, where they satisfy the conditions which they would be required to satisfy if they were entering that State at the time when they intended to take up such activities;

(e) by enabling a national of one Member State to acquire and use land and buildings situated in the territory of another Member State, in so far as this does not conflict with the principles laid down in Art. 39(2);

(f) by effecting the progressive abolition of restrictions on freedom of establishment in every branch of activity under consideration, both as regards the conditions for setting up agencies, branches or subsidiaries in the territory of a Member State and as regards the conditions governing the entry of personnel belonging to the main establishment into managerial or supervisory posts in such agencies, branches or subsidiaries;

(g) by coordinating to the necessary extent the safeguards which, for the protection of the interests of members and others, are required by Member States of companies or firms within the meaning of the second paragraph of Art. 58 with a view to making such safeguards equivalent throughout the Community;

(h) by satisfying themselves that the conditions of establishment are not distorted by aids granted by Member States.

Article 55. The provisions of this Chapter shall not apply, so far as any given Member State is concerned, to activities which in that State are connected, even occasionally, with the exercise of official authority.

The Council may, acting by a qualified majority on a proposal from the Commission, rule that the provisions of this Chapter shall not apply to certain activities.

Article 56. 1. The provisions of this Chapter and measures taken in pursuance thereof shall not prejudice the applicability of provisions laid down by law, regulation or administrative action providing for special treatment for foreign nationals on grounds of public policy, public security or public health.

2. Before the end of the transitional period, the Council shall, acting unanimously on a proposal from the Commission and after consulting the Assembly, issue directives for the coordination of the aforementioned provisions laid down by law, regulation or administrative action. After the end of the second stage, however, the Council shall, acting by a qualified majority on a proposal from the Commission and in co-operation with the European Parliament, issue directives for the co-ordination of such provisions as, in each Member State, are a matter for regulation or administrative action.

Article 57. 1. In order to make it easier for persons to take up and pursue activities as self-employed persons, the Council shall, on a proposal from the Commission and in co-operation with the European Parliament, acting unanimously during the first stage and by a qualified majority thereafter, issue directives for the mutual recognition of diplomas, certificates and other evidence of formal qualifications.

2. For the same purpose, the Council shall, before the end of the transitional period, acting on a proposal from the Commission and after consulting the Assembly, issue directives for the coordination of the pro-visions laid down by law, regulation or administrative action in Member States concerning the taking up and pursuit of activities as self-employed persons. Unanimity shall be required for directives the implementation of which involves in at least one Member State amendment of the existing principles laid down by law governing the professions with respect to training and conditions of access for natural persons. In other cases, the Council shall act by a qualified majority, in co-operation with the European Parliament.

3. In the case of the medical and allied, and pharmaceutical professions,

the progressive abolition of restrictions shall be dependent upon co-ordination of the conditions for their exercise in the various Member States.

Article 58.   Companies or firms formed in accordance with the law of a Member State and having their registered office, central administration or principal place of business within the Community shall, for the purposes of this Chapter, be treated in the same way as natural persons who are nationals of Member States.

'Companies or firms' means companies or firms constituted under civil or commercial law, including cooperative societies, and other legal persons governed by public or private law, save for those which are non-profit making.

CHAPTER 3. SERVICES

Article 59.   Within the framework of the provisions set out below, restrictions on freedom to provide services within the Community shall be progressively abolished during the transitional period in respect of nationals of Member States who are established in a State of the Community other than that of the person for whom the services are intended.

The Council may, acting by a qualified majority on a proposal from the Commission, extend the provisions of this Chapter to nationals of a third country who provide services and who are established within the Community.

Article 60.   Services shall be considered to be 'services' within the meaning of this Treaty where they are normally provided for remuneration, in so far as they are not governed by the provisions relating to freedom of movement for goods, capital and persons.

'Services' shall in particular include:

(a) activities of an industrial character;
(b) activities of a commercial character;
(c) activities of craftsmen;
(d) activities of the professions.

Without prejudice to the provisions of the Chapter relating to the right of establishment, the person providing a service may, in order to do so, temporarily pursue his activity in the State where the service is provided, under the same conditions as are imposed by that State on its own nationals.

Article 61.   1. Freedom to provide services in the field of transport shall be governed by the provisions of the Title relating to transport.

2. The liberalization of banking and insurance services connected with

movements of capital shall be effected in step with the progressive liberalization of movement of capital.

Article 62. Save as otherwise provided in this Treaty, Member States shall
not introduce any new restrictions on the freedom to provide services which
has in fact been attained at the date of the entry into force of this Treaty.

Article 63. 1. Before the end of the first stage, the Council shall, acting
unanimously on a proposal from the Commission and after consulting the
Economic and Social Committee and the Assembly, draw up a general
programme for the abolition of existing restrictions on freedom to provide
services within the Community. The Commission shall submit its proposal to
the Council during the first two years of the first stage.

The programme shall set out the general conditions under which and the
stages by which each type of service is to be liberalized.

2. In order to implement this general programme or, in the absence of
such programme, in order to achieve a stage in the liberalization of a specific
service, the Council shall, on a proposal from the Commission and after
consulting the Economic and Social Committee and the Assembly, issue
directives, acting unanimously until the end of the first stage and by a
qualified majority thereafter.

3. As regards the proposals and decision referred to in paragraphs 1 and
2, priority shall as a general rule be given to those services which directly
affect production costs or the liberalization of which helps to promote trade
in goods.

Article 64. The Member States declare their readiness to undertake the
liberalization of services beyond the extent required by the directives issued
pursuant to Art. 63 (2), if their general economic situation and the situation
of the economic sector concerned so permit.

To this end, the Commission shall make recommendations to the Member
States concerned.

Article 65. As long as restrictions on freedom to provide services have not
been abolished, each Member State shall apply such restrictions without
distinction on grounds of nationality or residence to all persons providing
services within the meaning of the first paragraph of Art. 59.

Article 66. The provisions of Arts. 55 to 58 shall apply to the matters
covered by this Chapter. . . .

Part Three. Policy of the Community

TITLE I. COMMON RULES

CHAPTER 3. APPROXIMATION OF LAWS

Article 100. The Council shall, acting unanimously on a proposal from the Commission, issue directives for the approximation of such provisions laid down by law, regulation or administrative action in Member States as directly affect the establishment or functioning of the common market.

The Assembly and the Economic and Social Committee shall be consulted in the case of directives whose implementation would, in one or more Member States, involve the amendment of legislation.

Article 100A. 1. By way of derogation from Article 100 and save where otherwise provided in this Treaty, the following provisions shall apply for the achievement of the objectives set out in Article 8A. The Council shall, acting by a qualified majority on a proposal from the Commission in co-operation with the European Parliament and after consulting the Economic and Social Committee, adopt the measures for the approximation of the provisions laid down by law, regulation or administrative action in Member States which have as their object the establishment and functioning of the internal market.

2. Paragraph 1 shall not apply to fiscal provisions, to those relating to the free movement of persons nor to those relating to the rights and interests of employed persons.

3. The Commission, in its proposals envisaged in paragraph 1 concering health, safety, environmental protection and consumer protection, will take as a base a high level of protection.

4. If, after the adoption of a harmonization measure by the Council acting by a qualified majority, a Member State deems it necessary to apply national provisions on grounds of major needs referred to in Article 36, or relating to protection of the environment or the working environment, it shall notify the Commission of these provisions.

The Commission shall confirm the provisions involved after having verified that they are not a means of arbitrary discrimination or a disguised restriction on trade between Member States.

By way of derogation from the procedure laid down in Articles 169 and 170, the Commission or any Member State may bring the matter directly before the Court of Justice if it considers that another Member State is making improper use of the powers provided for in this Article.

5. The harmonization measures referred to above shall, in appropriate cases, include a safeguard clause authorizing the Member States to take, for

one or more of the non-economic reasons referred to in Article 36, provisional measures subject to a Community control procedure.

Article 100B. 1. During 1992, the Commission shall, together with each Member State, draw up an inventory of national laws, regulations and administrative provisions which fall under Article 100A and which have not been harmonized pursuant to that Article.

The Council, acting in accordance with the provisions of Article 100A, may decide that the provisions in force in a Member State must be recognized as being equivalent to those applied by another Member State.

2. The provisions of Article 100A (4) shall apply by analogy.

3. The Commission shall draw up the inventory referred to in the first subparagraph of paragraph 1 and shall submit appropriate proposals in good time to allow the Council to act before the end of 1992. . . .

Part Five. Institutions of the Community

TITLE I. PROVISIONS GOVERNING THE INSTITUTIONS

CHAPTER 2. PROVISIONS COMMON TO SEVERAL INSTITUTIONS

Article 189. In order to carry out their task the Council and the Commission shall, in accordance with the provisions of this Treaty, make regulations, issue directives, take decisions, make recommendations or deliver opinions.

A regulation shall have general application. It shall be binding in its entirety and directly applicable in all Member States.

A directive shall be binding, as to the result to be achieved, upon each Member State to which it is addressed, but shall leave to the national authorities the choice of form and methods.

A decision shall be binding in its entirety upon those to whom it is addressed.

Recommendations and opinions shall have no binding force.

Article 190. Regulations, directives and decisions of the Council and of the Commission shall state the reasons on which they are based and shall refer to any proposals or opinions which were required to be obtained pursuant to this Treaty.

Article 191. Regulations shall be published in the Official Journal of the community. They shall enter into force on the date specified in them or, in the absence thereof, on the twentieth day following their publication.

Directives and decisions shall be notified to those to whom they are addressed and shall take effect upon such notification. . . .

Part Six. General and Final Provisions

Article 220.   Member States shall, so far as is necessary, enter into negotiations with each other with a view to securing for the benefit of their nationals:

— the protection of persons and the enjoyment and protection of rights under the same conditions as those accorded by each State to its own nationals;
— the abolition of double taxation within the Community;
— the mutual recognition of companies or firms within the meaning of the second paragraph of Art. 58, the retention of legal personality in the event of transfer of their seat from one country to another, and the possibility of mergers between companies or firms governed by the laws of different countries;
— the simplification of formalities governing the reciprocal recognition and enforcement of judgments of courts or tribunals and of arbitration awards. . . .

Article 235.   If action by the Community should prove necessary to attain, in the course of the operation of the common market, one of the objectives of the Community and this Treaty has not provided the necessary powers, the Council shall, acting unanimously on a proposal from the Commission and after consulting the Assembly, take the appropriate measures.

C

Company Law

First Council Directive

of 9 March 1968 on co-ordination of safeguards which,
for the protection of the interests of members and
others, are required by Member States of companies
within the meaning of the second paragraph of Article 58
of the Treaty, with a view to making such safeguards
equivalent throughout the Community

(68/151/EEC)

The Council of the European Communities,

Having regard to the Treaty establishing the European Economic Community, and in particular Article 54 (3) (g) thereof;

Having regard to the General Programme for the abolition of restrictions on freedom of establishment,[1] and in particular Title VI thereof;

Having regard to the proposal from the Commission;

Having regard to the Opinion of the European Parliament;[2]

Having regard to the Opinion of the Economic and Social Committee;[3]

Whereas the co-ordination provided for in Article 54 (3) (g) and in the General Programme for the abolition of restrictions on freedom of establishment is a matter of urgency, especially in regard to companies limited by shares or otherwise having limited liability, since the activities of such companies often extend beyond the frontiers of national territories;

Whereas the co-ordination of national provisions concerning disclosure, the validity of obligations entered into by, and the nullity of, such companies is of special importance, particularly for the purpose of protecting the interests of third parties;

Whereas in these matters Community provisions must be adopted in respect of such companies simultaneously, since the only safeguards they offer to third parties are their assets;

Whereas the basic documents of the company should be disclosed in order that third parties may be able to ascertain their contents and other information concerning the company, especially particulars of the persons who are authorised to bind the company;

Whereas the protection of third parties must be ensured by provisions which restrict to the greatest possible extent the grounds on which obligations entered into in the name of the company are not valid;

---

[1] OJ No 2, 15. 1. 1962, p. 36/62.   [2] OJ No 96, 28. 5. 1966, p. 1519/66.
[3] OJ No 194, 27. 11. 1964, p. 3248/64.

Whereas it is necessary, in order to ensure certainty in the law as regards relations between the company and third parties, and also between members, to limit the cases in which nullity can arise and the retroactive effect of a declaration of nullity, and to fix a short time limit within which third parties may enter objection to any such declaration;

Has adopted this directive:

Article 1. The co-ordination measures prescribed by this Directive shall apply to the laws, regulations and administrative provisions of the Member States relating to the following types of company:

— *In Germany;*
die Aktiengesellschaft, die Kommanditgesellschaft auf Aktien, die Gesellschaft mit beschränkter Haftung;
— *In Belgium:*
de naamloze vennootschap/la société anonyme,
de commanditaire vennootschap op aandelen/la société en commandite par actions,
de personenvennootschap met beperkte aansprakelijkheid/la société de personnes à responsabilité limitée;
— *In France:*
la société anonyme, la société en commandite par actions, la société à responsabilité limitée;
— *In Italy:*
società per azioni, società in accomandita per azioni, società a responsabilità limitata;
— *In Luxembourg:*
la société anonyme, la société en commandite par actions, la société à responsabilité limitée;
— *In the Netherlands:*
de naamloze vennootschap, de commanditaire vennootschap op aandelen;
— *In the United Kingdom:*
Companies incorporated with limited liability;
— *In Ireland:*
Companies incorporated with limited liability;
— *In Denmark:*
Aktieselskab; Kommandit-Aktieselskab.
— *In Greece:*
ἀνώνυμη ἑταιρία, ἑταιρία περιωρισμένης εὐθύνης, ἑτερόρρυθμη κατά μετοχές ἑταιρία;

— *In Spain:*
la sociedad anónima, la sociedad comanditaria por acciones, la sociedad de responsabilidad limitada;
— *In Portugal:*
a sociedade anónima de responsabilidade limitada, a sociedade em comandita por acções, a sociedade por quotas de responsabilidade limitada.

SECTION I. DISCLOSURE

Article 2.   1. Member States shall take the measures required to ensure compulsory disclosure by companies of at least the following documents and particulars:

(a) The instrument of constitution, and the statutes if they are contained in a separate instrument;

(b) Any amendments to the instruments mentioned in (a), including any extension of the duration of the company;

(c) After every amendment of the instrument of constitution or of the statutes, the complete text of the instrument or statutes as amended to date;

(d) The appointment, termination of office and particulars of the persons who either as a body constituted pursuant to law or as members of any such body:

(i) are authorized to represent the company in dealings with third parties and in legal proceedings;

(ii) take part in the administration, supervison or control of the company.

It must appear from the disclosure whether the persons authorized to represent the company may do so alone or must act jointly;

(e) At least once a year, the amount of the capital subscribed, where the instrument of constitution or the statutes mention in authorized capital, unless any increase in the capital subscribed necessitates an amendment of the statutes;

(f) The balance sheet and the profit and loss account for each financial year. The document containing the balance sheet must give details of the persons who are required by law to certify it. However, in respect of the Gesellschaft mit beschränkter Haftung, société de personnes à responsabilité limitée, personenvennootschap met beperkte aansprakelijkheid, société à responsabilité limitée, ἑταιρία περιορισμένησ εὐθύνης, società a responsabilità limitata and sociedade em comandita por acçoes under German, Belgian, French, Greek, Italian, Luxembourg or Portugese law referred to in Article 1, the besloten naamloze vennootschap under Netherlands law, the private company under the law of Ireland, and the private company under the law of Northern Ireland, the compulsory application of this provision shall be postponed until the date of implementation of a Directive concerning co-ordination of the contents of balance sheets and of profit and loss accounts and concerning exemption of such of those companies whose balance sheet total is less thant that specified in the Directive from the obligation to make disclosure in full or in part of the said documents. The Council will adopt such a Directive within two years following adoption of the present Directive.

(g) Any transfer of the seat of the company;

(h) The winding up of the company;

(i) Any declaration of nullity of the company by the courts;

(j) The appointment of liquidators, particulars concerning them, and their respective powers, unless such powers are expressly and exclusively derived from law or from the statutes of the company;

(k) The termination of the liquidation and, in Member States where striking off the register entails legal consequences, the fact of any such striking off.

2. For purposes of paragraph 1 (f), companies which fulfil the following conditions shall be considered as *besloten naamloze vennootschappen*:

(a) They cannot issue bearer shares;

(b) No bearer certificate of registered shares within the meaning of Article 42 (c) of the Netherlands Commercial Code can be issued by any person whatsoever:

(c) Their shares cannot be quoted on a stock exchange;

(d) Their statutes contain a clause requiring approval by the company before the transfer of shares to third parties, except in the case of transfer in the event of death and, if the statutes so provide, in the case of transfer to a spouse, forebears or issue; transfers shall not be in blank, but otherwise each transfer shall be in writing under hand, signed by the transferor and transferee or by notarial act;

(e) Their statutes specify that the company is a *besloten naamloze vennootschap*; the name of the company includes the words '*Besloten Naamloze Vennootschap*' or the initials '*BNV*'.

Article 3. 1. In each Member State a file shall be opened in a central register, commercial register or companies register, for each of the companies registered therein.

2. All documents and particulars which must be disclosed in pursuance of

Article 2 shall be kept in the file or entered in the register; the subject matter of the entries in the register must in every case appear in the file.

3. A copy of the whole or any part of the documents or particulars referred to in Article 2 must be obtainable by application in writing at a price not exceeding the administrative cost thereof.

Copies supplied shall be certified as 'true copies', unless the applicant dispenses with such certification.

4. Disclosure of the documents and particulars referred to in paragraph 2 shall be effected by publication in the national gazette appointed for that purpose by the Member State, either of the full or partial text, or by means of a reference to the document which has been deposited in the file or entered in the register.

5. The documents and particulars may be relied on by the company as against third parties only after they have been published in accordance with paragraph 4, unless the company proves that the third parties had knowledge thereof. However, with regard to transactions taking place before the sixteenth day following the publication, the documents and particulars shall not be relied on as against third parties who prove that it was impossible for them to have had knowledge thereof.

6. Member States shall take the necessary measures to avoid any discrepancy between what is disclosed by publication in the press and what appears in the register or file.

However, in cases of discrepancy, the text published in the press may not be relied on as against third parties; the latter may nevertheless rely thereon, unless the company proves that they had knowledge of the texts deposited in the file or entered in the register.

7. Third parties may, moreover, always rely on any documents and particulars in respect of which the disclosure formalities have not yet been completed, save where non-disclosure causes them not to have effect.

Article 4. Member States shall prescribe that letters and order forms shall state the following particulars:

— the register in which the file mentioned in Article 3 is kept, together with the number of the company in that register;
— the legal form of the company, the location of its seat and, where appropriate, the fact that the company is being wound up.

Where in these documents mention is made of the capital of the company, the reference shall be to the capital subscribed and paid up.

Article 5. Each Member State shall determine by which persons the disclosure formalities are to be carried out.

Article 6. Member States shall provide for appropriate penalties in case of:

— failure to disclose the balance sheet and profit and loss account as required by Article 2 (1) (f);

— omission from commercial documents of the compulsory particulars provided for in Article 4.

SECTION II. VALIDITY OF OBLIGATIONS ENTERED
INTO BY A COMPANY

Article 7. If, before a company being formed has acquired legal personality, action has been carried out in its name and the company does not assume the obligations arising from such action, the persons who acted shall, without limit, be jointly and severally liable therefore, unless otherwise agreed.

Article 8. Completion of the formalities of disclosure of the particulars concerning the persons who, as an organ of the company, are authorised to represent it shall constitute a bar to any irregularity in their appointment being relied upon as against third parties unless the company proves that such third parties had knowledge thereof.

Article 9. 1. Acts done by the organs of the company shall be binding upon it even if those acts are not within the objects of the company, unless such acts exceed the powers that the law confers or allows to be conferred on those organs.

However, Member States may provide that the company shall not be bound where such acts are outside the objects of the company, if it proves that the third party knew that the act was outside those objects or could not in view of the circumstances have been unaware of it; disclosure of the statutes shall not of itself be sufficient proof thereof.

2. The limits on the powers of the organs of the company, arising under the statutes or from a decision of the competent organs, may never be relied on as against third parties, even if they have been disclosed.

3. If the national law provides that authority to represent a company may, in derogation from the legal rules governing the subject, be conferred by the statutes on a single person or on several persons acting jointly, that law may provide that such a provision in the statutes may be relied on as against third parties on condition that it relates to the general power of representation; the question whether such a provision in the statutes can be relied on as against third parties shall be governed by Article 3.

SECTION III. NULLITY OF THE COMPANY

Article 10.   In all Member States whose laws do not provide for preventive control, administrative or judicial, at the time of formation of a company, the instrument of constitution, the company statutes and any amendments to those documents shall be drawn up and certified in due legal form.

Article 11.   The laws of the Member States may not provide for the nullity of companies otherwise than in accordance with the following provisions:
1. Nullity must be ordered by decision of a court of law;
2. Nullity may be ordered only on the following grounds:

   (a) that no instrument of constitution was executed or that the rules of preventive control or the requisite legal formalities were not complied with;
   (b) that the objects of the company are unlawful or contrary to public policy;
   (c) that the instrument of constitution or the statutes do not state the name of the company, the amount of the individual subscriptions of capital, the total amount of the capital subscribed or the objects of the company;
   (d) failure to comply with the provisions of the national law concerning the minimum amount of capital to be paid up;
   (e) the incapacity of all the founder members;
   (f) that, contrary to the national law governing the company, the number of founder members is less than two.

Apart from the foregoing grounds of nullity, a company shall not be subject to any cause of non-existence, nullity absolute, nullity relative or declaration of nullity.

Article 12.   1. The question whether a decision of nullity pronounced by a court of law may be relied on as against third parties shall be governed by Article 3. Where the national law entitles a third party to challenge the decision, he may do so only within six months of public notice of the decision of the court being given.
2. Nullity shall entail the winding up of the company, as may dissolution.
3. Nullity shall not of itself affect the validity of any commitments entered into by or with the company, without prejudice to the consequences of the company's being wound up.
4. The laws of each Member State may make provision for the consequences of nullity as between members of the company.
5. Holders of shares in the capital shall remain obliged to pay up the capital agreed to be subscribed by them but which has not been paid up, to the extent that commitments entered into with creditors so require.

SECTION IV. GENERAL PROVISIONS

Article 13.   Member States shall put into force, within eighteen months following notification of this Directive, all amendments to their laws, regulations or administrative provisions required in order to comply with provisions of this Directive and shall forthwith inform the Commission thereof.

The obligation of disclosure provided for in Article 2 (1) (f) shall not enter into force until thirty months after notification of this Directive in respect of *naamloze vennootschappen* under Netherlands law other than those referred to in the present Article 42 (c) of the Netherlands Commercial Code.

Member States may provide that initial disclosure of the full text of the statutes as amended since the formation of the company shall not be required until the statutes are next amended or until 31 December 1970, whichever shall be the earlier.

Member States shall ensure that they communicate to the Commission the text of the main provisions of national law which they adopt in the field covered by this Directive.

Article 14.   This Directive is addressed to the Member States.
Done at Brussels, 9 March 1968.

For the Council, The President, M. Couve de Murville

ADAPTATIONS

This Directive has been amended to reflect the accession of new members since the Directive was first adopted. Similar amendments have been made to the Second, Third, Fourth and Seventh Directives. See European Communities No. 18 (1979), Cmnd 7650 and European Communities No. 27 (1985), Cmnd. 9634.

Second Council Directive

of 13 December 1976 on coordination of safeguards which, for the protection of the interests of members and others, are required by Member States of companies within the meaning of the second paragraph of Article 58 of the Treaty, in respect of the formation of public limited liability companies and the maintenance and alteration of their capital, with a view to making such safeguards equivalent

(77/91/EEC)

The Council of the European Communities,

Having regard to the Treaty establishing the European Economic Community, and in particular Article 54 (3) (g) thereof,

Having regard to the proposal from the Commission,

Having regard to the opinion of the European Parliament,[1]

Having regard to the opinion of the Economic and Social Committee,[2]

Whereas the coordination provided for in Article 54 (3) (g) and in the General Programme for the abolition of restrictions on freedom of establishment, which was begun by Directive 68/151/EEC,[3] is especially important in relation to public limited liability companies, because their activities predominate in the economy of the Member States and frequently extend beyond their national boundaries;

Whereas in order to ensure minimum equivalent protection for both shareholders and creditors of public limited liability companies, the coordination of national provisions relating to their formation and to the maintenance, increase or reduction of their capital is particularly important;

Whereas in the territory of the Community, the statutes or instrument of incorporation of a public limited liability company must make it possible for any interested person to acquaint himself with the basic particulars of the company, including the exact composition of its capital;

Whereas Community provisions should be adopted for maintaining the capital, which constitutes the creditors' security, in particular by prohibiting any reduction thereof by distribution to shareholders where the latter are not entitled to it and by imposing limits on the company's right to acquire its own shares;

---

[1] OJ No C 114, 11. 11. 1971, p. 18.   [2] OJ No C 88, 6. 9. 1971, p. 1.
[3] OJ No L 65, 14. 3. 1968, p. 8.

Whereas it is necessary, having regard to the objectives of Article 54 (3) (g), that the Member States' laws relating to the increase or reduction of capital ensure that the principles of equal treatment of shareholders in the same position and of protection of creditors whose claims exist prior to the decision on reduction are observed and harmonized,

Has adopted this directive:

Article 1.   1. The coordination measures prescribed by this Directive shall apply to the provisions laid down by law, regulation or administrative action in Member States relating to the following types of company:

— *in Belgium:*
la société anonyme/de naamloze vennootschap;
— *in Denmark:*
aktieselskabet;
— *in France:*
la société anonyme;
— *in Germany;*
die Aktiengesellschaft;
— *in Ireland:*
the public company limited by shares, the public company limited by guarantee and having a share capital;
— *in Italy:*
la società per azioni;
— *in Luxembourg:*
la société anonyme;
— *in the Netherlands:*
de naamloze vennootschap;
— *in the United Kingdom:*
the public company limited by shares, the public company limited by guarantee and having a share capital.
— *In Greece:*
ἡ ἀνώνυμη ἑταιρία;
— *In Spain:*
la sociedad anónima;
— *In Portugal:*
a sociedade anónima de responsabilidade limitada.

The name for any company of the above types shall comprise or be accompanied by a description which is dinstict from the description required of other types of companies.

2. The Member States may decide not to apply this Directive to investment companies with variable capital and to cooperatives incorporated as one of the types of company listed in paragraph 1. In so far as the laws of the

Member States make use of this option, they shall require such companies to include the words 'investment company with variable capital' or 'cooperative' in all documents indicated in Article 4 of Directive 68/151/EEC.

The expression 'investment company with variable capital', within the meaning of this Directive, means only those companies:

— the exclusive object of which is to invest their funds in various stocks and shares, land or other assets with the sole aim of spreading investment risks and giving their shareholders the benefit of the results of the management of their assets,
— which offer their own shares for subscription by the public, and
— the statutes of which provide that, within the limits of a minimum and maximum capital, they may at any time issue, redeem or resell their shares.

Article 2.   The statutes or the instrument of incorporation of the company shall always give at least the following information:

(a) the type and name of the company;
(b) the objects of the company;
(c) when the company has no authorized capital, the amount of the subscribed capital,
      when the company has an authorized capital, the amount thereof and also the amount of the capital subscribed at the time the company is incorporated or is authorized to commence business, and at the time of any change in the authorized capital, without prejudice to Article 2 (1) (e) of Directive 68/151/EEC;
(d) in so far as they are not legally determined, the rules governing the number of and the procedure for appointing members of the bodies responsible for representing the company with regard to third parties, administration, management, supervision or control of the company and the allocation of powers among those bodies;
(e) the duration of the company, except where this is indefinite.

Article 3.   The following information at least must appear in either the statutes or the instrument of incorporation or a separate document published in accordance with the procedure laid down in the laws of each Member State in accordance with Article 3 of Directive 68/151/EEC.

(a) the registered office;
(b) the nominal value of the shares subscribed and, at least once a year, the number thereof;
(c) the number of shares subscribed without stating the nominal value, where such shares may be issued under national law;
(d) the special conditions if any limiting the transfer of shares;

(e) where there are several classes of shares, the information under (b), (c) and (d) for each class and the rights attaching to the shares of each class;

(f) whether the shares are registered or bearer, where national law provides for both types, and any provisions relating to the conversion of such shares unless the procedure is laid down by law;

(g) the amount of the subscribed capital paid up at the time the company is incorporated or is authorized to commence business;

(h) the nominal value of the shares or, where there is not nominal value, the number of shares issued for a consideration other than in cash, together with the nature of the consideration and the name of the person providing this consideration;

(i) the identity of the natural or legal persons or companies or firms by whom or in whose name the statutes or the instrument of incorporation, or where the company was not formed at the same time, the drafts of these documents, have been signed;

(j) the total amount, or at least an estimate, of all the costs payable by the company or chargeable to it by reason of its formation and, where appropriate, before the company is authorized to commence business;

(k) any special advantage granted, at the time the company is formed or up to the time it receives authorization to commence business, to anyone who has taken part in the formation of the company or in transactions leading to the grant of such authorization.

Article 4.   1. Where the laws of a Member State prescribe that a company may not commence business without authorization, they shall also make provision for responsibility for liabilities incurred by or on behalf of the company during the period before such authorization is granted or refused.

2. Paragraph 1 shall not apply to liabilities under contracts concluded by the company conditionally upon its being granted authorization to commence business.

Article 5.   1. Where the laws of a Member State require a company to be formed by more than one member, the fact that all the shares are held by one person or that the number of members has fallen below the legal minimum after incorporation of the company shall not lead to the automatic dissolution of the company.

2. If in the cases referred to in paragraph 1, the laws of a Member State permit the company to be wound up by order of the court, the judge having jurisdiction must be able to give the company sufficient time to regularize its position.

3. Where such a winding up order is made the company shall enter into liquidation.

Article 6.   1. The laws of the Member States shall require that, in order that a company may be incorporated or obtain authorization to commence business, a minimum capital shall be subscribed the amount of which shall be not less than 25 000 European units of account.

The European unit of account shall be that defined by Commission Decision No 3289/75/ECSC.[1] The equivalent in national currency shall be calculated initially at the rate applicable on the date of adoption of this Directive.

2. If the equivalent of the European unit of account in national currency is altered so that the value of the minimum capital in national currency remains less than 22 500 European units of account for a period of one year, the Commission shall inform the Member State concerned that it must amend its legislation to comply with paragraph 1 within 12 months following the expiry of that period. However, the Member State may provide that the amended legislation shall not apply to companies already in existence until 18 months after its entry into force.

Every five years the Council, acting on a proposal from the Commission, shall examine and, if need be, revise the amounts expressed in this Article in European units of account in the light of economic and monetary trends in the Community and of the tendency towards allowing only large and medium-sized undertakings to opt for the types of company listed in Article 1.

Article 7.   The subscribed capital may be formed only of assets capable of economic assessment. However, an undertaking to perform work or supply services may not form part of these assets.

Article 8.   1. Shares may not be issued at a price lower than their nominal value, or, where there is no nominal value, their accountable par.

2. However, Member States may allow those who undertake to place shares in the exercise of their profession to pay less than the total price of the shares for which they subscribe in the course of this transaction.

Article 9.   1. Shares issued for a consideration must be paid up at the time the company is incorporated or is authorized to commence business at not less than 25% of their nominal value or, in the absence of a nominal value, their accountable par.

2. However, where shares are issued for a consideration other than in cash at the time the company is incorporated or is authorized to commence business, the consideration must be transferred in full within five years of that time.

[1] OJ No L 327, 19. 12. 1975, p. 4.

Article 10.   1. A report on any consideration other than in cash shall be drawn up before the company is incoporated or is authorized to commence business, by one or more independent experts appointed or approved by an administrative or judicial authority. Such experts may be natural persons as well a legal persons and companies or firms under the laws of each Member State.

2. The experts' report shall contain at least a description of each of the assets comprising the consideration as well as of the methods of valuation used and shall state whether the values arrived at by the application of these methods correspond at least to the number and nominal value or, where there is no nominal value, to the accountable par and, where appropriate to the premium on the shares to be issued for them.

3. The experts' report shall be published in the manner laid down by the laws of each Member State, in accordance with Article 3 of Directive 68/151/EEC.

4. Member States may decide not to apply this Article where 90% of the nominal value, or where there is no nominal value, of the accountable par, of all the shares is issued to one or more companies for a consideration other than in cash, and where the following requirements are met:

(a) with regard to the company in receipt of such consideration, the persons referred to in Article 3 (i) have agreed to dispense with the experts' report;

(b) such agreement has been published as provided for in paragraph 3;

(c) the companies furnishing such consideration have reserves which may not be distributed under the law or the statutes and which are at least equal to the nominal value or, where there is no nominal value, the accountable par of the shares issued for consideration other than in cash;

(d) the companies furnishing such consideration guarantee, up to an amount equal to that indicated in paragraph (c), the debts of the recipient company arising between the time the shares are issued for a consideration other than in cash and one year after the publication of that company's annual accounts for the financial year during which such consideration was furnished. Any transfer of these shares is prohibited within this period;

(e) the guarantee referred to in (d) has been published as provided for in paragraph 3;

(f) the companies furnishing such consideration shall place a sum equal to that indicated in (c) into a reserve which may not be distributed until three years after publication of the annual accounts of the recipient company for the financial year during which such consideration was furnished or, if necessary, until such later date as all claims relating to the guarantee referred to in (d) which are submitted during this period have been settled.

Article 11. 1. If, before the expiry of a time limit laid down by national law of at least two years from the time the company is incorporated or is authorized to commence business, the company acquires any asset belonging to a person or company or firm referred to in Article 3 (i) for a consideration of not less than one-tenth of the subscribed capital, the acquisition shall be examined and details of it published in the manner provided for in Article 10 and it shall be submitted for the approval of the general meeting.

Member States may also require these provisions to be applied when the assets belong to a shareholder or to any other person.

2. Paragraph 1 shall not apply to acquisitions effected in the normal course of the company's business, to acquisitions effected at the instance or under the supervision of an administrator or judicial authority, or to stock exchange acquisitions.

Article 12. Subject to the provisions relating to the reduction of subscribed capital, the shareholders may not be released from the obligation to pay up their contributions.

Article 13. Pending coordination of national laws at a subsequent date, Member States shall adopt the measures necessary to require provision of at least the same safeguards as are laid down in Articles 2 to 12 in the event of the conversion of another type of company into a public limited liability company.

Article 14. Articles 2 to 13 shall not prejudice the provisions of Member States on competence and procedure relating to the modification of the statutes or of the instrument of incorporation.

Article 15. 1

(a) Except for cases of reductions of subscribed capital, no distribution to shareholders may be made when on the closing date of the last financial year the net assets as set out in the company's annual accounts are, or following such a distribution would become, lower than the amount of the subscribed capital plus those reserves which may not be distributed under the law or the statutes.

(b) Where the uncalled part of the subscribed capital is not included in the assets shown in the balance sheet, this amount shall be deducted from the amount of subscribed capital referred to in paragraph (a).

(c) The amount of a distribution to shareholders may not exceed the amount of the profits at the end of the last financial year plus any profits brought forward and sums drawn from reserves available for this purpose, less any losses brought forward and sums placed to reserve in accordance with the law or the statutes.

(d) The expression 'distribution' used in subparagraphs (a) and (c) includes in particular the payment of dividends and of interest relating to shares.

2. When the laws of a Member State allow the payment of interim dividends, the following conditions at least shall apply:

(a) interim accounts shall be drawn up showing that the funds available for distribution are sufficient,

(b) the amount to be distributed may not exceed the total profits made since the end of the last financial year for which the annual accounts have been drawn up, plus any profits brought forward and sums drawn from reserves available for this purpose, less losses brought forward and sums to be placed to reserve pursuant to the requirements of the law or the statutes.

3. Paragraphs 1 and 2 shall not affect the provisions of the Member States as regards increases in subscribed capital by capitalization of reserves.

4. The laws of a Member State may provide for derogations from paragraph 1 (a) in the case of investment companies with fixed capital.

The expression 'investment company with fixed capital', within the meaning of this paragraph means only those companies:

— the exclusive object of which is to invest their funds in various stocks and shares, land or other assets with the sole aim of spreading investment risks and giving their shareholders the benefit of the results of the management of their assets, and

— which offer their own shares for subscription by the public.

In so far as the laws of Member States make use of this option they shall:

(a) require such companies to include the expression 'investment company' in all documents indicated in Article 4 of Directive 68/151/EEC;

(b) not permit any such company whose net assets fall below the amount specified in paragraph 1 (a) to make a distribution to shareholders when on the closing date of the last financial year the company's total assets as set out in the annual accounts are, or following such distribution would become, less than one-and-a-half times the amount of the company's total liabilities to creditors as set out in the annual accounts;

(c) require any such company which makes a distribution when its net assets fall below the amount specified in paragraph 1 (a) to include in its annual accounts a note to that effect.

Article 16.   Any distribution made contrary to Article 15 must be returned by shareholders who have received it if the company proves that these shareholders knew of the irregularity of the distributions made to them, or could not in view of the circumstances have been unaware of it.

Article 17.   1. In the case of a serious loss of the subscribed capital, a general meeting of shareholders must be called within the period laid down by the laws of the Member States, to consider whether the company should be wound up or any other measures taken.

2. The amount of a loss deemed to be serious within the meaning of paragraph 1 may not be set by the laws of Member States at a figure higher than half the subscribed capital.

Article 18.   1. The shares of a company may not be subscribed for by the company itself.

2. If the shares of a company have been subscribed for by a person acting in his own name, but on behalf of the company, the subscriber shall be deemed to have subscribed for them for his own account.

3. The persons or companies or firms referred to in Article 3 (i) or, in cases of an increase in subscribed capital, the members of the administrative or management body shall be liable to pay for shares subscribed in contravention of this Article.

However, the laws of a Member State may provide that any such person may be released from his obligation if he proves that no fault is attributable to him personally.

Article 19.   1. Where the laws of a Member State permit a company to acquire its own shares, either itself or through a person acting in his own name but on the company's behalf, they shall make such acquisitions subject to at least the following conditions:

(a) authorization shall be given by the general meeting, which shall determine the terms and conditions of such acquisitions, and in particular the maximum number of shares to be acquired, the duration of the period for which the authorization is given and which may not exceed 18 months, and, in the case of acquisition for value, the maximum and minimum consideration. Members of the administrative or management body shall be required to satisfy themselves that at the time when each authorized acquisition is effected the conditions referred to in subparagraphs (b), (c) and (d) are respected;

(b) the nominal value or, in the absence thereof, the accountable par of the acquired shares, including shares previously acquired by the company and held by it, and shares acquired by a person acting in his own name but on the company's behalf, may not exceed 10% of the subscribed capital;

(c) the acquisitions may not have the effect of reducing the net assets below the amount mentioned in Article 15 (1) (a);

(d) only fully paid-up shares may be included in the transaction.

2. The laws of a Member State may provide for derogations from the first sentence of paragraph 1 (a) where the acquisition of a company's own shares is necessary to prevent serious and immiment harm to the company. In such a case, the next general meeting must be informed by the administrative or management body of the reasons for and nature of the acquisitions effected, of the number and nominal value or, in the absence of a nominal value, the accountable par, of the shares acquired, of the proportion of the subscribed capital which they represent, and of the consideration for these shares.

3. Member States may decide not to apply the first sentence of paragraph 1 (a) to shares acquired by either the company itself or by a person acting in his own name but on the company's behalf, for distribution to that company's employees or to the employees of an associate company. Such shares must be distributed within 12 months of their acquisition.

Article 20. 1. Member States may decide not to apply Article 19 to:

(a) shares acquired in carrying out a decision to reduce capital, or in the circumstances referred to in Article 39;

(b) shares acquired as a result of a universal transfer of assets;

(c) fully paid-up shares acquired free of charge or by banks and other financial institutions as purchasing commission;

(d) shares acquired by virtue of a legal obligation or resulting from a court ruling for the protection of minority shareholders in the event, particularly, of a merger, a change in the company's object or form, transfer abroad of the registered office, or the introduction of restrictions on the transfer of shares;

(e) shares acquired from a shareholder in the event of failure to pay them up;

(f) shares acquired in order to indemnify minority shareholders in associated companies;

(g) fully paid-up shares acquired under a sale enforced by a court order for the payment of a debt owed to the company by the owner of the shares;

(h) fully paid-up shares issued by an investment company with fixed capital, as defined in the second subparagraph of Article 15 (4), and acquired at the investor's request by that company or by an associate company. Artile 15 (4) (a) shall apply. These acquisitions may not have the effect of reducing the net assets below the amount of the subscribed capital plus any reserves the distribution of which is forbidden by law.

2. Shares acquired in the cases listed in paragraph 1 (b) to (g) above must, however, be disposed of within not more than three years of their acquisition unless the nominal value or, in the absence of a nominal value, the accountable par of the shares acquired, including shares which the company may have acquired through a person acting in his own name but on the company's behalf, does not exceed 10% of the subscribed capital.

3. If the shares are not disposed of within the period laid down in paragraph 2, they must be cancelled. The laws of a Member State may make this cancellation subject to a corresponding reduction in the subscribed capital. Such a reduction must be prescribed where the acquisition of shares to be cancelled results in the net assets having fallen below the amount specified in Article 15 (1) (a).

Article 21. Shares acquired in contravention of Articles 19 and 20 shall be disposed of within one year of their acquisition. Should they not be disposed of within that period, Article 20 (3) shall apply.

Article 22. 1. Where the laws of a Member State permit a company to acquire its own shares, either itself or through a person acting in his own name but on the company's behalf, they shall make the holding of these shares at all times subject to at least the following conditions:

(a) among the rights attaching to the shares, the right to vote attaching to the company's own shares shall in any event be suspended;
(b) if the shares are included among the assets shown in the balance sheet, a reserve of the same amount, unavailable for distribution, shall be included among the liabilities.

2. Where the laws of a Member State permit a company to acquire its own shares, either itself or through a person acting in his own name but on the company's behalf, they shall require the annual report to state at least:

(a) the reasons for acquisition made during the financial year;
(b) the number and nominal value or, in the absence of a nominal value, the accountable par of the shares acquired and disposed of during the financial year and the proportion of the subscribed capital which they represent;
(c) in the case of acquisition or disposal for a value, the consideration for the shares;
(d) the number and nominal value or, in the absence of a nominal value, the accountable par of all the shares acquired and held by the company and the proportion of the subscribed capital which they represent.

Article 23. 1. A company may not advance funds, nor make loans, nor provide security, with a view to the acquisition of its shares by a third party.

2. Paragraph 1 shall not apply to transactions concluded by banks and other financial institutions in the normal course of business, nor to transactions effected with a view to the acquisition of shares by or for the company's employees or the employees of an associate company. However, these transactions may not have the effect of reducing the net assets below the amount specified in Article 15 (1) (a).

3. Paragraph 1 shall not apply to transactions effected with a view to acquisition of shares as described in Article 20 (1) (h).

Article 24.   1. The acceptance of the company's own shares as security, either by the company itself or through a person acting in his own name but on the company's behalf, shall be treated as an acquisition for the purposes of Articles 19, 20 (1), 22 and 23.

2. The Member States may decide not to apply paragraph 1 to transactions concluded by banks and other financial institutions in the normal course of business.

Article 25.   1. Any increase in capital must be decided upon by the general meeting. Both this decision and the increase in the subscribed capital shall be published in the manner laid down by the laws of each Member State, in accordance with Article 3 of Directive 68/151/EEC.

2. Nevertheless, the statutes or instrument of incorporation or the general meeting, the decision of which must be published in accordance with the rules referred to in paragraph 1, may authorize an increase in the subscribed capital up to a maximum amount which they shall fix with due regard for any maximum amount provided for by law. Where appropriate, the increase in the subscribed capital shall be decided on within the limits of the amount fixed, by the company body empowered to do so. The power of such body in this respect shall be for a maximum period of five years and may be renewed one or more times by the general meeting, each time for a period not exceeding five years.

3. Where there are several classes of shares, the decision by the general meeting concerning the increase in capital referred to in paragraph 1 or the authorization to increase the capital referred to in paragraph 2, shall be subject to a separate vote at least for each class of shareholder whose rights are affected by the transaction.

4. This Article shall apply to the issue of all securities which are convertible into shares or which carry the right to subscribe for shares, but not to the conversion of such securities, nor to the exercise of the right to subscribe.

Article 26.   Shares issued for a consideration, in the course of an increase in subscribed capital, must be paid up to at least 25% of their nominal value or, in the absence of a nominal value, of their accountable par. Where provision is made for an issue premium, it must be paid in full.

Article 27.   1. Where shares are issued for a consideration other than in cash in the course of an increase in the subscribed capital the consideration must be transferred in full within a period of five years from the decision to increase the subscribed capital.

2. The consideration referred to in paragraph 1 shall be the subject of a report drawn up before the increase in capital is made by one or more experts who are independent of the company and appointed or approved by an administrative or judicial authority. Such experts may be natural persons as well as legal persons and companies and firms under the laws of each Member State.

Article 10 (2) and (3) shall apply.

3. Member States may decide not to apply paragraph 2 in the event of an increase in subscribed capital made in order to give effect to a merger or a public offer for the purchase or exchange of shares and to pay the shareholders of the company which is being absorbed or which is the object of the public offer for the purchase or exchange of shares.

4. Member States may decide not to apply paragraph 2 if all the shares issued in the course of an increase in subscribed capital are issued for a consideration other than in cash to one or more companies, on condition that all the shareholders in the company which receive the consideration have agreed not to have an experts' report drawn up and that the requirements of Article 10 (4) (b) to (f) are met.

Article 28.   Where an increase in capital is not fully subscribed, the capital will be increased by the amount of the subscriptions received only if the conditions of the issue so provide.

Article 29.   1. Whenever the capital is increased by consideration in cash, the shares must be offered on a pre-emptive basis to shareholders in proportion to the capital represented by their shares.

2. The laws of a Member State:

(a) need not apply paragraph 1 above to shares which carry a limited right to participate in distributions within the meaning of Article 15 and/or in the company's assets in the event of liquidation; or

(b) may permit, where the subscribed capital of a company having several classes of shares carrying different rights with regard to voting, or participation in distributions within the meaning of Article 15 or in assets in the event of liquidation, is increased by issuing new shares in only one of these classes, the right of pre-emption of shareholders of the other classes to be exercised only after the exercise of this right by the shareholders of the class in which the new shares are being issued.

3. Any offer of subscription on a pre-emptive basis and the period within which this right must be exercised shall be published in the national gazette appointed in accordance with Directive 68/151/EEC. However, the laws of a Member State need not provide for such publication where all a company's shares are registered. In such case, all the company's shareholders must be informed in writing. The right of pre-emption must be exercised within a period which shall not be less than 14 days from the date of publication of the offer or from the date of dispatch of the letters to the shareholders.

4. The right of pre-emption may not be restricted or withdrawn by the statutes or instrument of incorporation. This may, however, be done by decision of the general meeting. The administrative or management body shall be required to present to such a meeting a written report indicating the reasons for restriction or withdrawal of the right of pre-emption, and justifying the proposed issue price. The general meeting shall act in accordance with the rules for a quorum and a majority laid down in Article 40. Its decision shall be published in the manner laid down by the laws of each Member State, in accordance with Article 3 of Directive 68/151/EEC.

5. The laws of a Member State may provide that the statutes, the instrument of incorporation or the general meeting, acting in accordance with the rules for a quorum, a majority and publication set out in paragraph 4, may give the power to restrict or withdraw the right of pre-emption to the company body which is empowered to decide on an increase in subscribed capital within the limits of the authorized capital. This power may not be granted for a longer period than the power for which provision is made in Article 25 (2).

6. Paragraphs 1 to 5 shall apply to the issue of all securities which are convertible into shares or which carry the right to subscribe for shares, but not to the conversion of such securities, nor to the exercise of the right to subscribe.

7. The right of pre-emption is not excluded for the purposes of paragraphs 4 and 5 where, in accordance with the decision to increase the subscribed capital, shares are issued to banks or other financial institutions with a view to their being offered to shareholders of the company in accordance with paragraphs 1 and 3.

Article 30.   Any reduction in the subscribed capital, except under a court order, must be subject at least to a decision of the general meeting acting in accordance with the rules for a quorum and a majority laid down in Article 40 without prejudice to Articles 36 and 37. Such decision shall be published in the manner laid down by the laws of each Member State in accordance with Article 3 of Directive 68/151/EEC.

The notice convening the meeting must specify at least the purpose of the reduction and the way in which it is to be carried out.

Article 31.   Where there are several classes of shares, the decision by the general meeting concerning a reduction in the subscribed capital shall be subject to a separate vote, at least for each class of shareholders whose rights are affected by the transaction.

Article 32.   1. In the event of a reduction in the subscribed capital, at least the creditors whose claims antedate the publication of the decision to make the reduction shall be entitled at least to have the right to obtain security for claims which have not fallen due by the date of that publication. The laws of a Member State shall lay down the conditions for the exercise of this right. They may not set aside such right unless the creditor has adequate safeguards, or unless the latter are not necessary in view of the assets of the company.

2. The laws of the Member States shall also stipulate at least that the reduction shall be void or that no payment may be made for the benefit of the shareholders, until the creditors have obtained satisfaction or a court has decided that their application should not be acceded to.

3. This Article shall apply where the reduction in the subscribed capital is brought about by the total or partial waiving of the payment of the balance of the shareholder's contributions.

Article 33.   1. Member States need not apply Article 32 to a reduction in the subscribed capital whose purpose is to offset losses incurred or to include sums of money in a rescue provided that, following this operation, the amount of such reserve is not more than 10% of the reduced subscribed capital. Except in the event of a reduction in the subscribed capital, this reserve may not be distributed to shareholders; it may be used only for offsetting losses incurred or for increasing the subscribed capital by the capitalization of such reserve, in so far as the Member States permit such an operation.

2. In the cases referred to in paragraph 1 the laws of the Member States must at least provide for the measures necessary to ensure that the amounts deriving from the reduction of subscribed capital may not be used for making payments or distributions to shareholders or discharging shareholders from the obligation to make their contributions.

Article 34.   The subscribed capital may not be reduced to an amount less than the minimum capital laid down in accordance with Article 6. However,

Member States may permit such a reduction if they also provide that the decision to reduce the subscribed capital may take effect only when the subscribed capital is increased to an amount at least equal to the prescribed minimum.

Article 35. Where the laws of a Member State authorize total or partial redemption of the subscribed capital without reduction of the latter, they shall at least require that the following conditions are observed:

(a) where the statutes or instrument of incorporation provide for redemption, the latter shall be decided on by the general meeting voting at least under the usual conditions of quorum and majority. Where the statutes or instrument of incorporation do not provide for redemption, the latter shall be decided upon by the general meeting acting at least under the conditions of quorum and majority laid down in Article 40. The decision must be published in the manner prescribed by the laws of each Member State, in accordance with Article 3 of Directive 68/151/EEC;

(b) only sums which are available for distribution within the meaning of Article 15 (1) may be used for redemption purposes;

(c) shareholders whose shares are redeemed shall retain their rights in the company, with the exception of their rights to the repayment of their investment and participation in the distribution of an initial dividend on unredeemed shares.

Article 36. 1. Where the laws of a Member State may allow companies to reduce their subscribed capital by compulsory withdrawal of shares, they shall require that at least the following conditions are observed:

(a) compulsory withdrawal must be prescribed or authorized by the statutes or instrument of incorporation before subscription of the shares which are to be withdrawn are subscribed for;

(b) where the compulsory withdrawal is merely authorized by the statutes or instrument of incorporation, it shall be decided upon by the general meeting unless it has been unanimously approved by the shareholders concerned;

(c) the company body deciding on the compulsory withdrawal shall fix the terms and manner thereof, where they have not already been fixed by the statutes or instrument of incorporation;

(d) Article 32 shall apply except in the case of fully paid-up shares which are made available to the company free of charge or are withdrawn using sums available for distribution in accordance with Article 15 (1); in these cases, an amount equal to the nominal value or, in the absence thereof, to the accountable par of all the withdrawn shares must be included in a reserve. Except in the event of a reduction in the subscribed capital this reserve may not be distributed to shareholders. It can be used only for offsetting losses incurred or for increasing the subscribed capital by the capitalization of such reserve, in so far as Member States permit such an operation;

(e) the decision on compulsory withdrawal shall be published in the manner laid down by the laws of each Member State in accordance with Article 3 of Directive 68/151/EEC.

2. Articles 30 (1), 31, 33 and 40 shall not apply to the cases to which paragraph 1 refers.

Article 37. 1. In the case of a reduction in the subscribed capital by the withdrawal of shares acquired by the company itself or by a person acting in his own name but on behalf of the company, the withdrawal must always be decided on by the general meeting.

2. Article 32 shall apply unless the shares are fully paid up and are acquired free of charge or using sums available for distribution in accordance with Article 15 (1); in these cases an amount equal to the nominal value or, in the absence thereof, to the accountable par of all the shares withdrawn must be included in a reserve. Except in the event of a reduction in the subscribed capital, this reserve may not be distributed to shareholders. It may be used only for offsetting losses incurred or for increasing the subscribed capital by the capitalization of such reserve, in so far as the Member States permit such an operation.

3. Articles 31, 33 and 40 shall not apply to the cases to which paragraph 1 refers.

Article 38. In the cases covered by Articles 35, 36 (1) (b) and 37 (1), when there are several classes of shares, the decision by the general meeting concerning redemption of the subscribed capital or its reduction by withdrawal of shares shall be subject to a separate vote, at least for each class of shareholders whose rights are affected by the transaction.

Article 39. Where the laws of a Member State authorize companies to issue redeemable shares, they shall require that the following conditions, at least, are complied with for the redemption of such shares:

(a) redemption must be authorized by the company's statutes or instrument of incorporation before the redeemable shares are subscribed for;
(b) the shares must be fully paid up;
(c) the terms and the manner of redemption must be laid down in the company's statutes or instrument of incorporation;
(d) redemption can be only effected by using sums available for distribution in accordance with Article 15 (1) or the proceeds of a new issue made with a view to effecting such redemption;

(e) an amount equal to the nominal value or, in the absence thereof, to the accountable par of all the redeemed shares must be included in a reserve which cannot be distributed to the shareholders, except in the event of a reduction in the subscribed capital; it may be used only for the purpose of increasing the subscribed capital by the capitalization of reserves;

(f) subparagraph (e) shall not apply to redemption using the proceeds of a new issue made with a view to effecting such redemption;

(g) where provision is made for the payment of a premium to shareholders in consequence of a redemption, the premium may be paid only from sums available for distribution in accordance with Article 15 (1), or from a reserve other than that referred to in (e) which may not be distributed to shareholders except in the event of a reduction in the subscribed capital; this reserve may be used only for the purposes of increasing the subscribed capital by the capitalization of reserves or for covering the costs referred to in Article 3 (j) or the cost of issuing shares or debentures or for the payment of a premium to holders of redeemable shares or debentures;

(h) notification of redemption shall be published in the manner laid down by the laws of each Member State in accordance with Article 3 of Directive 68/151/EEC.

Article 40. 1. The laws of the Member States shall provide that the decisions referred to in Articles 29 (4) and (5), 30, 31, 35 and 38 must be taken at least by a majority of not less than two-thirds of the votes attaching to the securities or the subscribed capital represented.

2. The laws of the Member States may, however, lay down that a simple majority of the votes specified in paragraph 1 is sufficient when at least half the subscribed capital is represented.

Article 41. 1. Member States may derogate from Article 9 (1), Article 19 (1) (a), first sentence, and (b) and from Articles 25, 26 and 29 to the extent that such derogations are necessary for the adoption or application of provisions designed to encourage the participation of employees, or other groups of persons defined by national law, in the capital of undertakings.

2. Member States may decide not to apply Article 19 (1) (a), first sentence, and Articles 30, 31, 36, 37, 38 and 39 to companies incorporated under a special law which issue both capital shares and workers' shares, the latter being issued to the company's employees as a body, who are represented at general meetings of shareholders by delegates having the right to vote.

Article 42.   For the purposes of the implementation of this Directive, the laws of the Member States shall ensure equal treatment to all shareholders who are in the same position.

Article 43.   1. Member States shall bring into force the laws, regulations and administrative provisions needed in order to comply with this Directive within two years of its notification. They shall forthwith inform the Commission thereof.

2. Member States may decide not to apply Article 3 (g), (i), (j) and (k) to companies already in existence at the date of entry into force of the provisions referred to in paragraph 1.

They may provide that the other provisions of this Directive shall not apply to such companies until 18 months after that date.

However, this time limit may be three years in the case of Articles 6 and 9 and five years in the case of unregistered companies in the United Kingdom and Ireland.

3. Member States shall ensure that they communicate to the Commission the text of the main provisions of national law which they adopt in the field covered by this Directive.

Article 44.   This Directive is addressed to the Member States.

Done at Brussels, 13 December 1976.

For the Council, The President, M. van der Stoel

Third Council Directive

of 9 October 1978 based on Article 54 (3) (g) of the
Treaty concerning mergers of public limited liability
companies

(78/855/EEC)

The Council of the European Communities,

Having regard to the Treaty establishing the European Economic Community, and in particular Article 54 (3) (g) thereof,

Having regard to the proposal from the Commission,[1]

Having regard to the opinion of the European Parliament,[2]

Having regard to the opinion of the Economic and Social Committee,[3]

Whereas the coordination provided for in Article 54 (3) (g) and in the general programme for the abolition of restrictions on freedom of establishment[4] was begun with Directive 68/151/EEC;[5]

Whereas this coordination was continued as regards the formation of public limited liability companies and the maintenance and alteration of their capital with Directive 77/91/EEC,[6] and as regards the annual accounts of certain types of companies with Directive 78/660/EEC;[7]

Whereas the protection of the interests of members and third parties requires that the laws of the Member States relating to mergers of public limited liability companies be coordinated and that provision for mergers should be made in the laws of all the Member States;

Whereas in the context of such coordination it is particularly important that the shareholders of merging companies be kept adequately informed in as objective a manner as possible and that their rights be suitably protected;

Whereas the protection of employees' rights in the event of transfers of undertakings, businesses or parts of businesses is at present regulated by Directive 77/187/EEC;[8]

Whereas creditors, including debenture holders, and persons having other claims on the merging companies must be protected so that the merger does not adversely affect their interests;

Whereas the disclosure requirements of Directive 68/151/EEC must be extended to include mergers so that third parties are kept adequately informed;

---

[1] OJ No C 89, 14. 7. 1970, p. 20.
[2] OJ No C 129, 11. 12. 1972, p. 50; OJ No C 95, 28. 4. 1975, p. 12.
[3] OJ No C 88, 6. 9. 1971, p. 18.   [4] OJ No 2, 15. 1. 1962, p. 36/62.
[5] OJ No L 65, 14. 3. 1968, p. 8.   [6] OJ No L 26, 31. 1. 1977, p. 1.
[7] OJNo L 222, 14. 8. 1978, p. 11.   [8] OJ No L 61, 5. 3. 1977, p. 26.

Whereas the safeguards afforded to members and third parties in connection with mergers must be extended to cover certain legal practices which in important respects are similar to merger, so that the obligation to provide such protection cannot be evaded;

Whereas to ensure certainty in the law as regards relations between the companies concerned, between them and third parties, and between the members, the cases in which nullity can arise must be limited by providing that defects be remedied wherever that is possible and by restricting the period within which nullification proceedings may be commenced,

Has adopted this directive:

Article 1.

Scope

1. The coordination measures laid down by this Directive shall apply to the laws, regulations and administrative provisions of the Member States relating to the following types of company:

— Germany:
die Aktiengesellschaft,
— Belgium:
la société anonyme/de naamloze vennootschap,
— Denmark:
aktieselskaber,
— France:
la société anonyme,
— Ireland:
public companies limited by shares, and public companies limited by guarantee having a share capital,
— Italy:
la società per azioni,
— Luxembourg:
la société anonyme,
— the Netherlands:
da naamloze vennootschap,
— the United Kingdom:
public companies limited by shares, and public companies limited by guarantee having a share capital.
— In Greece:
ἡ ἀνώνυμη ἑταιρία,
— In Spain:
la sociedad anónima,
— In Portugal:
a sociedade anónima de responsabilidade limitada.

2. The Member States need not apply this Directive to cooperatives incorporated as one of the types of company listed in paragraph 1. In so far as the laws of the Member States make use of this option, they shall require such companies to include the word 'cooperative' in all the documents referred to in Article 4 of Directive 68/151/EEC.

3. The Member States need not apply this Directive in cases where the company or companies which are being acquired or will cease to exist are the subject of bankruptcy proceedings, proceedings relating to the winding-up of insolvent companies, judicial arrangements, compositions and analogous proceedings.

CHAPTER I. REGULATION OF MERGER BY THE ACQUISITION OF ONE OR MORE COMPANIES BY ANOTHER AND OF MERGER BY THE FORMATION OF A NEW COMPANY

Article 2. The Member States shall, as regards companies governed by their national laws, make provision for rules governing merger by the acquisition of one or more companies by another and merger by the formation of a new company.

Article 3. 1. For the purposes of this Directive, 'merger by acquisition' shall mean the operation whereby one or more companies are wound up without going into liquidation and transfer to another all their assets and liabilities in exchange for the issue to the shareholders of the company or companies being acquired of shares in the acquiring company and a cash payment, if any, not exceeding 10% of the nominal value of the shares so issued or, where they have no nominal value, of their accounting par value.

2. A Member State's laws may provide that merger by acquisition may also be effected where one or more of the companies being acquired is in liquidation, provided that this option is restricted to companies which have not yet begun to distribute their assets to their shareholders.

Article 4. 1. For the purposes of this Directive, 'merger by the formation of a new company' shall mean the operation whereby several companies are wound up without going into liquidation and transfer to a company that they set up all their assets and liabilities in exchange for the issue of their shareholders of shares in the new company and a cash payment, if any, not exceeding 10% of the nominal value of the shares so issued or, where they have no nominal value, of their accounting par value.

2. A Member State's laws may provide that merger by the formation of a new company may also be effected where one or more of the companies which are ceasing to exist is in liquidation, provided that this option is

restricted to companies which have not yet begun to distribute their assets to their shareholders.

CHAPTER II. MERGER BY ACQUISITION

Article 5. 1. The administrative or management bodies of the merging companies shall draw up draft terms of merger in writing.

2. Draft terms of merger shall specify at least:

(a) the type, name and registered office of each of the merging companies;
(b) the share exchange ratio and the amount of any cash payment;
(c) the terms relating to the allotment of shares in the acquiring company;
(d) the date from which the holding of such shares entitles the holders to participate in profits and any special conditions affecting that entitlement;
(e) the date from which the transactions of the company being acquired shall be treated for accounting purposes as being those of the acquiring company;
(f) the rights conferred by the acquiring company on the holders of shares to which special rights are attached and the holders of securities other than shares, or the measures proposed concerning them;
(g) any special advantage granted to the experts referred to in Article 10(1) and members of the merging companies' administrative, management, supervisory or controlling bodies.

Article 6. Draft terms of merger must be published in the manner prescribed by the laws of each Member State in accordance with Article 3 of Directive 68/151/EEC, for each of the merging companies, at least one month before the date fixed for the general meeting which is to decide thereon.

Article 7. 1. A merger shall require at least the approval of the general meeting of each of the merging companies. The laws of the Member States shall provide that this decision shall require a majority of not less than two thirds of the votes attaching either to the shares or to the subscribed capital represented.

The laws of a Member State may, however, provide that a simple majority of the votes specified in the first subparagraph shall be sufficient when at least half of the subscribed capital is represented. Moreover, where appropriate, the rules governing alterations to the memorandum and articles of association shall apply.

2. Where there is more than one class of shares, the decision concerning a merger shall be subject to a separate vote by at least each class of shareholders whose rights are affected by the transaction.

3. The decision shall cover both the approval of the draft terms of merger and any alterations to the memorandum and articles of association necessitated by the merger.

Article 8.   The laws of a Member State need not require approval of the merger by the general meeting of the acquiring company if the following conditions are fulfilled:

(a) the publication provided for in Article 6 must be effected, for the acquiring company, at least one month before the date fixed for the general meeting of the company or companies being acquired which are to decide on the draft terms of merger;

(b) at least one month before the date specified in (a), all shareholders of the acquiring company must be entitled to inspect the documents specified in Article 11 (1) at the registered office of the acquiring company;

(c) one or more shareholders of the acquiring company holding a minimum percentage of the subscribed capital must be entitled to require that a general meeting of the acquiring company be called to decide whether to approve the merger. This minimum percentage may not be fixed at more than 5%. The Member States may, however, provide for the exclusion of non-voting shares from this calculation.

Article 9.   The administration or management bodies of each of the merging companies shall draw up a detailed written report explaining the draft terms of merger and setting out the legal and economic grounds for them, in particular the share exchange ratio.

The report shall also describe any special valuation difficulties which have arisen.

Article 10.   1. One or more experts, acting on behalf of each of the merging companies but independent of them, appointed or approved by a judicial or administrative authority, shall examine the draft terms of merger and draw up a written report to the shareholders. However, the laws of a Member State may provide for the appointment of one or more independent experts for all the merging companies, if such appointment is made by a judicial or administrative authority at the joint request of those companies. Such experts may, depending on the laws of each Member State, be natural or legal persons or companies or firms.

2. In the report mentioned in paragraph 1 the experts must in any case state whether in their opinion the share exchange ratio is fair and reasonable. Their statement must at least:

(a) indicate the method or methods used to arrive at the share exchange ratio proposed;

(b) state whether such method or methods are adequate in the case in question, indicate the values arrived at using each such method and give an opinion on the relative importance attributed to such methods in arriving at the value decided on.

The report shall also describe any special valuation difficulties which have arisen.

3. Each expert shall be entitled to obtain from the merging companies all relevant information and documents and to carry out all necessary investigations.

Article 11. 1. All shareholders shall be entitled to inspect at least the following documents at the registered office at least one month before the date fixed for the general meeting which is to decide on the draft terms of merger:

(a) the draft terms of merger;
(b) the annual accounts and annual reports of the merging companies for the preceding three financial years;
(c) an accounting statement drawn up as at a date which must not be earlier than the first day of the third month preceding the date of the draft terms of merger, if the latest annual accounts relate to a financial year which ended more than six months before that date;
(d) the reports of the administrative or management bodies of the merging companies provided for in Article 9;
(e) the reports provided for in Article 10.

2. The accounting statement provided for in paragraph 1 (c) shall be drawn up using the same methods and the same layout as the last annual balance sheet.

However, the laws of a Member State may provide that:

(a) it shall not be necessary to take a fresh physical inventory;
(b) the valuations shown in the last balance sheet shall be altered only to reflect entries in the books of account; the following shall nevertheless be taken into account:

— interim depreciation and provisions,
— material changes in actual value not shown in the books.

3. Every shareholder shall be entitled to obtain, on request and free of charge, full or, if so desired, partial copies of the documents referred to in paragraph 1.

Article 12. Protection of the rights of the employees of each of the merging companies shall be regulated in accordance with Directive 77/187/EEC.

Article 13. 1. The laws of the Member States must provide for an adequate system of protection of the interests of creditors of the merging companies whose claims antedate the publication of the draft terms of merger and have not fallen due at the time of such publication.

2. To this end, the laws of the Member States shall at least provide that such creditors shall be entitled to obtain adequate safeguards where the financial situation of the merging companies makes such protection necessary and where those creditors do not already have such safeguards.

3. Such protection may be different for the creditors of the acquiring company and for those of the company being acquired.

Article 14. Without prejudice to the rules governing the collective exercise of their rights, Article 13 shall apply to the debenture holders of the merging companies, except where the merger has been approved by a meeting of the debenture holders, if such a meeting is provided for under national laws, or by the debenture holders individually.

Article 15. Holders of securities, other than shares, to which special rights are attached, must be given rights in the acquiring company at least equivalent to those they possessed in the company being acquired, unless the alteration of those rights has been approved by a meeting of the holders of such securities, if such a meeting is provided for under national laws, or by the holders of those securities individually, or unless the holders are entitled to have their securities repurchased by the acquiring company.

Article 16. 1. Where the laws of a Member State do not provide for judicial or administrative preventive supervision of the legality of mergers, or where such supervision does not extend to all the legal acts required for a merger, the minutes of the general meetings which decide on the merger and, where appropriate, the merger contract subsequent to such general meetings shall be drawn up and certified in due legal form. In cases where the merger need not be approved by the general meetings of all the merging companies, the draft terms of merger must be drawn up and certified in due legal form.

2. The notary or the authority competent to draw up and certify the document in due legal form must check and certify the existence and validity of the legal acts and formalities required of the company for which he or it is acting and of the draft terms of merger.

Article 17. The laws of the Member States shall determine the date on which a merger takes effect.

Article 18. 1. A merger must be publicized in the manner prescribed by the laws of each Member State, in accordance with Article 3 of Directive 68/151/EEC, in respect of each of the merging companies.

2. The acquiring company may itself carry out the publication formalities relating to the company or companies being acquired.

Article 19. 1. A merger shall have the following consequences *ipso jure* and simultaneously:

(a) the transfer, both as between the company being acquired and the acquiring company and as regards third parties, to the acquiring company of all the assets and liabilities of the company being acquired;
(b) the shareholders of the company being acquired become shareholders of the acquiring company;
(c) the company being acquired ceases to exist.

2. No shares in the acquiring company shall be exchanged for shares in the company being acquired held either:

(a) by the acquiring company itself or through a person acting in his own name but on its behalf; or
(b) by the company being acquired itself or through a person acting in his own name but on its behalf.

3. The foregoing shall not affect the laws of Member States which require the completion of special formalities for the transfer of certain assets, rights and obligations by the acquired company to be effective as against third parties. The acquiring company may carry out these formalities itself; however, the laws of the Member States may permit the company being acquired to continue to carry out these formalities for a limited period which cannot, save in exceptional cases, be fixed at more than six months from the date on which the merger takes effect.

Article 20. The laws of the Member States shall at least lay down rules governing the civil liability towards the shareholders of the company being acquired of the members of the administrative or management bodies of that company in respect of misconduct on the part of members of those bodies in preparing and implementing the merger.

Article 21. The laws of the Member States shall at least lay down rules governing the civil liability towards the shareholders of the company being acquired of the experts responsible for drawing up on behalf of that company the report referred to in Article 10 (1) in respect of misconduct on the part of those experts in the performance of their duties.

Article 22. 1. The laws of the Member States may lay down nullity rules for mergers in accordance with the following conditions only:

(a) nullity must be ordered in a court judgment;

(b) mergers which have taken effect pursuant to Article 17 may be declared void only if there has been no judicial or administrative preventive supervision of their legality, or if they have not been drawn up and certified in due legal form, or if it is shown that the decision of the general meeting is void or voidable under national law;

(c) nullification proceedings may not be initiated more than six months after the date on which the merger becomes effective as against the person alleging nullity or if the situation has been rectified;

(d) where it is possible to remedy a defect liable to render a merger void, the competent court shall grant the companies involved a period of time within which to rectify the situation;

(e) a judgment declaring a merger void shall be published in the manner prescribed by the laws of each Member State in accordance with Article 3 of Directive 68/151/EEC;

(f) where the laws of a Member State permit a third party to challenge such a judgment, he may do so only within six months of publication of the judgment in the manner prescribed by Directive 68/151/EEC;

(g) a judgment declaring a merger void shall not of itself affect the validity of obligations owed by or in relation to the acquiring company which arose before the judgment was published and after the date referred to in Article 17;

(h) companies which have been parties to a merger shall be jointly and severally liable in respect of the obligations of the acquiring company referred to in (g).

2. By way of derogation from paragraph 1 (a), the laws of a Member State may also provide for the nullity of a merger to be ordered by an administrative authority if an appeal against such a decision lies to a court. Sub-paragraphs (b), (d), (e), (f), (g) and (h) shall apply by analogy to the administrative authority. Such nullification proceedings may not be initiated more than six months after the date referred to in Article 17.

3. The foregoing shall not affect the laws of the Member States on the nullity of a merger pronounced following any supervision other than judicial or administrative preventive supervision of legality.

CHAPTER III. MERGER BY FORMATION OF A NEW COMPANY

Article 23. 1. Articles 5, 6, 7 and 9 to 22 shall apply, without prejudice to Articles 11 and 12 of Directive 68/151/EEC, to merger by formation of a new company. For this purpose, 'merging companies' and 'company being acquired' shall mean the companies which will cease to exist, and 'acquiring company' shall mean the new company.

2. Article 5 (2) (a) shall also apply to the new company.

3. The draft terms of merger and, if they are contained in a separate document, the memorandum or draft memorandum of association and the articles or draft articles of association of the new company shall be approved at a general meeting of each of the companies that will cease to exist.

4. The Member States need not apply to the formation of a new company the rules governing the verification of any consideration other than cash which are laid down in Article 10 of Directive 77/91/EEC.

CHAPTER IV. ACQUISITION OF ONE COMPANY BY ANOTHER WHICH HOLDS 90% OR MORE OF ITS SHARES

Article 24. The Member States shall make provision, in respect of companies governed by their laws, for the operation whereby one or more companies are wound up without going into liquidation and transfer all their assets and liabilities to another company which is the holder of all their shares and other securities conferring the right to vote at general meetings. Such operations shall be regulated by the provisions of Chapter II, with the exception of Articles 5 (2) (b), (c) and (d), 9, 10, 11 (1) (d) and (e), 19 (1) (b), 20 and 21.

Article 25. The Member States need not apply Article 7 to the operations specified in Article 24 if the following conditions at least are fulfilled:

(a) the publication provided for in Article 6 must be effected, as regards each company involved in the operation, at least one month before the operation takes effect;

(b) at least one month before the operation takes effect, all shareholders of the acquiring company must be entitled to inspect the documents specified in Article 11 (1) (a), (b) and (c) at the company's registered office. Article 11 (2) and (3) must apply;

(c) Article 8 (c) must apply.

Article 26. The Member States may apply Articles 24 and 25 to operations whereby one or more companies are wound up without going into liquidation and transfer all their assets and liabilities to another company, if all the shares and other securities specified in Article 24 of the company or companies being acquired are held by the acquiring company and/or by persons holding those shares and securities in their own names but on behalf of that company.

Article 27. In cases of merger where one or more companies are acquired by another company which holds 90% or more, but not all, of the shares and other securities of each of those companies the holding of which confers the right to vote at general meetings, the Member States need not require approval of the merger by the general meeting of the acquiring company, provided that the following conditions at least are fulfilled:

(a) the publication provided for in Article 6 must be effected, as regards the acquiring company, at least one month before the date fixed for the general meeting of the company or companies being acquired which is to decide on the draft terms of merger;

(b) at least one month before the date specified in (a), all shareholders of the acquiring company must be entitled to inspect the documents specified in Article 11 (1) (a), (b) and (c) at the company's registered office. Article 11 (2) and (3) must apply;

(c) Article 8 (c) must apply.

Article 28. The Member States need not apply Articles 9 to 11 to a merger within the meaning of Article 27 if the following conditions at least are fulfilled:

(a) the minority shareholders of the company being acquired must be entitled to have their shares acquired by the acquiring company;

(b) if they exercise that right, they must be entitled to receive consideration corresponding to the value of their shares;

(c) in the event of disagreement regarding such consideration, it must be possible for the value of the consideration to be determined by a court.

Article 29. The Member States may apply Articles 27 and 28 to operations whereby one or more companies are wound up without going into liquidation and transfer all their assets and liabilities to another company if 90% or more, but not all, of the shares and other securities referred to in Article 27 of the company or companies being acquired are held by that acquiring company and/or by persons holding those shares and securities in their own names but on behalf of that company.

CHAPTER V. OTHER OPERATIONS TREATED AS MERGERS

Article 30. Where in the case of one of the operations referred to in Article 2 the laws of a Member State permit a cash payment to exceed 10%, Chapters II and III and Articles 27, 28 and 29 shall apply.

Article 31. Where the laws of a Member State permit one of the operations referred to in Articles 2, 24 and 30, without all of the transferring companies thereby ceasing to exist, Chapter II, except for Article 19 (1) (c), Chapter III or Chapter IV shall apply as appropriate.

CHAPTER VI. FINAL PROVISIONS

Article 32.   1. The Member States shall bring into force the laws, regulations and administrative provisions necessary for them to comply with this Directive within three years of its notification. They shall forthwith inform the Commission thereof.

2. However, provision may be made for a delay of five years from the entry into force of the provisions referred to in paragraph 1 for the application of those provisions to unregistered companies in the United Kingdom and Ireland.

3. The Member States need not apply Articles 13, 14 and 15 as regards the holders of convertible debentures and other convertible securities if, at the time when the laws, regulations and administrative provisions referred to in paragraph 1 come into force, the position of these holders in the event of a merger has previously been determined by the conditions of issue.

4. The Member States need not apply this Directive to mergers or to operations treated as mergers for the preparation or execution of which an act or formality required by national law has already been completed when the provisions referred to in paragraph 1 enter into force.

Article 33.   This Directive is addressed to the Member States.
Done at Luxembourg, 9 October 1978.

For the Council, The President, H.-J. Vogel

Fourth Council Directive

of 25 July 1978 based on Article 54 (3) (g) of the Treaty
on the annual accounts of certain types of companies

(78/660/EEC)

The Council of the European Communities,

Having regard to the Treaty establishing the European Economic Community, and in particular Article 54 (3) (g) thereof,

Having regard to the proposal from the Commission,

Having regard to the opinion of the European Parliament,[1]

Having regard to the opinion of the Economic and Social Committee,[2]

Whereas the coordination of national provisions concerning the presentation and content of annual accounts and annual reports, the valuation methods used therein and their publication in respect of certain companies with limited liability is of special importance for the protection of members and third parties;

Whereas simultaneous coordination is necessary in these fields for these forms of company because, on the one hand, these companies' activities frequently extend beyond the frontiers of their national territories and, on the other, they offer no safeguards to third parties beyond the amounts of their net assets; whereas, moreover, the necessity for and the urgency of such coordination have been recognized and confirmed by Article 2 (1) (f) of Directive 68/151/EEC;[3]

Whereas it is necessary, moreover, to establish in the Community minimum equivalent legal requirements as regards the extent of the financial information that should be made available to the public by companies that are in competition with one another;

Whereas annual accounts must give a true and fair view of a company's assets and liabilities, financial position and profit or loss; whereas to this end a mandatory layout must be prescribed for the balance sheet and the profit and loss account and whereas the minimum content of the notes on the accounts and the annual report must be laid down; whereas, however, derogations may be granted for certain companies of minor economic or social importance;

Whereas the different methods for the valuation of assets and liabilities must be coordinated to the extent necessary to ensure that annual accounts disclose comparable and equivalent information.

---

[1] OJ No C 129, 11. 12. 1972, p. 38. [2] OJ No C 39, 7. 6. 1973, p. 31.
[3] OJ No L 65, 14. 3. 1968, p. 8.

Whereas the annual accounts of all companies to which this Directive applies must be published in accordance with Directive 68/151/EEC; whereas, however, certain derogations may likewise be granted in this area for small and medium-sized companies;

Whereas annual accounts must be audited by authorized persons whose minimum qualifications will be the subject of subsequent coordination; whereas only small companies may be relieved of this audit obligation;

Whereas, when a company belongs to a group, it is desirable that group accounts giving a true and fair view of the activities of the group as a whole be published; whereas, however, pending the entry into force of a Council Directive on consolidated accounts, derogations from certain provisions of this Directive are necessary;

Whereas, in order to meet the difficulties arising from the present position regarding legislation in certain Member States, the period allowed for the implementation of certain provisions of this Directive must be longer than the period generally laid down in such cases,

Has adopted this directive:

Article 1. 1. The coordination measures prescribed by this Directive shall apply to the laws, regulations and administrative provisions of the Member States relating to the following types of companies:

— in Germany:
  die Aktiengesellschaft, die Kommanditgesellschaft auf Aktien, die Gesellschaft mit beschränkter Haftung;
— in Belgium:
  la société anonyme/de naamloze vennootschap, la société en commandite par actions/de commanditaire vennootschap op aandelen, la société de personnes à responsabiliteé limitée/de personenvennootschap met beperkte aansprakelijkheid;
— in Denmark:
  aktieselskaber, kommanditaktieselskaber, anpartsselskaber;
— in France:
  la société anonyme, la société en commandite par actions, la société à responsabilité limitée;
— in Ireland:
  public companies limited by shares or by guarantee, private companies limited by shares or by guarantee;
— in Italy:
  la società per azioni, la società in accomandita per azioni, la società a responsabilità limitata;
— in Luxembourg:
  la société anonyme, la société en commandite par actions, la société à responsabilité limitée;

— in the Netherlands:

de naamloze vennootschap, de besloten vennootschap met beperkte aansprakelijkheid;

— in the United Kingdom:

public companies limited by shares or by guarantee, private companies limited by shares or by guarantee.

— in Greece:

ἡ ἀνώνυμος ἑταιρία

ἡ ἑταιρία περιωρισμένης εὐθύνης

ἡ ἑτερόρρυθμος κατά μετοχάς ἑταιρία

— in Spain:

la sociedad anónima, la sociedad comanditaria por acciones, la sociedad de responsabilidad limitada;

— in Portugal:

a sociedade anónima de responsabilidade limitada, a sociedade em comandita por acções, a sociedade por quotas de responsabilidade limitada.

2. Pending subsequent coordination, the Member States need not apply the provisions of this Directive to banks and other financial institutions or to insurance companies.

SECTION I. GENERAL PROVISIONS

Article 2. 1. The annual accounts shall comprise the balance sheet, the profit and loss account and the notes on the accounts. These documents shall constitute a composite whole.

2. They shall be drawn up clearly and in accordance with the provisions of this Directive.

3. The annual accounts shall give a true and fair view of the company's assets, liabilities, financial position and profit or loss.

4. Where the application of the provisions of this Directive would not be sufficient to give a true and fair view within the meaning of paragraph 3, additional information must be given.

5. Where in exceptional cases the application of a provision of this Directive is incompatible with the obligation laid down in paragraph 3, that provision must be departed from in order to give a true and fair view within the meaning of paragraph 3. Any such departure must be disclosed in the notes on the accounts together with an explanation of the reasons for it and a statement of its effect on the assets, liabilities, financial position and profit or loss. The Member States may define the exceptional cases in question and lay down the relevant special rules.

6. The Member States may authorize or require the disclosure in the

annual accounts of other information as well as that which must be disclosed in accordance with this Directive.

SECTION 2.GENERAL PROVISIONS CONCERNING THE BALANCE SHEET AND THE PROFIT AND LOSS ACCOUNT

Article 3. The layout of the balance sheet and of the profit and loss account, particularly as regards the form adopted for their presentation, may not be changed from one financial year to the next. Departures from this principle shall be permitted in exceptional cases. Any such departure must be disclosed in the notes on the accounts together with an explanation of the reasons therefor.

Article 4. 1. In the balance sheet and in the profit and loss account the items prescribed in Articles 9, 10 and 23 to 26 must be shown separately in the order indicated. A more detailed subdivision of the items shall be authorized provided that the layouts are complied with. New items may be added provided that their contents are not covered by any of the items prescribed by the layouts. Such subdivision or new items may be required by the Member States.

2. The layout, nomenclature and terminology of items in the balance sheet and profit and loss account that are preceded by Arabic numerals must be adapted where the special nature of an undertaking so requires. Such adaptations may be required by the Member States of undertakings forming part of a particular economic sector.

3. The balance sheet and profit and loss account items that are preceded by Arabic numerals may be combined where:

(a) they are immaterial in amount for the purposes of Article 2 (3); or
(b) such combination makes for greater clarity, provided that the items so combined are dealt with separately in the notes on the accounts. Such combination may be required by the Member States.

4. In respect of each balance sheet and profit and loss account item the figure relating to the corresponding item for the preceding financial year must be shown. The Member States may provide that, where these figures are not comparable, the figure for the preceding financial year must be adjusted. In any case, non-comparability and any adjustment of the figures must be disclosed in the notes on the accounts, with relevant comments.

5. Save where there is a corresponding item for the preceding financial year within the meaning of paragraph 4, a balance sheet or profit and loss account item for which there is no amount shall not be shown.

Article 5. 1. By way of derogation from Article 4 (1) and (2), the Member

States may prescribe special layouts for the annual accounts of investment companies and of financial holding companies provided that these layouts give a view of these companies equivalent to that provided for in Article 2 (3).

2. For the purposes of this Directive, 'investment companies' shall mean only:

(a) those companies the sole object of which is to invest their funds in various securities, real property and other assets with the sole aim of spreading investment risks and giving their shareholders the benefit of the results of the management of their assets:

(b) those companies associated with investment companies with fixed capital if the sole object of the companies so associated is to acquire fully paid shares issued by those investment companies without prejudice to the provisions of Article 20 (1) (h) of Directive 77/91/EEC.[1]

3. For the purposes of this Directive, 'financial holding companies' shall mean only those companies the sole object of which is to acquire holdings in other undertakings, and to manage such holdings and turn them to profit, without involving themselves directly or indirectly in the management of those undertakings, the aforegoing without prejudice to their rights as a shareholders. The limitations imposed on the activities of these companies must be such that compliance with them can be supervised by an administrative or judicial authority.

Article 6.   The Member States may authorize or require adaptation of the layout of the balance sheet and profit and loss account in order to include the appropriation of profit or the treatment of loss.

Article 7.   Any set-off between asset and liability items, or between income and expenditure items, shall be prohibited.

SECTION 3. LAYOUT OF THE BALANCE SHEET

Article 8.   For the presentation of the balance sheet, the Member States shall prescribe one or both of the layouts prescribed by Articles 9 and 10. If a Member State prescribes both, it may allow companies to choose between them.

Article 9.

Assets

A. Subscribed capital unpaid   of which there has been called (unless national law provides that called-up capital be shown under 'Liabilities'. In

---

[1] OJ No L 26, 31. 1. 1977, p. 1.

that case, the part of the capital called but not yet paid must appear as an asset either under A or under D (II) (5)).

B. Formation expenses as defined by national law, and in so far as national law permits their being shown as an asset. National law may also provide for formation expenses to be shown as the first item under 'Intangible assets'.

C. Fixed assets

I. *Intangible assets*

1. Costs of research and development, in so far as national law permits their being shown as assets.
2. Concessions, patents, licences, trade marks and similar rights and assets, if they were:

(a) acquired for valuable consideration and need not be shown under C (I) (3); or
(b) created by the undertaking itself, in so far as national law permits their being shown as assets.

3. Goodwill, to the extent that it was acquired for valuable consideration.
4. Payments on account.

II. *Tangible assets*

1. Land and buildings.
2. Plant and machinery.
3. Other fixtures and fittings, tools and equipment.
4. Payments on account and tangible assets in course of construction.

III. *Financial assets*

1. Shares in affiliated undertakings.
2. Loans to affiliated undertakings.
3. Participating interests.
4. Loans to undertakings with which the company is linked by virtue of participating interests.
5. Investments held as fixed assets.
6. Other loans.
7. Own shares (with an indication of their nominal value or, in the absence of a nominal value, their accounting par value) to the extent that national law permits their being shown in the balance sheet.

D. Current Assets

I. *Stocks*

1. Raw materials and consumables.
2. Work in progress.
3. Finished goods and goods for resale.
4. Payments on account.

II. *Debtors*

(Amounts becoming due and payable after more than one year must be shown separately for each item.)

1. Trade debtors.
2. Amounts owned by affiliated undertakings.
3. Amounts owed by undertakings with which the company is linked by virtue of participating interests.
4. Other debtors.
5. Subscribed capital called but not paid (unless national law provides that called-up capital be shown as an asset under A).
6. Prepayments and accrued income (unless national law provides for such items to be shown as an asset under E).

III. *Investments*

1. Shares in affiliated undertakings.
2. Own shares (with an indication of their nominal value or, in the absence of a nominal value, their accounting par value) to the extent that national law permits their being shown in the balance sheet.
3. Other investments

IV *Cash at bank and in hand*

E. Prepayments and accrued income   (unless national law provides for such items to be shown as an asset under D (II) (6)).

F. Loss for the financial year   (unless national law provides for it to be shown under A (VI) under 'Liabilities').

Liabilities

A. Capital and reserves

I. *Subscribed capital*

(unless national law provides for called-up capital to be shown under this item. In that case, the amounts of subscribed capital and paid-up capital must be shown separately).

II. *Share premium account*

III. *Revaluation reserve*

IV. *Reserves*

1. Legal reserve, in so far as national law requires such a reserve.
2. Reserve for own shares, in so far as national law requires such a reserve, without prejudice to Article 22 (1) (b) of Directive 77/91/EEC.
3. Reserves provided for by the articles of association.
4. Other reserves.

V. *Profit or loss brought forward*

VI. *Profit or loss for the financial year*
(unless national law requires that this item be shown under F under 'Assets' or under E under 'Liabilities').

B. Provisions for liabilities and charges
1. Provisions for pensions and similar obligations.
2. Provisions for taxation.
3. Other provisions.

C. Creditors (Amounts becoming due and payable within one year and amounts becoming due and payable after more than one year must be shown separately for each item and for the aggregate of these items.)
1. Debenture loans, showing convertible loans separately.
2. Amounts owed to credit institutions.
3. Payments received on account of orders in so far as they are not shown separately as deductions from stocks.
4. Trade creditors.
5. Bills of exchange payable.
6. Amounts owed to affiliated undertakings.
7. Amounts owed to undertakings with which the company is linked by virtue of participating interests.
8. Other creditors including tax and social security.
9. Accruals and deferred income (unless national law provides for such items to be shown under D under 'Liabilities').

D. Accruals and deferred income (unless national law provides for such items to be shown under C (9) under 'Liabilities').

E. Profit for the financial year (unless national law provides for it to be shown under A (VI) under 'Liabilities').

Article 10.

A. Subscribed capital unpaid of which there has been called (unless national law provides that called-up capital be shown under L. In that case, the part of the capital called but not yet paid must appear either under A or under D (II) (5)).

B. Formation expenses as defined by national law, and in so far as national law permits their being shown as an asset. National law may also provide for formation expenses to be shown as the first item under 'Intangible assets'.

C. Fixed assets
I. *Intangible assets*
1. Costs of research and development, in so far as national law permits their being shown as assets.

2. Concessions, patents, licences, trade marks and similar rights and assets, if they were:
   (a) acquired for valuable consideration and need not be shown under C (I) (3); or
   (b) created by the undertaking itself, in so far as national law permits their being shown as assets.
3. Goodwill, to the extent that it was acquired for valuable consideration.
4. Payments on account.

II. *Tangible assets*
1. Land and buildings.
2. Plant and machinery.
3. Other fixtures and fittings, tools and equipment.
4. Payments on account and tangible assets in course of construction.

III. *Financial assets*
1. Shares in affiliated undertakings.
2. Loans to affiliated undertakings.
3. Participating interests.
4. Loans to undertakings with which the company is linked by virtue of participating interests.
5. Investments held as fixed assets.
6. Other loans.
7. Own shares (with an indication of their nominal value or, in the absence of a nominal value, their accounting par value) to the extent that national law permits their being shown in the balance sheet.

D. Current assets
I. *Stocks*
1. Raw materials and consumables.
2. Work in progress.
3. Finished goods and goods for resale.
4. Payments on account.

II. *Debtors*
(amounts becoming due and payable after more than one year must be shown separately for each item.)
1. Trade debtors.
2. Amounts owed by affiliated undertakings.
3. Amounts owed by undertakings with which the company is linked by virtue of participating interests.
4. Other debtors.
5. Subscribed capital called but not paid (unless national law provides that called-up capital be shown under A).

6. Prepayments and accrued income (unless national law provides that such items be shown under E).

III. *Investments*
1. Shares in affiliated undertakings.
2. Own shares (with an indication of their nominal value or, in the absence of a nominal value, their accounting par value) to the extent that national law permits their being shown in the balance sheet.
3. Other investments.

IV. *Cash at bank and in hand*

E. Prepayments and accrued income   (unless national law provides for such items to be shown under D (II) (6)).

F. Creditors: amounts becoming due and payable within one year
1. Debenture loans, showing convertible loans separately.
2. Amounts owed to credit institutions.
3. Payments received on account of orders in so far as they are not shown separately as deductions from stocks.
4. Trade creditors.
5. Bills of exchange payable.
6. Amounts owed to affiliated undertakings.
7. Amounts owed to undertakings with which the company is linked by virtue of participating interests.
8. Other creditors including tax and social security.
9. Accruals and deferred income (unless national law provides for such items to be shown under K).

G. Net current assets/liabilities   (taking into account prepayments and accrued income when shown under E and accruals and deferred income when shown under K).

H. Total assets less current liabilities

I. Creditors: amounts becoming due and payable after more than one year
1. Debenture loans, showing convertible loans separately.
2. Amounts owed to credit institutions.
3. Payments received on account of orders in so far as they are not shown separately as deductions from stocks.
4. Trade creditors.
5. Bills of exchange payable.
6. Amounts owed to affiliated undertakings.
7. Amounts owed to undertakings with which the company is linked by virtue of participating interests.
8. Other creditors including tax and social security

9. Accruals and deferred income (unless national law provides for such items to be shown under K).

J. Provisions for liabilities and charges
1. Provisions for pensions and similar obligations.
2. Provisions for taxation.
3. Other provisions.

K. Accruals and deferred income   (unless national law provides for such items to be shown under F (9) or I (9) or both).

L. Capital and reserves
I. *Subscribed capital*
(unless national law provides for called-up capital to be shown under this item. In that case, the amounts of subscribed capital and paid-up capital must be shown separately).

II. *Share premium account*

III. *Revaluation reserve*

IV. *Reserves*
1. Legal reserve, in so far as national law requires such a reserve.
2. Reserve for own shares, in so far as national law requires such a reserve, without prejudice to Article 22 (1) (b) of Directive 77/91/EEC.
3. Reserves provided for by the articles of association.
4. Other reserves.

V. *Profit or loss brought forward*

VI. *Profit or loss for the financial year*

Article 11.   The Member States may permit companies which on their balance sheet dates do not exceed the limits of two of the three following criteria:
— balance sheet total: 1 000 000 EUA,
— net turnover: 2 000 000 EUA.
— average number of employees during the financial year: 50
to draw up abridged balance sheets showing only those items preceded by letters and roman numerals in Articles 9 and 10, disclosing separately the information required in brackets in D (II) under 'Assets' and C under 'Liabilities' in Article 9 and in D (II) in Article 10, but in total for each.

Article 12.   1. Where on its balance sheet date, a company exceeds or ceases to exceed the limits of two of the three criteria indicated in Article 11, that fact shall affect the application of the derogation provided for in that Article only if it occurs in two consecutive financial years.

2. For the purposes of translation into national currencies, the amounts in European units of account specified in Article 11 may be increased by not more than 10%.

3. The balance sheet total referred to in Article 11 shall consist of the assets in A to E under 'Assets' in the layout prescribed in Article 9 or those in A to E in the layout prescribed in Article 10.

Article 13. 1. Where an asset or liability relates to more than one layout item, its relationship to other items must be disclosed either under the item where it appears or in the notes on the accounts, if such disclosure is essential to the comprehension of the annual accounts.

2. Own shares and shares in affiliated undertakings may be shown only under the items prescribed for that purpose.

Article 14. All commitments by way of guarantee of any kind must, if there is no obligation to show them as liabilities, be clearly set out at the foot of the balance sheet or in the notes on the accounts, and a distinction made between the various types of guarantee which national law recognizes; specific disclosure must be made of any valuable security which has been provided. Commitments of this kind existing in respect of affiliated under-takings must be shown separately.

SECTION 4. SPECIAL PROVISIONS RELATING TO CERTAIN BALANCE SHEET ITEMS

Article 15. 1. Whether particular assets are to be shown as fixed assets or current assets shall depend upon the purpose for which they are intended.

2. Fixed assets shall comprise those assets which are intended for use on a continuing basis for the purposes of the undertaking's activities.

3. (a) Movements in the various fixed asset items shall be shown in the balance sheet or in the notes on the accounts. To this end there shall be shown separately, starting with the purchase price or production cost, for each fixed asset item, on the one hand, the additions, disposals and transfers during the financial year and, on the other, the cumulative value adjustments at the balance sheet date and the rectifications made during the financial year to the value adjustments of previous financial years. Value adjustments shall be shown either in the balance sheet, as clear deductions from the relevant items, or in the notes on the accounts.

(b) If, when annual accounts are drawn up in accordance with this

Directive for the first time, the purchase price or production cost of a fixed asset cannot be determined without undue expense or delay, the residual value at the beginning of the financial year may be treated as the purchase price or production cost. Any application of this provision must be disclosed in the notes on the accounts.

(c) Where Article 33 is applied, the movements in the varius fixed asset items referred to in subparagraph (a) of this paragraph shall be shown starting with the purchase price or production cost resulting from revaluation.

4. Paragraph 3 (a) and (b) shall apply to the presentation of 'Formation expenses'.

Article 16. Rights to immovables and other similar rights as defined by national law must be shown under 'Land and buildings'.

Article 17. For the purposes of this Directive, 'participating interest' shall mean rights in the capital of other undertakings, whether or not represented by certificates, which, by creating a durable link with those undertakings, are intended to contribute to the company's activities. The holding of part of the capital of another company shall be presumed to constitute a participating interest where it exceeds a percentage fixed by the Member States which may not exceed 20%.

Article 18. Expenditure incurred during the financial year but relating to a subsequent financial year, together with any income which, though relating to the financial year in question, is not due until after its expiry must be shown under 'Prepayments and accrued income'. The Member States may, however, provide that such income shall be included in 'Debtors'. Where such income is material, it must be disclosed in the notes on the accounts.

Article 19. Value adjustments shall comprise all adjustments intended to take account of reductions in the values of individual assets established at the balance sheet date whether that reduction is final or not.

Article 20. 1. Provisions for liabilities and charges are intended to cover losses or debts the nature of which is clearly defined and which at the date of the balance sheet are either likely to be incurred, or certain to be incurred but uncertain as to amount or as to the date on which they will arise.

2. The Member States may also authorize the creation of provisions intended to cover charges which have their origin in the financial year under review or in a previous financial year, the nature of which is clearly defined

and which at the date of the balance sheet are either likely to be incurred, or certain to be incurred but uncertain as to amount or as to the date on which they will arise.

3. Provisions for liabilities and charges may not be used to adjust the values of assets.

Article 21.   Income receivable before the balance sheet date but relating to a subsequent financial year, together with any charges which, though relating to the financial year in question, will be paid only in the course of a subsequent financial year, must be shown under 'Accruals and deferred income'. The Member States may, however, provide that such charges shall be included in 'Creditors'. Where such charges are material, they must be disclosed in the notes on the accounts.

SECTION 5. LAYOUT OF THE PROFIT AND LOSS ACCOUNT

Article 22.   For the presentation of the profit and loss account, the Member States shall prescribe one or more of the layouts provided for in Articles 23 to 26. If a Member State prescribes more than one layout, it may allow companies to choose from among them.

Article 23.   1. Net turnover.

2. Variation in stocks of finished goods and in work in progress.

3. Work performed by the undertaking for its own purposes and capitalized.

4. Other operating income.

5.

(a) Raw materials and consumables.

(b) other external charges.

6. Staff costs:

(a) wages and salaries;

(b) social security costs, with a separate indication of those relating to pensions.

7.

(a) Value adjustments in respect of formation expenses and of tangible and intangible fixed assets.

(b) Value adjustments in respect of current assets, to the extent that they exceed the amount of value adjustments which are normal in the undertaking concerned.

8. Other operating charges.

9. Income from participating interests, with a separate indication of that derived from affiliated undertakings.

10. Income from other investments and loans forming part of the fixed assets, with a separate indication of that derived from affiliated undertakings.

11. Other interest receivable and similar income, with a separate indication of that derived from affiliated undertakings.

12. Value adjustments in respect of financial assets and of investments held as current assets.

13. Interest payable and similar charges, with a separate indication of those concerning affiliated undertakings.

14. Tax on profit or loss on ordinary activities.

15. Profit or loss on ordinary activities after taxation.

16. Extraordinary income.

17. Extraordinary charges.

18. Extraordinary profit or loss.

19. Tax on extraordinary profit or loss.

20. Other taxes not shown under the above items.

21. Profit or loss for the financial year.

Article 24.

A. Charges

1. Reduction in stocks of finished goods and in work in progress:

2.

(a) raw materials and consumables;

(b) other external charges.

3. Staff costs:

(a) wages and salaries;

(b) social security costs, with a separate indication of those relating to pensions.

4.

(a) Value adjustments in respect of formation expenses and of tangible and intangible fixed assets.

(b) Value adjustments in respect of current assets, to the extent that they exceed the amount of value adjustments which are normal in the undertaking concerned.

5. Other operating charges.

6. Value adjustments in respect of financial assets and of investments held as current assets.

7. Interest payable and similar charges, with a separate indication of those concerning affiliated undertakings.

8. Tax on profit or loss on ordinary activities.

9. Profit or loss on ordinary activities after taxation.

10. Extraordinary charges.

11. Tax on extraordinary profit or loss.

12. Other taxes not shown under the above items.

13. Profit or loss for the financial year.

B. Income

1. Net turnover.

2. Increase in stocks of finished goods and in work in progress.

3. Work performed by the undertaking for its own purposes and capitalized.

4. Other operating income.

5. Income from participating interests, with a separate indication of that derived from affiliated undertakings.

6. Income from other investments and loans forming part of the fixed assets, with a separate indication of that derived from affiliated undertakings.

7. Other interest receivable and similar income, with a separate indication of that derived from affiliated undertakings.

8. Profit or loss on ordinary activities after taxation.

9. Extraordinary income.

10. Profit or loss for the financial year.

Article 25.   1. Net turnover.

2. Cost of sales (including value adjustments).

3. Gross profit or loss.

4. Distribution costs (including value adjustments).

5. Administrative expenses (including value adjustments).

6. Other operating income.

7. Income from participating interests, with a separate indication of that derived from affiliated undertakings.

8. Income from other investments and loans forming part of the fixed assets, with a separate indication of that derived from affiliated undertakings.

9. Other interest receivable and similar income, with a separate indication of that derived from affiliated undertakings.

10. Value adjustments in respect of financial assets and of investments held as current assets.

11. Interest payable and similar charges, with a separate indication of those concerning affiliated undertakings.

12. Tax on profit or loss on ordinary activities.

13. Profits or loss on ordinary activities after taxation.

14. Extraordinary income.

15. Extraordinary charges.

16. Extraordinary profit or loss.

17. Tax on extraordinary profit or loss.

18. Other taxes not shown under the above items.

19. Profit or loss for the financial year.

Article 26.

A. Charges

1. Cost of sales (including value adjustments).

2. Distribution costs (including value adjustments).

3. Administrative expenses (including value adjustments).

4. Value adjustments in respect of financial assets and of investments held as current assets.

5. Interest payable and similar charges, with a separate indication of those concerning affiliated undertakings.

6. Tax on profit or loss on ordinary activities.

7. Profit or loss on ordinary activities after taxation.

8. Extraordinary charges.

9. Tax on extraordinary profit or loss.

10. Other taxes not shown under the above items.

11. Profit or loss for the financial year.

B. Income

1. Net turnover.

2. Other operating income.

3. Income from participating interests, with a separate indication of that derived from affiliated undertakings.

4. Income from other investments and loans forming part of the fixed assets, with a separate indication of that derived from affiliated undertakings.

5. Other interest receivable and similar income, with a separate indication of that derived from affiliated undertakings.

6. Profit or loss on ordinary activities after taxation.

7. Extraordinary income.

8. Profit or loss for the financial year.

Article 27. The Member States may permit companies which on their balance sheet dates do not exceed the limits of two of the three following criteria:

— balance sheet total: 4 million EUA,

— net turnover: 8 million EUA,

— average number of employees during the financial year: 250

to adopt layouts different from those prescribed in Articles 23 to 26 within the following limits:

(a) in Article 23: 1 to 5 inclusive may be combined under one item called 'Gross profit or loss';
(b) in Article 24: A (1), A (2) and B (1) to B (4) inclusive may be combined under one item called 'Gross profit or loss';
(c) in Article 25: (1), (2), (3) and (6) may be combined under one item called 'Gross profit or loss';
(d) in Article 26, A (1) and B (2) may be combined under one item called 'Gross profit or loss'.

Article 12 shall apply.

SECTION 6. SPECIAL PROVISIONS RELATING TO CERTAIN ITEMS IN THE PROFIT AND LOSS ACCOUNT

Article 28.   The net turnover shall comprise the amounts derived from the sale of products and the provision of services falling within the company's ordinary activities, after deduction of sales rebates and of value added tax and other taxes directly linked to the turnover.

Article 29.   1. Income and charges that arise otherwise than in the course of the company's ordinary activities must be shown under 'Extraordinary income and extraordinary charges'.

2. Unless the income and charges referred to in paragraph 1 are immaterial for the assessment of the results, explanations of their amount and nature must be given in the notes on the accounts. The same shall apply to income and charges relating to another financial year.

Article 30.   The Member States may permit taxes on the profit or loss on ordinary activities and taxes on the extraordinary profit or loss to be shown in total as one item in the profit and loss account before 'Other taxes not shown under the above items'. In that case, 'Profit or loss on ordinary activities after taxation' shall be omitted from the layouts prescribed in Articles 23 to 26.

Where this derogation is applied, companies must disclose in the notes on the accounts the extent to which the taxes on the profit or loss affect the profit or loss on ordinary activities and the 'Extraordinary profit or loss'.

SECTION 7. VALUATION RULES

Article 31.   1. The Member States shall ensure that the items shown in the annual accounts are valued in accordance with the following general principles:

(a) the company must be presumed to be carrying on its business as a going concern;
(b) the methods of valuation must be applied consistently from one financial year to another;
(c) valuation must be made on a prudent basis, and in particular:
    (aa) only profits made at the balance sheet date may be included,
    (bb) account must be taken of all foreseeable liabilities and potential losses arising in the course of the financial year concerned or of a previous one, even if such liabilities or losses become apparent only between the date of the balance sheet and the date on which it is drawn up,
    (cc) account must be taken of all depreciation, whether the result of the financial year is a loss or a profit;
(d) account must be taken of income and charges relating to the financial year, irrespective of the date of receipt or payment of such income or charges;
(e) the components of asset and liability items must be valued separately;
(f) the opening balance sheet for each financial year must correspond to the closing balance sheet for the preceding financial year.

2. Departures from these general principles shall be permitted in exceptional cases. Any such departures must be disclosed in the notes on the accounts and the reasons for them given together with an assessment of their effect on the assets, liabilities, financial position and profit or loss.

Article 32. The items shown in the annual accounts shall be valued in accordance with Articles 34 to 42, which are based on the principle of purchase price or production cost.

Article 33. 1. The Member States may declare to the Commission that they reserve the power, by way of derogation from Article 32 and pending subsequent coordination, to permit or require in respect of all companies or any classes of companies:

(a) valuation by the replacement value method for tangible fixed assets with limited useful economic lives and for stocks;
(b) valuation by methods other than that provided for in (a) which are designed to take account of inflation for the items shown in annual accounts, including capital and reserves;
(c) revaluation of tangible fixed assets and financial fixed assets.

Where national law provides for valuation methods as indicated in (a), (b) and (c), it must define their content and limits and the rules for their application.

The application of any such method, the balance sheet and profit and loss account items concerned and the method by which the values shown are calculated shall be disclosed in the notes on the accounts.

2.

(a) Where paragraph 1 is applied, the amount of the difference between valuation by the method used and valuation in accordance with the general rule laid down in Article 32 must be entered in the revaluation reserve under 'Liabilities'. The treatment of this item for taxation purposes must be explained either in the balance sheet or in the notes on the accounts.

For purposes of the application of the last subparagraph of paragraph 1, companies shall, whenever the amount of the reserve has been changed in the course of the financial year, publish in the notes on the accounts *inter alia* a table showing:

— the amount of the revaluation reserve at the beginning of the financial year,
— the revaluation differences transferred to the revaluation reserve during the financial year,
— the amounts capitalized or otherwise transferred from the revaluation reserve during the financial year, the nature of any such transfer being disclosed,
— the amount of the revaluation reserve at the end of the financial year.

(b) The revaluation reserve may be capitalized in whole or in part at any time.

(c) The revaluation reserve must be reduced to the extent that the amounts transferred thereto are no longer necessary for the implementation of the valuation method used and the achievement of its purpose.

The Member States may lay down rules governing the application of the revaluation reserve, provided that transfers to the profit and loss account from the revaluation reserve may be made only to the extent that the amounts transferred have been entered as charges in the profit and loss account or reflect increases in value which have been actually realized. These amounts must be disclosed separately in the profit and loss account. No part of the revaluation reserve may be distributed, either directly or indirectly, unless it represents gains actually realized.

(d) Save as provided under (b) and (c) the revaluation reserve may not be reduced.

3. Value adjustments shall be calculated each year on the basis of the value adopted for the financial year in question, save that by way of derogation from Articles 4 and 22, the Member States may permit or require

that only the amount of the value adjustments arising as a result of the application of the general rule laid down in Article 32 be shown under the relevant items in the layouts prescribed in Articles 23 to 26 and that the difference arising as a result of the valuation method adopted under this Article be shown separately in the layouts. Furthermore, Articles 34 to 42 shall apply *mutatis mutandis*.

4. Where paragraph 1 is applied, the following must be disclosed, either in the balance sheet or in the notes on the accounts, separately for each balance sheet item as provided for in the layouts prescribed in Articles 9 and 10, except for stocks, either:

(a) the amount at the balance sheet date of the valuation made in accordance with the general rule laid down in Article 32 and the amount of the cumulative value adjustments; or

(b) the amount at the balance sheet date of the difference between the valuation made in accordance with this Article and that resulting from the application of Article 32 and, where appropriate, the cumulative amount of the additional value adjustments.

5. Without prejudice to Article 52 the Council shall, on a proposal from the Commission and within seven years of the notification of this Directive, examine and, where necessary, amend this Article in the light of economic and monetary trends in the Community.

Article 34.   1.

(a) Where national law authorizes the inclusion of formation expenses under 'Assets', they must be written off within a maximum period of five years.

(b) In so far as formation expenses have not been completely written off, no distribution of profits shall take place unless the amount of the reserves available for distribution and profits brought forward is at least equal to that of the expenses not written off.

2. The amounts entered under 'Formation expenses' must be explained in the notes on the accounts.

Article 35.   1.

(a) Fixed assets must be valued at purchase price or production cost, without prejudice to (b) and (c) below.

(b) The purchase price or production cost of fixed assets with limited useful economic lives must be reduced by value adjustments calculated to write off the value of such assets systematically over their useful economic lives.

(c) (aa) Value adjustments may be made in respect of financial fixed assets, so that they are valued at the lower figure to be attributed to them at the balance sheet date.

(bb) Value adjustments must be made in respect of fixed assets, whether their useful economic lives are limited or not, so that they are valued at the lower figure to be attributed to them at the balance sheet date if it is expected that the reduction in their value will be permanent.

(cc) The value adjustments referred to in (aa) and (bb) must be charged to the profit and loss account and disclosed separately in the notes on the accounts if they have not been shown separately in the profit and loss account.

(dd) Valuation at the lower of the values provided for in (aa) and (bb) may not be continued if the reasons for which the value adjustments were made have ceased to apply.

(d) If fixed assets are the subject of exceptional value adjustments for taxation purposes alone, the amount of the adjustments and the reasons for making them shall be indicated in the notes on the accounts.

2. The purchase price shall be calculated by adding to the price paid the expenses incidental thereto.

3.

(a) The production cost shall be calculated by adding to the purchasing price of the raw materials and consumables the costs directly attributable to the product in question.

(b) A reasonable proportion of the costs which are only indirectly attributable to the product in question may be added into the production costs to the extent that they relate to the period of production.

4. Interest on capital borrowed to finance the production of fixed assets may be included in the production costs to the extent that it relates to the period of production. In that event, the inclusion of such interest under 'Assets' must be disclosed in the notes on the accounts.

Article 36. By way of derogation from Article 35 (1) (c) (cc), the Member States may allow investment companies within the meaning of Article 5 (2) to set off value adjustments to investments directly against 'Capital and reserves'. The amounts in question must be shown separately under 'Liabilities' in the balance sheet.

Article 37. 1. Article 34 shall apply to costs of research and development. In exceptional cases, however, the Member States may permit derogations from Article 34 (1) (a). In that case, they may also provide for derogations from Article 34 (1) (b). Such derogations and the reasons for them must be disclosed in the notes on the accounts.

2. Article 34 (1) (a) shall apply to goodwill. The Member States may, however, permit companies to write goodwill off systematically over a limited period exceeding five years provided that this period does not exceed the useful economic life of the asset and is disclosed in the notes on the accounts together with the supporting reasons therefore.

Article 38.   Tangible fixed assets, raw materials and consumables which are constantly being replaced and the overall value of which is of secondary importance to the undertaking may be shown under 'Assets' at a fixed quantity and value, if the quantity, value and composition thereof do not vary materially.

Article 39.   1.

(a) Current assets must be valued at purchase price or production cost, without prejudice to (b) and (c) below.
(b) Value adjustments shall be made in respect of current assets with a view to showing them at the lower market value or, in particular circumstances, another lower value to be attributed to them at the balance sheet date.
(c) The Member States may permit exceptional value adjustments where, on the basis of a reasonable commercial assessment, these are necessary if the valuation of these items is not to be modified in the near future because of fluctuations in value. The amount of these value adjustments must be disclosed separately in the profit and loss account or in the notes on the accounts.
(d) Valuation at the lower value provided for in (b) and (c) may not be continued if the reasons for which the value adjustments were made have ceased to apply.
(e) If current assets are the subject of exceptional value adjustments for taxation purposes alone, the amount of the adjustments and the reasons for making them must be disclosed in the notes on the accounts.

2. The definitions of purchase price and of production cost given in Article 35 (2) and (3) shall apply. The Member States may also apply Article 35 (4). Distribution costs may not be included in production costs.

Article 40.   1. The Member States may permit the purchase price or production cost of stocks of goods of the same category and all fungible items including investments to be calculated either on the basis of weighted average prices or by the 'first in, first out' (FIFO) method, the 'last in, first out' (LIFO) method, or some similar method.

2. Where the value shown in the balance sheet, following application of the methods of calculation specified in paragraph 1, differs materially, at the

balance sheet date, from the value on the basis of the last known market value prior to the balance sheet date, the amount of that difference must be disclosed in total by category in the notes on the accounts.

Article 41. 1. Where the amount repayable on account of any debt is greater than the amount received, the difference may be shown as an asset. It must be shown separately in the balance sheet or in the notes on the accounts.

2. The amount of this difference must be written off by a reasonable amount each year and completely written off no later than the time of repayment of the debt.

Article 42. Provisions for liabilities and charges may not exceed in amount the sums which are necessary.

The provisions shown in the balance sheet under 'Other provisions' must be disclosed in the notes on the accounts if they are material.

SECTION 8. CONTENTS OF THE NOTES ON THE ACCOUNTS

Article 43. 1. In addition to the information required under other provisions of this Directive, the notes on the accounts must set out information in respect of the following matters at least:

(1) the valuation methods applied to the various items in the annual accounts, and the methods employed in calculating the value adjustments. For items included in the annual accounts which are or were originally expressed in foreign currency, the bases of conversion used to express them in local currency must be disclosed;

(2) the name and registered office of each of the undertakings in which the company, either itself or through a person acting in his own name but on the company's behalf, holds at least a percentage of the capital which the Member States cannot fix at more than 20%, showing the proportion of the capital held, the amount of capital and reserves, and the profit or loss for the latest financial year of the undertaking concerned for which accounts have been adopted. This information may be omitted where for the purposes of Article 2 (3) it is of negligible importance only. The information concerning capital and reserves and the profit or loss may also be omitted where the undertaking concerned does not publish its balance sheet and less than 50% of its capital is held (directly or indirectly) by the company;

(3) the number and the nominal value or, in the absence of a nominal value, the accounting par value of the shares subscribed during the financial year within the limits of an authorized capital, without prejudice as far as the

amount of this capital is concerned to Article 2 (1) (e) of Directive 68/151/EEC or to Article 2 (c) of Directive 77/91/EEC;

(4) where there is more than one class of shares, the number and the nominal value or, in the absence of a nominal value, the accounting par value for each class;

(5) the existence of any participation certificates, convertible debentures or similar securities or rights, with an indication of their number and the rights they confer;

(6) amounts owed by the company becoming due and payable after more than five years as well as the company's entire debts covered by valuable security furnished by the company with an indication of the nature and form of the security. This information must be disclosed separately for each creditors item, as provided for in the layouts prescribed in Articles 9 and 10;

(7) the total amount of any financial commitments that are not included in the balance sheet, in so far as this information is of assistance in assessing the financial position. Any commitments concerning pensions and affiliated undertakings must be disclosed separately;

(8) the net turnover within the meaning of Article 28, broken down by categories of activity and into geographical markets in so far as, taking account of the manner in which the sale of products and the provision of services falling within the company's ordinary activities are organized, these categories and markets differ substantially from one another;

(9) the average number of persons employed during the financial year, broken down by categories and, if they are not disclosed separately in the profit and loss account, the staff costs relating to the financial year, broken down as provided for in Article 23 (6);

(10) the extent to which the calculation of the profit or loss for the financial year has been affected by a valuation of the items which, by way of derogation from the principles enunciated in Articles 31 and 34 to 42, was made in the financial year in question or in an earlier financial year with a view to obtaining tax relief. Where the influence of such a valuation on future tax charges is material, details must be disclosed;

(11) the difference between the tax charged for the financial year and for earlier financial years and the amount of tax payable in respect of those years, provided that this difference is material for purposes of future taxation. This amount may also be disclosed in the balance sheet as a cumulative amount under a separate item with an appropriate heading;

(12) the amount of the emoluments granted in respect of the financial year to the members of the administrative, managerial and supervisory bodies by reason of their responsibilities, and any commitments arising or entered into in respect of retirement pensions for former members of those bodies, with an indication of the total for each category;

(13) the amount of advances and credits granted to the members of the

administrative, managerial and supervisory bodies, with indications of the interest rates, main conditions and any amounts repaid, as well as commitments entered into on their behalf by way of guarantees of any kind, with an indication of the total for each category.

2. Pending subsequent coordination, the Member States need not apply paragraph 1 (2) to financial holding companies within the meaning of Article 5 (3).

Article 44. The Member States may permit the companies referred to in Article 11 to draw up abridged notes on their accounts without the information required in Article 43 (1) (5) to (12). However, the notes must disclose the information specified in Article 43 (1) (6) in total for all the items concerned.

Article 12 shall apply.

Article 45. 1. The Member States may allow the disclosures prescribed in Article 43 (1) (2):

(a) to take the form of a statement deposited in accordance with Article 3 (1) and (2) of Directive 68/151/EEC; this must be disclosed in the notes on the accounts;

(b) to be omitted when their nature is such that they would be seriously prejudicial to any of the undertakings to which Article 43 (1) (2) relates. The Member States may make such omissions subject to prior administrative or judicial authorization. Any such omission must be disclosed in the notes on the accounts.

2. Paragraph 1 (b) shall also apply to the information prescribed by Article 43 (1) (8).

The Member States may permit the companies referred to in Article 27 to omit the disclosures prescribed by Article 43 (1) (8). Article 12 shall apply.

SECTION 9. CONTENTS OF THE ANNUAL REPORT

Article 46. 1. The annual report must include at least a fair review of the development of the company's business and of its position.

2. The report shall also give an indication of:

(a) any important events that have occurred since the end of the financial year;

(b) the company's likely future development;

(c) activities in the field of research and development;

(d) the information concerning acquisitions of own shares prescribed by Article 22 (2) of Directive 77/91/EEC.

SECTION 10. PUBLICATION

Article 47.   1. The annual accounts, duly approved, and the annual report, together with the opinion submitted by the person responsible for auditing the accounts, shall be published as laid down by the laws of each Member State in accordance with Article 3 of Directive 68/151/EEC.

The laws of a Member State may, however, permit the annual report not to be published as stipulated above. In that case, it shall be made available to the public at the company's registered office in the Member State concerned. It must be possible to obtain a copy of all or part of any such report free of charge upon request.

2. By way of derogation from paragraph 1, the Member States may permit the companies referred to in Article 11 to publish:

(a) abridged balance sheets showing only those items preceded by letters and roman numerals in Articles 9 and 10, disclosing separately the information required in brackets in D (II) under 'Assets' and C under 'Liabilities' in Article 9 and in D (II) in Article 10, but in total for all the items concerned; and

(b) abridged notes on their accounts without the explanations required in Article 43 (1) (5) to (12). However, the notes must disclose the information specified in Article 43 (1) (6) in total for all the items concerned.

Article 12 shall apply.

In addition, the Member States may relieve such companies from the obligation to publish their profit and loss accounts and annual reports and the opinions of the persons responsible for auditing the accounts.

3. The Member States may permit the companies mentioned in Article 27 to publish:

(a) abridged balance sheets showing only those items preceded by letters and roman numerals in Articles 9 and 10 disclosing separately, either in the balance sheet or in the notes on the accounts:

— C (I) (3), C (II) (1), (2), (3) and (4), C (III) (1), (2), (3), (4) and (7), D (II) (2), (3) and (6) and D (III) (1) and (2) under 'Assets' and C (1), (2), (6), (7) and (9) under 'Liabilities' in Article 9,

— C (I) (3), C (II) (1), (2), (3) and (4), C (III) (1), (2), (3), (4) and (7), D (II) (2), (3) and (6), D (III) (1) and (2), F (1), (2), (6), (7) and (9) and (I) (1), (2), (6), (7) and (9) in Article 10,

— the information required in brackets in D (II) under 'Assets' and C under 'Liabilities' in Article 9, in total for all the items concerned and separately for D (II) (2) and (3) under 'Assets' and C (1), (2), (6), (7) and (9) under 'Liabilities',

— the information required in brackets in D (II) in Article 10, in total for all the items concerned, and separately for D (II) (2) and (3);

(b) abridged notes on their accounts without the information required in Article 43 (I) (5), (6), (8), (10) and (11). However, the notes on the accounts must give the information specified in Article 43 (1) (6) in total for all the items concerned.

This paragraph shall be without prejudice to paragraph 1 in so far as it relates to the profit and loss account, the annual report and the opinion of the person responsible for auditing the accounts.

Article 12 shall apply.

Article 48.   Whenever the annual accounts and the annual report are published in full, they must be reproduced in the form and text on the basis of which the person responsible for auditing the accounts has drawn up his opinion. They must be accompanied by the full text of his report. If the person responsible for auditing the accounts has made any qualifications or refused to report upon the accounts, that fact must be disclosed and the reasons given.

Article 49.   If the annual accounts are not published in full, it must be indicated that the version published is abridged and reference must be made to the register in which the accounts have been filed in accordance with Article 47 (1). Where such filing has not yet been effected, the fact must be disclosed. The report issued by the person responsible for auditing the accounts may not accompany this publication, but it must be disclosed whether the report was issued with or without qualification, or was refused.

Article 50.   The following must be published together with the annual accounts, and in like manner:

— the proposed appropriation of the profit or treatment of the loss,
— the appropriation of the profit or treatment of the loss,

where these items do not appear in the annual accounts.

SECTION 11. AUDITING

Article 51.   1.

(a) Companies must have their annual accounts audited by one or more persons authorized by national law to audit accounts.
(b) The person or persons responsible for auditing the accounts must also verify that the annual report is consistent with the annual accounts for the same financial year.

2. The Member States may relieve the companies referred to in Article 11 from the obligation imposed by paragraph 1.

Article 12 shall apply.

3. Where the exemption provided for in paragraph 2 is granted the Member States shall introduce appropriate sanctions into their laws for cases in which the annual accounts or the annual reports of such companies are not drawn up in accordance with the requirements of this Directive.

SECTION 12. FINAL PROVISIONS

Article 52.   1. A Contact Committee shall be set up under the auspices of the Commission. Its function shall be:

(a) to facilitate, without prejudice to the provisions of Articles 169 and 170 of the Treaty, harmonized application of this Directive through regular meetings dealing in particular with practical problems arising in connection with its application;

(b) to advise the Commission, if necessary, on additions or amendments to this Directive.

2. The Contact Committee shall be composed of representatives of the Member States and representatives of the Commission. The chairman shall be a representative of the Commission. The Commission shall provide the secretariat.

3. The Committee shall be convened by the chairman either on his own initiative or at the request of one of its members.

Article 53.   1. For the purposes of this Directive, the European unit of account shall be that defined by Commission Decision No 3289/75/ECSC of 18 December 1975.[1] The equivalent in national currency shall be calculated initially at the rate obtaining on the date of adoption of this Directive.

2. Every five years the Council, acting on a proposal from the Commission, shall examine and, if need be, revise the amounts expressed in European units of account in this Directive, in the light of economic and monetary trends in the Community.

Article 54.   This Directive shall not affect laws in the Member States requiring that the annual accounts of companies not falling within their jurisdiction be filed in a register in which branches of such companies are listed.

Article 55.   1. The Member States shall bring into force the laws, regulations and administrative provisions necessary for them to comply with this

[1] OJ No L 327, 19. 12. 1975, p. 4.

Directive within two years of its notification. They shall forthwith inform the Commission thereof.

2. The Member States may stipulate that the provisions referred to in paragraph 1 shall not apply until 18 months after the end of the period provided for in that paragraph.

That period of 18 months may, however, be five years:

(a) in the case of unregistered companies in the United Kingdom and Ireland;

(b) for purposes of the application of Articles 9 and 10 and Articles 23 to 26 concerning the layouts for the balance sheet and the profit and loss account, where a Member State has brought other layouts for these documents into force not more than three years before the notification of this Directive;

(c) for purposes of the application of this Directive as regards the calculation and disclosure in balance sheets of depreciation relating to assets covered by the asset items mentioned in Article 9, C (II) (2) and (3), and Article 10, C (II) (2) and (3);

(d) for purposes of the application of Article 47 (1) of this Directive except as regards companies already under an obligation of publication under Article 2 (1) (f) of Directive 68/151/EEC. In this case the second subparagraph of Article 47 (1) of this Directive shall apply to the annual accounts and to the opinion drawn up by the person responsible for auditing the accounts;

(e) for purposes of the application of Article 51 (1) of this Directive.

Furthermore, this period of 18 months may be extended to eight years for companies the principal object of which is shipping and which are already in existence on the entry into force of the provisions referred to in paragraph 1.

3. The Member States shall ensure that they communicate to the Commission the texts of the main provisions of national law which they adopt in the field covered by this Directive.

Article 56. The obligation to show in the annual accounts the items prescribed by Articles 9, 10 and 23 to 26 which relate to affiliated undertakings, and the obligation to provide information concerning these undertakings in accordance with Article 13 (2), 14 or 43 (1) (7), shall enter into force at the same time as a Council Directive on consolidated accounts.

Article 57. 1. Until the entry into force of a Council Directive on consolidated accounts, and without prejudice to the provisions of Directives 68/151/EEC and 77/91/EEC, the Member States need not apply to the dependent companies of any group governed by their national laws the provisions of this Directive concerning the content, auditing and publication of the annual accounts of such dependent companies where the following conditions are fulfilled:

(a) the dominant company must be subject to the laws of a Member State;
(b) all shareholders or members of the dependent company must have declared their agreement to the exemption from such obligation; this declaration must be made in respect of every financial year;
(c) the dominant company must have declared that it guarantees the commitments entered into by the dependent company;
(d) the declarations referred to in (b) and (c) must be published by the dependent company in accordance with the first subparagraph of Article 47 (1);
(e) the annual accounts of the dependent company must be consolidated in the group's annual accounts;
(f) the exemption concerning the preparation, auditing and publication of the annual accounts of the dependent company must be disclosed in the notes on the group's annual accounts.

2. Articles 47 and 51 shall apply to the group's annual accounts.

3. Articles 2 to 46 shall apply as far as possible to the group's annual accounts.

Article 58. 1. Until the entry into force of a Council Directive on consolidated accounts, and without prejudice to the provisions of Directive 77/91/EEC, the Member States need not apply to the dominant companies of groups governed by their national laws the provisions of this Directive concerning the auditing and publication of the profit and loss accounts of such dominant companies where the following conditions are fulfilled:

(a) this exemption must be published by the dominant company in accordance with Article 47 (1);
(b) the annual accounts of the dominant company must be consolidated in the group's annual accounts;
(c) the exemption concerning the auditing and publication of the profit and loss account of the dominant company must be mentioned in the notes on the group's annual accounts;
(d) the profit or loss of the dominant company, determined in accordance with the principles of this Directive, must be shown in the balance sheet of the dominant company.

2. Articles 47 and 51 shall apply to the group's annual accounts.

3. Articles 2 to 46 shall apply as far as possible to the group's annual accounts.

Article 59. Pending subsequent coordination, the Member States may permit the valuation of holdings in affiliated undertakings by the equity method provided the following conditions are fulfilled:

(a) the use of this method of valuation must be disclosed in the notes on the accounts of a company having such holdings;

(b) the amount of any differences existing when such holdings were acquired between their purchase price and the percentage of the capital which they represent, including the affiliated undertaking's reserves, profit and loss and profits and losses brought forward, must be shown separately in the balance sheet or in the notes on the accounts of a company having such holdings;

(c) the purchase price of these holdings shall be increased or reduced in the balance sheet of a company having such holdings by the profits or losses realized by the affiliated undertaking according to the percentage of capital held;

(d) the amounts specified in subparagraph (c) shall be shown each year in the profit and loss account of a company having such holdings as a separate item with an appropriate heading;

(e) when an affiliated undertaking distributes dividends to a company having such holdings, their book values shall be reduced accordingly;

(f) when the amounts shown in the profit and loss account in accordance with subparagraph (d) exceed the amounts of dividends already received or the payment of which can be claimed, the amount of the differences must be placed in a reserve which cannot be distributed to shareholders.

Article 60. Pending subsequent coordination, the Member States may prescribe that investments in which investment companies within the meaning of Article 5 (2) have invested their funds shall be valued on the basis of their market value.

In that case, the Member States may also waive the obligation on investment companies with variable capital to show separately the value adjustments referred to in Article 36.

Article 61. Until the entry into force of a Council Directive on consolidated accounts, the Member States need not apply to the dominant companies of groups governed by their national laws the provisions of Article 43 (1) (2) concerning the amount of capital and reserves and the profits and losses of the undertakings concerned if the annual accounts of such undertakings are consolidated into the group's annual accounts or if the holdings in those undertakings are valued by the equity method.

Article 62. This Directive is addressed to the Member States.
Done at Brussels, 25 July 1978.

For the Council, The President, K. von Dohnanyi

Council Directive

of 27 November 1984 revising the amounts expressed in ECU in Directive 78/660/EEC

(84/569/EEC)

The Council of the European Communities,

Having regard to the Treaty establishing the European Economic Community,

Having regard to Council Directive 78/660/EEC of 25 July 1978 based on Article 54 (3) (g) of the Treaty on the annual accounts of certain types of companies,[1] and in particular Article 53 (2) thereof,

Having regard to the proposal from the Commission,

Whereas Regulation (EEC) No 3180/78,[2] as amended by Regulation (EEC) No 2626/84,[3] defined a new unit of account, known as the ECU;

Whereas Regulation (EEC, Euratom) No 3308/80[4] replaced 'European unit of account' by 'ECU' in all Community legal instruments applying at the time of its entry into force;

Whereas Articles 11 and 27 of Directive 78/660/EEC and, by reference thereto, Article 6 of Directive 83/349/EEC[5] and Articles 20 and 21 of Directive 84/253/EEC[6] lay down limits in ECU for the balance sheet total and net turnover within which the Member States may grant certain derogations from the provisions of those Directives;

Whereas Article 53 (2) of Directive 78/660/EEC stipulates that every five years the Council, acting on a proposal from the Commission, shall examine and, if need be, revise the amounts expressed in ECU in that Directive, in the light of economic and monetary trends in the community;

Whereas, when measured in real terms, the ECU has not retained the value it had at the time of the adoption of Directive 78/660/EEC;

Whereas, to take account of monetary trends with relation to the ECU

[1] OJ No L 222, 14. 8. 1978, p. 11.
[2] OJ No L 379, 30. 12. 1978, p. 1.   [3] OJ No L 247, 16. 9. 1984, p. 1.
[4] OJ No L 345, 20. 12. 1980, p. 1.   [5] OJ No L 193, 18. 7. 1983, p. 1.
[6] OJ No L 126, 12. 5. 1984, p. 20.

since that time, equivalents in national currency should be recalculated on the date, fixed in Article 53 (2) of Directive 78/660/EEC;

Has adopted this directive.

Article 1. Directive 78/660/EEC is hereby amended as follows:

1. Article 11:

— the first indent: 'balance sheet total: 1 000 000 ECU' is replaced by: 'balance sheet total: 1 550 000 ECU';

— the second indent: 'net turnover: 2 000 000 ECU' is replaced by 'net turnover: 3 200 000 ECU';

2. In Article 27:

— the first indent: 'balance sheet total: 4 000 000 ECU' is replaced by 'balance sheet total 6 200 000 ECU';

— The second indent: 'net turnover: 8 000 000 ECU' is replaced by 'net turnover: 12 800 000 ECU'.

3.

(a) Article 53 (1) is replaced by the following: '1. For the purpose of this Directive, the ECU shall be that defined by Regulation (EEC) No 3180/78,[1] as amended by Regulation (EEC) No 2626/84.[2] The equivalent in national currency shall be calculated at the rate obtaining on 25 July 1983.';

(b) Footnote [1] shall be replaced by the following footnotes: [1]OJ No L 379, 30. 12. 1978, p. 1. [2]OJ No L 247, 16. 9. 1984, p. 1.

Article 2. Member States shall forthwith inform the Commission of any laws, regulations or administrative provisions which they bring into force pursuant to this Directive.

Article 3. This Directive is addressed to the Member States.

Done at Brussels, 27 November 1984.

For the Council, The President, P. Barry

Council Directive of

8 November 1990 amending Directive 78/660/EEC on annual accounts and Directive 83/349/EEC on consolidated accounts as concerns the exemptions for small and medium-sized companies and the publication of accounts in ECUs

90/604/EEC

The Council of the European Communities,

Having regard to the Treaty establishing the European Economic Community, and in particular Article 54 thereof,

Having regard to the proposal from the Commission,[1]

In co-operation with the European Parliament,[2]

Having regard to the opinion of the Economic and Social Committee,[3]

Whereas the harmonization of the national provisions concerning the presentation and content of annual accounts and of the annual report, the valuation methods and the publication of these documents as concerns, in particular, public and private limited liability companies was the subject of Directive 78/660/EEC,[4] as last amended by the Act of Accession of Spain and Portugal;

Whereas the administrative procedures imposed on small and medium-sized undertakings should be simplified in accordance with the Council resolution of 3 November 1986 on the action programme for small and medium-sized undertakings (SMUs)[5] and the Council resolution of 30 June 1988 on the improvement of the business environment and action to promote the development of enterprises, especially small and medium-sized enterprises in the Community[6] which calls more especially for a substantial simplification of the obligations arising from Directive 78/660/EEC;

Whereas, on the basis of Article 53 (2) of Directive 78/660/EEC, it is appropriate that a second review of the thresholds defining small and medium-sized undertakings should be carried out;

Whereas the derogations as regards establishment, audit and publication of accounts which Member States may provide for under Directive 78/660/EEC should be increased as far as small companies are concerned;

Whereas Member States should be afforded the possibility of allowing

---

[1] OJ No C 287, 11. 11. 1986, p. 5, and OJ No C 318, 20. 12. 1989, p. 12.
[2] OJ No C 158, 26. 6. 1989, p. 257, and Decision of . . . (not yet publ. in OJ).
[3] OJ No C 139, 5. 6. 1989, p. 42.   [4] OJ No L 222, 14. 8. 1978, p. 11.
[5] OJ No C 287, 14. 11. 1986, p. 1.
[6] OJ No C 197, 27. 7. 1988, p. 6.

companies not to include in the notes to the accounts certain information concerning remuneration granted to members of the company's administrative or management body where such information enables the position of a given member of such bodies to be identified;

Whereas it is also appropriate to enable Member States to render less stringent the obligations imposed on small companies as regards the drawing up and publication of the notes to the accounts; whereas Member States should be able to exempt such companies from the obligation to supply, in the notes to the accounts, certain data which may be deemed of less importance for small companies; whereas, with the same interests in view, Member States should have the possibility of exempting such companies from the obligation to draw up an annual report providing they include, in the notes to the accounts, the data referred to in Article 22 (2) of Directive 77/91/EEC[7] concerning the acquisition of own shares;

Whereas it is important to promote European monetary integration by allowing companies, at least, to publish their accounts in ecus; whereas this is simply an additional facility which does not change the position of companies which can at present already draw up and publish accounts in ecus; whereas, on this point, the provisions of Directives 78/660/EEC and 83/349/EEC,[8] as amended by the Act of Accession of Spain and Portugal should be clarified by obliging companies which have recourse to this facility to indicate the conversion rate used in the notes to the accounts,

Has adopted this directive:

Article 1. Article 11 of Directive 78/660/EEC is hereby amended as follows:

1. 'balance sheet total: ECU 1550000' is hereby replaced by 'balance sheet total: ECU 2000000';

2. 'net turnover: ECU 3200000' is hereby replaced by 'net turnover: ECU 4000000';

3. the following paragraph is hereby added: 'Member States may waive the application of Article 15 (3) (*a*) and (4) to the abridged balance sheet'. The revision of the above amounts in ecus shall constitute the second five-yearly revision provided for in Article 53 (2) of Directive 78/660/EEC.

Article 2. Article 27 of Directive 78/660/EEC is hereby amended as follows:

1. 'balance sheet total: ECU 6200000' is hereby replaced by 'balance sheet total: ECU 8000000';

2. 'net turnover: ECU 12800000' is hereby replaced by 'net turnover: ECU 16000000'.

---

[7] OJ No L 26, 31. 1. 1977, p. 1.   [8] OJ No L 193, 18. 7. 1983, p. 1.

The revision of the above amounts in ecus shall constitute the second five-yearly revision provided for in Article 53 (2) of Directive 78/660/EEC.

Article 3.   Article 53 (1) of Directive 78/660/EEC shall be replaced by the following:

1. For the purposes of this Directive, the ecu shall be that defined in Regulation (EEC) No 3180/78,* as amended by Regulation (EEC) No 2626/84**, and by Regulation (EEC) No 1971/89.***

The equivalent in national currency shall be that applying on 8 November 1990.[1]

Article 4.   The following paragraph is hereby added to Article 43 of Directive 78/660/EEC:

3. Member States may waive the requirement to provide the information referred to in paragraph 1 point 12 where such information makes it possible to identify the position of a specific member of such a body.

Article 5.   Article 44 of Directive 78/660/EEC is hereby replaced by the following:

Article 44.   1. Member States may permit companies covered by Article 11 to draw up abridged notes on their accounts without the information prescribed in Article 43 (1) points 5 to 12. However, the notes must disclose the information prescribed in Article 43 (1) point 6 in total for all the items concerned.

2. Member States may also permit the companies referred to in paragraph 1 to be exempted from the obligation to disclose in the notes on their accounts the information prescribed in Article 15 (3) (a) and (4), Articles 18, 21 and 29 (2), the second subparagraph of Article 30, Article 34 (2), Article 40 (2) and the second subparagraph of Article 42.

3. Article 12 shall apply.

Article 6.   The following paragraph is hereby added to Article 46 of Directive 78/660/EEC:

3. Member States may waive the obligation on companies covered by Article 11 to prepare annual reports, provided that the information referred to in Article 22 (2) of Directive 77/91/EEC concerning the acquisition by a company of its own shares is given in the notes to their accounts.

---

* OJ No L 379, 30. 12. 1978, p. 1.   ** OJ No L 247, 16. 9. 1984, p. 1.
*** OJ No L 189, 4. 7. 1989, p. 1.   [1] Date of adoption of the Directive.

Article 7.   Article 47 (2) (*b*) of Directive 78/660/EEC is hereby replaced by the following: '(b) abridged notes on their accounts in accordance with Article 44.'

Article 8. The following Article is hereby inserted in Directive 78/660/EEC:

*Article 50*a.   Annual accounts may be published in the currency in which they were drawn up and in ecus, translated at the exchange rate prevailing on the balance sheet date. That rate shall be disclosed in the notes on the accounts.

Article 9. The following Article is hereby inserted in Directive 83/349/EEC:

*Article 38*a.   Consolidated accounts may be published in the currency in which they were drawn up and in ecus, translated at the exchange rate prevailing on the consolidated balance sheet date. That rate shall be disclosed in the notes on the accounts.

Article 10.   1. Member States shall bring into force the laws, regulations and administrative provisions necessary for them to comply with this Directive by 1 January 1993. They shall forthwith inform the Commission thereof.

2. Member States may provide that this Directive shall only apply for the first time to accounts for the financial year beginning on 1 January 1995 or during the calendar year 1995.

3. Member States shall communicate to the Commission the texts of the main provisions of national law which they adopt in the field covered by this Directive.

Article 11.   This Directive is addressed to the Member States.
   Done at Brussels, 8 November 1990.

For the Council, The President, P. ROMITA

Council Directive

of 8 November 1990 amending Directive 78/660/EEC
on annual accounts and Directive 83/349/EEC
on consolidated accounts as regards the scope
of those Directives

90/605/EEC

The Council of the European Communities,

Having regard to the Treaty establishing the European Economic Community, and in particular Article 54 thereof,

Having regard to the proposal from the Commission,[1]

In co-operation with the European Parliament,[2]

Having regard to the opinion of the Economic and Social Committee,[3]

Whereas Directive 78/660/EEC,[4] as last amended by Directive 90/604/EEC[5], applies to the annual accounts of public and private limited liability companies in particular because those types of company offer no safeguards to third parties beyond the amounts of their net assets;

Whereas, in accordance with Directive 83/349/EEC,[6] as amended by the Directive 90/604/EEC, Member States need require only companies covered by Directive 78/660/EEC to draw up consolidated accounts;

Whereas, within the Community, there is a substantial and constantly growing number of partnerships and limited partnerships all of the fully liable members of which are constituted either as public or as private limited liability companies;

Whereas these fully liable members may also be companies which do not fall within the law of a Member State but which have a legal status comparable to that referred to in Directive 68/151/EEC;[7]

Whereas it would run counter to the spirit and aims of those Directives to allow such partnerships and partnerships with limited liability not to be subject to Community rules;

Whereas the provisions covering the scope of the two Directives in question should therefore be explicitly supplemented;

Whereas it is of importance that the name, head office and legal status of any undertaking of which a limited liability company is a fully liable member should be indicated in the notes to the accounts of such member;

Whereas the obligation to draw up, publish and to have audited the

---

[1] OJ No C 144, 11. 6. 1986, p. 10.
[2] OJ No C 125, 11. 5. 1987, p. 140, and Decision of . . . (not yet publ. in OJ).
[3] OJ No C 328, 22. 12. 1986, p. 43   [4] OJ No L 222, 14. 8. 1978, p. 11.
[6] OJ No L 193, 18. 7. 1983, p. 1.   [5] See page 57 of this Official Journal.
[7] OJ No L 65, 14. 3. 1968, p. 8.

accounts of partnerships and limited liability partnerships may also be imposed on the fully liable member; whereas it should also be possible to include these companies in consolidated accounts, drawn up by such member or established at a higher level;

Whereas some of the partnerships covered by this Directive are not subject, in the Member State where they have their head office, to entry in a register, which makes it difficult to apply accounting obligations to them; whereas, in particular in these cases, special rules are necessary according to whether the fully liable members are undertakings which fall within the law of the same Member State, another Member State or a third country,

Has adopted this Directive:

Article 1. Directive 78/660/EEC is hereby amended as follows:

1. The following subparagraphs are added to Article 1 (1):

The co-ordination measures prescribed by this Directive shall also apply to the Member States' laws, regulations and administrative provisions relating to the following types of company:

(a) in Germany:
die offene Handelsgesellschaft, die Kommanditgesellschaft;
(b) in Belgium:
la société en nom collectif/de vennootschap onder firma,
la société en commandité simple/de gewone commanditaire vennootschap;
(c) in Denmark:
interessentskaber, kommanditselskaber;
(d) in France:
la société en nom collectif, la société en commandite simple;
(e) in Greece:
ἡ ὁμόρρυθμος ἑταιρία, ἡ ἑτερόρρυθμος ἑταιρία;
(f) in Spain:
sociedad colectiva, sociedad en comandita simple;
(g) in Ireland:
partnerships, limited partnerships, unlimited companies;
(h) in Italy:
la società in nome collettivo, la società in accomandita semplice;
(i) in Luxembourg:
la société en nom collectif, la société en commandite simple;
(j) in the Netherlands:
de vennootschap onder firma, de commanditaire vennootschap;
(k) in Portugal:
sociedade em nome colectivo, sociedade em comandita simples;
(l) in the United Kingdom:
partnerships, limited partnerships, unlimited companies;

where all members having unlimited liability are companies of the types set out in the first subparagraph or companies which are not governed by the laws of a Member

State but which have a legal form comparable to those referred to in Directive 68/151/EEC.

This Directive shall also apply to the types of companies or firms referred to in the second subparagraph where all members having unlimited liability are themselves companies of the types set out in that or the first subparagraph.

2. The following subparagraph is added in Article 43 (1), point 2:

the name, the head or registered office and the legal form of each of the undertakings of which the company or firm is a member having unlimited liability. This information may be omitted where for the purposes of Article 2 (3) it is of negligible importance only.

3. The following paragraph is inserted in Article 47:

1a. The Member State of a company or firm referred to in Article 1 (1), second and third subparagraphs (entity concerned) may exempt that entity from publishing its accounts in accordance with Article 3 of Directive 68/151/EEC, provided that those accounts are available to the public at its head office, where:

(a) all the members having unlimited liability of the entity concerned are the companies referred to in the first subparagraph of Article 1 (1) governed by the laws of Member States other than the Member State whose law governs that entity and none of those companies publishes the accounts of the entity concerned with its own accounts; or

(b) all the members having unlimited liability are companies which are not governed by the laws of a Member State but which have a legal form comparable to those referred to in Directive 68/151/EEC.

Copies of the accounts must be obtainable upon request. The price of such a copy may not exceed its administrative cost. Appropriate sanctions must be provided for failure to comply with the publication obligation imposed in this paragraph.

4. The following Article is inserted:

Article 57a.   1. Member States may require the companies referred to in the first subparagraph of Article 1 (1) governed by their law, which are members having unlimited liability of any of the companies and firms listed in Article 1 (1), second and third subparagraphs (entity concerned), to draw up, have audited and publish, with their own accounts, the accounts of the entity concerned in conformity with the provisions of this Directive.

In this case, the requirements of this Directive do not apply to the entity concerned.

2. Member States need not apply the requirements of this Directive to the entity concerned where:

(a) the accounts of this entity are drawn up, audited and published in conformity with the provisions of this Directive by a company which is a member having unlimited liability of the entity and is governed by the law of another Member State;

(b) the entity concerned is included in consolidated accounts drawn up, audited and published in accordance with Directive 83/349/EEC by a member having unlimited liability or where the entity concerned is included in the consolidated accounts of a larger body of undertakings drawn up, audited and published in conformity with Council Directive 83/349/EEC by a parent undertaking governed by the law of a Member State. The exemption must be disclosed in the notes on the consolidated accounts.

3. In these cases, the entity concerned must reveal to whomsoever so requests the name of the entity publishing the accounts.

Article 2. Directive 83/349/EEC is hereby amended as follows:

1. The following subparagraph is inserted in Article 4 (1):

The first subparagraph shall also apply where either the parent undertaking or one or more subsidiary undertakings is constituted as one of the types of company mentioned in Article 1 (1), second or third subparagraph of Directive 78/660/EEC.

2. In Article 4, paragraph 2 is replaced by the following:

2. The Member States may, however, grant exemption from the obligation imposed in Article 1 (1) where the parent undertaking is not constituted as one of the types of company mentioned in Article 4 (1) of this Directive or in Article 1 (1), second or third subparagraph of Directive 78/660/EEC.

Article 3. 1. Member States shall bring into force the laws, regulations and administrative provisions necessary for them to comply with this Directive before 1 January 1993. They shall forthwith inform the Commission thereof.

2. Member States may provide that the provisions referred to in paragraph 1 shall first apply to the annual accounts and consolidated accounts for financial years beginning on 1 January 1995 or during the 1995 calendar year.

3. The Member States shall communicate to the Commission the texts of the main provisions of national law which they adopt in the field covered by this Directive.

Article 4. This Directive is addressed to the Member States.
Done at Brussels, 8 November 1990.

For the Council, The President, P. ROMITA

Sixth Council Directive

of 17 December 1982 based on Article 54 (3) (g) of the
Treaty, concerning the division of public limited liability
companies

(82/891/EEC)

The Council of the European Communities,

Having regard to the Treaty establishing the European Economic
Community, and in particular Article 54 (3) (g) thereof,

Having regard to the proposal from the Commission,[1]

Having regard to the opinion of the European Parliament,[2]

Having regard to the opinion of the Economic and Social Committee,[3]

Whereas the coordination provided for in Article 54 (3) (g) and in
the general programme for the abolition of restrictions on freedom of
establishment[4] was begun with Directive 68/151/EEC[5].

Whereas that coordination was continued as regards the formation of
public limited liability companies and the maintenance and alteration of
their capital with Directive 77/91/EEC,[6] as regards the annual accounts
of certain types of companies with Directive 78/660/EEC,[7] and as regards
mergers of public limited liability companies with Directive 78/885/EEC;[8]

Whereas Directive 78/855/EEC dealt only with mergers of public limited
liability companies and certain operations treated as mergers; whereas,
however, the Commission proposal also covered division operations;
whereas the opinions of the European Parliament and of the Economic and
Social Committee were in favour of the regulation of such operation;

Whereas, because of the similarities which exist between merger and
division operations, the risk of the guarantees given with regard to mergers
by Directive 78/855/EEC being circumvented can be avoided only if
provision is made for equivalent protection in the event of division;

Whereas the protection of the interests of members and third parties
requires that the laws of the Member States relating to divisions of public
limited liability companies be coordinated where the Member states permit
such operations;

Whereas, in the context of such coordination, it is particularly important
that the shareholders of the companies involved in a division be kept

[1] OJ No C 89, 14. 7. 1970, p. 20.
[2] OJ No C 129, 11. 12. 1972, p. 50, and OJ No C 95, 28. 4. 1975, p. 12.
[3] OJ No C 88, 6. 9. 1971, p. 18   [4] OJ No 2, 15. 1. 1962, p. 36/62.
[5] OJ No L 65, 14. 3. 1968, p. 8.   [6] OJ No L 26, 31. 1. 1977, p. 1.
[7] OJ No L 222, 14. 8. 1978, p. 11.   [8] OJ No L 295, 20. 10. 1978, p. 36.

adequately informed in as objective a manner as possible and that their rights be suitably protected;

Whereas the protection of employees' rights in the event of transfers of undertakings, businesses or parts of businesses is at present regulated by Directive 77/187/EEC;[9]

Whereas creditors, including debenture holders, and persons having other claims on the companies involved in a division, must be protected so that the division does not adversely affect their interests;

Whereas the disclosure requirements of Directive 68/151/EEC must be extended to include divisions so that third parties are kept adequately informed;

Whereas the safeguards afforded to members and third parties in connection with divisions must be extended to cover certain legal practices which in important respects are similar to division, so that the obligation to provide such protection cannot be evaded;

Whereas to ensure certainty in the law as regards relations between the companies involved in the division, between them and third parties, and between the members, the cases in which nullity can arise must be limited by providing that defects be remedied wherever that is possible and by restricting the period within which nullification proceedings may be commenced,

Has adopted this directive:

Article 1. 1. Where Member States permit the companies referred to in Article 1 (1) of Directive 78/855/EEC coming under their laws to carry out division operations by acquisition as defined in Article 2 of this Directive, they shall subject those operations to the provisions of Chapter 1 of this Directive.

2. Where Member States permit the companies referred to in paragraph 1 to carry out division operations by the formation of new companies as defined in Article 21, they shall subject those operations to the provisions of Chapter II of this Directive.

3. Where Member States permit the companies referred to in paragraph 1 to carry out operations, whereby a division by acquisition as defined in Article 2 (1) is combined with a division by the formation of one or more new companies as defined in Article 21 (1), they shall subject operation to the provisions of Chapter 1 and Article 22.

4. Article 1 (2) and (3) of Directive 78/855/EEC shall apply.

CHAPTER I. DIVISION BY ACQUISITION

Article 2. 1. For the purposes of this Directive, 'division by acquisition' shall mean the operation whereby, after being wound up without going into

[9] OJ No L 61, 5. 3. 1977, p. 26.

liquidation, a company transfers to more than one company all its assets and liabilities in exchange for the allocation to the shareholders of the company being divided of shares in the companies receiving contributions as a result of the division (hereinafter referred to as 'recipient companies') and possibly a cash payment not exceeding 10% of the nominal value of the shares allocated or, where they have no nominal value, of their accounting par value.

2. Article 3 (2) of Directive 78/855/EEC shall apply.

3. In so far as this Directive refers to Directive 78/855/EEC, the expression 'merging companies' shall mean 'the companies involved in a division', the expression 'company being acquired' shall mean 'the company being divided', the expression 'acquiring company' shall mean 'each of the recipient companies' and the expression 'draft terms of merger', shall mean 'draft terms of division'.

Article 3.   1. The administrative or management bodies of the companies involved in a division shall draw up draft terms of division in writing.

2. Draft terms of division shall specify at least:

(a) the type, name and registered office of each of the companies involved in the division;
(b) the share exchange ratio and the amount of any cash payment;
(c) the terms relating to the allotment of shares in the recipient companies;
(d) the date from which the holding of such shares entitles the holders to participate in profits and any special conditions affecting that entitlement;
(e) the date from which the transactions of the company being divided shall be treated for accounting purposes as being those of one or other of the recipient companies;
(f) the rights conferred by the recipient companies on the holders of shares to which special rights are attached and the holders of securities other than shares, or the measures proposed concerning them;
(g) any special advantage granted to the experts referred to in Article 8 (1) and members of the administrative, management, supervisory or controlling bodies of the companies involved in the division;
(h) the precise description and allocation of the assets and liabilities to be transferred to each of the recipient companies;
(i) the allocation to the shareholders of the company being divided of shares in the recipient companies and the criterion upon which such allocation is based.

3.

(a) Where an asset is not allocated by the draft terms of division and where the interpretation of these terms does not make a decision on its allocation possible, the asset or the consideration therefor shall be allocated to all the recipient companies in proportion to the share of the net assets allocated to each of those companies under the draft terms of division.

(b) Where a liability is not allocated by the draft terms of division and where the interpretation of these terms does not make a decision on its allocation possible, each of the recipient companies shall be jointly and severally liable for it. Member States may provide that such joint and several liability be limited to the net assets allocated to each company.

Article 4. Draft terms of division must be published in the manner prescribed by the laws of each Member State in accordance with Article 3 of Directive 68/151/EEC[1] for each of the companies involved in a division, at least one month before the date of the general meeting which is to decide thereon.

Article 5. 1. A division shall require at least the approval of a general meeting of each company involved in the division. Article 7 of Directive 78/855/EEC shall apply with regard to the majority required for such decisions, their scope and the need for separate votes.

2. Where shares in the recipient companies are allocated to the shareholders of the company being divided otherwise than in proportion to their rights in the capital of that company, Member States may provided that the minority shareholders of that company may exercise the right to have their shares purchased. In such case, they shall be entitled to receive consideration corresponding to the value of their shares. In the event of a dispute concerning such consideration, it must be possible for the consideration to be determined by a court.

Article 6. The laws of a Member State need not require approval of a division by a general meeting of a recipient company if the following conditions are fulfilled:

(a) the publication provided for in Article 4 must be effected, for each recipient company, at least one month before the date fixed for the general meeting of the company being divided which is to decide on the draft terms of division;

(b) at least one month before the date specified in point (a), all shareholders of each recipient company must be entitled to inspect the documents specified in Article 9 (1) at the registered office of that company;

(c) one or more shareholders of any recipient company holding a minimum percentage of the subscribed capital must be entitled to require that a general meeting of such recipient company be called to decide whether

[1] OJ No L 65, 14. 3. 1968, p. 9.

to approve the division. This minimum percentage may not be fixed at more than 5%. Member States may, however, provide for the exclusion of non-voting shares from this calculation.

Article 7. 1. This administration or management bodies of each of the companies involved in the division shall draw up a detailed written report explaining the draft terms of division and setting out the legal and economic grounds for them, in particular the share exchange ratio and the criterion determining the allocation of shares.

2. The report shall also describe any special valuation difficulties which have arisen.

It shall disclose the preparation of the report on the consideration other than in cash referred to in Article 27 (2) of Directive 77/91/EEC[2] for recipient companies and the register where that report must be lodged.

3. The administrative or management bodies of a company being divided must inform the general meeting of that company and the administrative or management bodies of the recipient companies so that they can inform their respective general meetings of any material change in the assets and liabilities between the date of preparation of the draft terms of division and the date of the general meeting of the company being divided which is to decide on the draft terms of division.

Article 8. 1. One or more experts acting on behalf of each of the companies involved in the division but independent of them, appointed or approved by a judicial or administrative authority, shall examine the draft terms of division and draw up a written report to the shareholders. However, the laws of a Member State may provide for the appointment of one or more independent experts for all of the companies involved in a division if such appointment is made by a judicial or administrative authority at the joint request of those companies. Such experts may, depending on the laws of each Member State, be natural or legal persons or companies or firms.

2. Article 10 (2) and (3) of Directive 78/855/EEC shall apply.

3. Member States may provide that the report on the consideration other than in cash referred to in Article 27 (2) of Directive 77/91/EEC and the report on the draft terms of division drawn up in accordance with paragraph 1 shall be drawn up by the same expert or experts.

Article 9. 1. All shareholders shall be entitled to inspect at least the following documents at the registered office at least one month before the date of the general meeting which is to decide on the draft terms of division:

(a) the draft terms of division.

[2] OJ No L 26, 31. 1. 1977, p. 1.

(b) the annual accounts and annual reports of the companies involved in the division for the preceding three financial years;

(c) an accounting statement drawn up as at a date which must not be earlier than the first day of the third month preceding the date of the draft terms of division, if the latest annual accounts relate to a financial year which ended more than six months before that date;

(d) the reports of the administrative or management bodies of the companies involved in the division provided for in Article 7 (1);

(e) the reports provided for in Article 8.

2. The accounting statement provided for in paragraph 1 (c) shall be drawn up using the same methods and the same layout as the last annual balance sheet.

However, the laws of a Member State may provide that:

(a) it shall not be necessary to take a fresh physical inventory;

(b) the valuations shown in the last balance sheet shall be altered only to reflect entries in the books of account; the following shall nevertheless be taken into account:

— interim depreciation and provisions,
— material changes in actual value not shown in the books.

3. Every shareholder shall be entitled to obtain, on request and free of charge, full or, if so desired, partial copies of the documents referred to in paragraph 1.

Article 10. Member States may permit the non-application of Articles 7 and 8 (1) and (2), and of Article 9 (1) (c), (d) and (e) if all the shareholders and the holders of other securities giving the right to vote of the companies involved in a division have so agreed.

Article 11. Protection of the rights of the employees of each of the companies involved in a division shall be regulated in accordance with Directive 77/187/EEC.[1]

Article 12. 1. The laws of Member States must provide for an adequate system of protection for the interests of the creditors of the companies involved in a division whose claims antedate publication of the draft terms of division and have not yet fallen due at the time of such publication.

2. To that end, the laws of Member States shall at least provide that such creditors shall be entitled to obtain adequate safeguards where the financial situation of the company being divided and that of the company to which the obligation will be transferred in accordance with the draft terms of division make such protection necessary and where those creditors do not already have such safeguards.

[1] OJ No L 61, 5. 3. 1977, p. 26.

3. In so far as a creditor of the company to which the obligation has been transferred in accordance with the draft terms of division has not obtained satisfaction, the recipient companies shall be jointly and severally liable for that obligation. Member States may limit that liability to the net assets allocated to each of those companies other than the one to which the obligation has been transferred. However, they need not apply this paragraph where the division operation is subject to the supervision of a judicial authority in accordance with Article 23 and a majority in number representing three-fourths in value of the creditors or any class of creditors of the company being divided have agreed to forego such joint and several liability at a meeting held pursuant to Article 23 (1) (c).

4. Article 13 (3) of Directive 78/855/EEC shall apply.

5. Without prejudice to the rules governing the collective exercise of their rights, paragraphs 1 to 4 shall apply to the debenture holders of the companies involved in the division except where the division has been approved by a meeting of the debenture holders, if such a meeting is provided for under national laws, or by the debenture holders individually.

6. Member States may provide that the recipient companies shall be jointly and severally liable for the obligations of the company being divided. In such case they need not apply the foregoing paragraphs.

7. Where a Member State combines the system of creditor protection set out in paragraph 1 to 5 with the joint and several liability of the recipient companies as referred to in paragraph 6, it may limit such joint and several liability to the net assets allocated to each of those companies.

Article 13.   Holders of securities, other than shares, to which special rights are attached, must be given rights in the recipient companies against which such securities may be invoked in accordance with the draft terms of division, at least equivalent to the rights they possessed in the company being divided, unless the alteration of those rights has been approved by a meeting of the holders of such securities, if such a meeting is provided for under national laws, or by the holders of those securities individually, or unless the holders are entitled to have their securities repurchased.

Article 14.   Where the laws of a Member State do not provide for judicial or administrative preventive supervision of the legality of divisions or where such supervision does not extend to all the legal acts required for a division, Article 16 of Directive 78/855/EEC shall apply.

Article 15.   The laws of Member States shall determine the date on which a division takes effect.

Article 16.   1. A division must be published in the manner prescribed by the laws of each Member State in accordance with Article 3 of Directive

68/151/EEC in respect of each of the companies involved in a division.

2. Any recipient company may itself carry out the publication formalities relating to the company being divided.

Article 17. 1. A division shall have the following consequences *ipso jure* and simultaneously:

(a) the transfer, both as between the company being divided and the recipient companies and as regards third parties, to each of the recipient companies of all the assets and liabilities of the company being divided; such transfer shall take effect with the assets and liabilities being divided in accordance with the allocation laid down in the draft terms of division or in Article 3 (3);

(b) the shareholders of the company being divided become shareholders of one or more of the recipient companies in accordance with the allocation laid down in the draft terms of division;

(c) the company being divided ceases to exist.

2. No shares in a recipient company shall be exchanged for shares held in the company being divided either:

(a) by that recipient company itself or by a person acting in his own name but on its behalf; or

(b) by the company being divided itself or by a person acting in his own name but on its behalf.

3. The foregoing shall not affect the laws of Member States which require the completion of special formalities for the transfer of certain assets, rights and obligations by a company being divided to be effective as against third parties. The recipient company or companies to which such assets, rights or obligations are transferred in accordance with the draft terms of division or with Article 3 (3) may carry out these formalities themselves; however, the laws of Member States may permit a company being divided to continue to carry out these formalities for a limited period which may not, save in exceptional circumstances, be fixed at more than six months from the date on which the division takes effect.

Article 18. The laws of Member States shall at least lay down rules governing the civil liability of members of the administrative or management bodies of a company being divided towards the shareholders of that company in respect of misconduct on the part of members of those bodies in preparing and implementing the division and the civil liability of the experts responsible for drawing up for that company the report provided for in Article 8 in respect of misconduct on the part of those experts in the performance of their duties.

Article 19. 1. The laws of Member States may lay down nullity rules for divisions in accordance with the following conditions only:

(a) nullity must be ordered in a court judgment;

(b) divisions which have taken effect pursuant to Article 15 may be declared void only if there has been no judicial or administrative preventive supervision of their legality, or if they have not been drawn up and certified in due legal form, or if it is shown that the decision of the general meeting is void or voidable under national law;

(c) nullification proceedings may not be initiated more than six months after the date on which the division becomes effective as against the person alleging nullity or if the situation has been rectified;

(d) where it is possible to remedy a defect liable to render a division void, the competent court shall grant the companies involved a period of time within which to rectify the situation;

(e) a judgment declaring a division void shall be published in the manner prescribed by the laws of each Member State in accordance with Article 3 of Directive 68/151/EEC;

(f) where the laws of a Member State permit a third party to challenge such a judgment, he may do so only within six months of publication of the judgment in the manner prescribed by Directive 68/151/EEC;

(g) a judgment declaring a division void shall not of itself affect the validity of obligations owed by or in relation to the recipient companies which arose before the judgment was published and after the date referred to in Article 15;

(h) each of the recipient companies shall be liable for its obligations arising after the date on which the division took effect and before the date on which the decision pronouncing the nullity of the division was published. The company being divided shall also be liable for such obligations; Member States may provide that this liability be limited to the share of net assets transferred to the recipient company on whose account such obligations arose.

2. By way of derogation from paragraph 1 (a), the laws of a Member State may also provide for the nullity of a division to be ordered by an administrative authority if an appeal against such a decision lies to a court. Subparagraphs (b), (d), (e), (f), (g), and (h) shall apply by analogy to the administrative authority. Such nullification proceedings may not be initiated more than six months after the date referred to in Article 15.

3. The foregoing shall not affect the laws of the Member States on the nullity of a division pronounced following any supervision of legality.

Article 20. Without prejudice to Article 6, Member States need not require the division to be approved by the general meeting of the company being divided where the recipient companies together hold all the shares of the company being divided and all other securities conferring the right to vote at general meetings of the company being divided, and the following conditions, at least, are fulfilled:

(a) each of the companies involved in the operation must carry out the publication provided for in Article 4 at least one month before the operation takes effect;

(b) at least one month before the operation takes effect, all shareholders of companies involved in the operation must be entitled to inspect the documents specified in Article 9 (1), at their company's registered office. Article 9 (2) and (3) shall also apply;

(c) one or more shareholders of the company being divided holding a minimum percentage of the subscribed capital must be entitled to require that a general meeting of the company being divided be called to decide whether to approve the division. This minimum percentage may not be fixed at more than 5%. Member States may, however, provide for the exclusion of non-voting shares from this calculation;

(d) where a general meeting of the company being divided, required for the approval of the division, is not summoned, the information provided for by Article 7 (3) covers any material change in the asset and liabilities after the date of preparation of the draft terms of division.

CHAPTER II. DIVISION BY THE FORMATION OF NEW COMPANIES

Article 21. 1. For the purposes of this Directive, 'division by the formation of new companies' means the operation whereby, after being wound up without going into liquidation, a company transfers to more than one newly-formed company all its assets and liabilities in exchange for the allocation to the shareholders of the company being divided of shares in the recipient companies, and possibly a cash payment not exceeding 10% of the nominal value of the shares allocated or, where they have no nominal value, of their accounting par value.

2. Article 4 (2) of Directive 78/855/EEC shall apply.

Article 22. 1. Articles 3, 4, 5 and 7, 8 (1) and (2) and 9 to 19 of this Directive shall apply, without prejudice to Articles 11 and 12 of Directive 68/151/EEC, to division by the formation of new companies. For this purpose, the expression 'companies involved in a division' shall refer to the company being divided and the expression 'recipient companies' shall refer to each of the new companies.

2. In addition to the information specified in Article 3 (2), the draft terms of division shall indicate the form, name and registered office of each of the new companies.

3. The draft terms of division and, if they are contained in a separate document, the memorandum or draft memorandum of association and the articles or draft articles of association of each of the new companies shall be approved at a general meeting of the company being divided.

4. Member States may provide that the report on the consideration other than in cash as referred to in Article 10 of Directive 77/91/EEC and the report on the draft terms of division as referred to in Article 8 (1) shall be drawn up the same expert or experts.

5. Member States may provide that neither Article 8, nor Article 9 as regards the expert's report, shall apply where the shares in each of the new companies are allocated to the shareholders of the company being divided in proportion to their rights in the capital of that company.

CHAPTER III. DIVISION UNDER THE SUPERVISION OF A JUDICIAL AUTHORITY

Article 23. 1. Member States may apply paragraph 2 where division operations are subject to the supervision of a judicial authority having the power:

(a) to call a general meeting of the shareholders of the company being divided in order to decide upon the division;
(b) to ensure that the shareholders of each of the companies involved in a division have received or can obtain at least the documents referred to in Article 9 in time to examine them before the date of the general meeting of their company called to decide upon the division. Where a Member State makes use of the option provided for in Article 6 the period must be long enough for the shareholders of the recipient companies to be able to exercise the rights conferred on them by that Article;
(c) to call any meeting of creditors of each of the companies involved in a division in order to decide upon the division;
(d) to ensure that the creditors of each of the companies involved in a division have received or can obtain at least the draft terms of division in time to examine them before the date referred to in (b);
(e) to approve the draft terms of division.

2. Where the judicial authority establishes that the conditions referred to in paragraph 1 (b) and (d) have been fulfilled and that no prejudice would be caused to shareholders or creditors, it may relieve the companies involved in the division from applying:

(a) Article 4, on condition that the adequate system of protection of the interest of the creditors referred to in Article 12 (1) covers all claims regardless of their date;

(b) the conditions referred to in Article 6 (a) and (b) where a Member State makes use of the option provided for in Article 6;

(c) Article 9, as regards the period and the manner prescribed for the inspection of the documents referred to therein.

CHAPTER IV. OTHER OPERATIONS TREATED AS DIVISIONS

Article 24. Where, in the case of one of the operations specified in Article 1, the laws of a Member State permit the cash payment to exceed 10%, Chapters I, II and III shall apply.

Article 25. Where the laws of a Member State permit one of the operations specified in Article 1 without the company being divided ceasing to exist, Chapters I, II and III shall apply, except for Article 17 (1) (c).

CHAPTER V. FINAL PROVISIONS

Article 26. 1. The Member States shall bring into force before 1 January 1986, the laws, regulations and administrative provisions necessary for them to comply with this Directive provided that on that date they permit the operations to which this Directive applies. They shall immediately inform the Commission thereof.

2. Where, after the date mentioned in paragraph 1, a Member State permits division operations, it shall bring into force the provisions mentioned in that paragraph on the date on which it permits such operations. It shall immediately inform the Commission thereof.

3. However, provision may be made for a period of five years from the entry into force of the provisions referred to in paragraph 1 for the application of those provisions to unregistered companies in the United Kingdom and Ireland.

4. Member States need not apply Articles 12 and 13 as regards the holders of convertible debentures and other securities convertible into shares if, at the time when the provisions referred to in paragraph 1 or 2 come into force, the position of these holders in the event of a division has previously been determined by the conditions of issue.

5. Member States need not apply this Directive to divisions or to operations treated as divisions for the preparation or execution of which an act or formality required by national law has already been completed when the provisions referred to in paragraph 1 or 2 enter into force.

Article 27. This Directive is addressed to the Member States.
Done at Brussels, 17 December 1982.

For the Council, The President, H. Christophersen

Seventh Council Directive

of 13 June 1983 based on the Article 54 (3) (g) of the
Treaty on consolidated accounts

(83/349/EEC)

The Council of the European Communities,

Having regard to the Treaty establishing the European Economic Community, and in particular Article 54 (3) (g) thereof,

Having regard to the proposal from the Commission,[1]

Having regard to the opinion of the European Parliament,[2]

Having regard to the opinion of the Economic and Social Committee,[3]

Whereas on 25 July 1978 the Council adopted Directive 78/660/EEC[4] on the coordination of national legislation governing the annual accounts of certain types of companies; whereas many companies are members of bodies of undertakings; whereas consolidated accounts must be drawn up so that financial information concerning such bodies of undertakings may be conveyed to members and third parties; whereas national legislation governing consolidated accounts must therefore be coordinated in order to achieve the objectives of comparability and equivalence in the information which companies must publish within the Community;

[Whereas, in order to determine the terms of consolidation, account must be taken not only of cases in]* which the power of control is based on a majority of voting rights but also of those in which it is based on agreements, where these are permitted; whereas, furthermore, Member States in which the possibility occurs must be permitted to cover cases in which in certain circumstances control has been effectively exercised on the basis of a minority holding; whereas the Member States must be permitted to cover the case of bodies of undertakings in which the undertakings exist on an equal footing with each other;

Whereas the aim of coordinating the legislation governing consolidated accounts is to protect the interests subsisting in companies with share capital; whereas such protection implies the principle of the preparation of consolidated accounts where such a company is a member of a body of undertakings, and that such accounts must be drawn up at least where such a

---

[1] OJ No C 121, 2. 6. 1976, p. 2.   [2] OJ No C 163, 10. 7. 1978, p. 60.
[3] OJ No C 75, 26. 3. 1977, p. 5.   [4] OJ No L 222, 14. 8. 1978, p. 11.

* The English text here is defective, repeating the opening lines of the previous paragraph. The text in square brackets has been supplied from the French, which reads: 'considérant que, pour determiner les conditions de consolidation, il faut avoir égard non seulement aux cas où . . .'.

company is a parent undertaking; whereas, furthermore, the cause of full information also requires that a subsidiary undertaking which is itself a parent undertaking draw up consolidated accounts; whereas, nevertheless, such a parent undertaking may, and, in certain circumstances, must be exempted from the obligation to draw up such consolidated accounts provided that its members and third parties are sufficiently protected;

Whereas, for bodies of undertakings not exceeding a certain size, exemption from the obligation to prepare consolidated accounts may be justified; whereas, accordingly, maximum limits must be set for such exemptions; whereas it follows therefrom that the Member States may either provide that it is sufficient to exceed the limit of one only of the three criteria for the exemption not to apply or adopt limits lower than those prescribed in the Directive;

Whereas consolidated accounts must give a true and fair view of the assets and liabilities, the financial position and the profit and loss of all the undertakings consolidated taken as a whole; whereas, therefore, consolidation should in principle include all of those undertakings; whereas such consolidation requires the full incorporation of the assets and liabilities and of the income and expenditure of those undertakings and the separate disclosure of the interests of persons outwith such bodies; whereas, however, the necessary corrections must be made to eliminate the effects of the financial relations between the undertakings consolidated;

Whereas a number of principles relating to the preparation of consolidated accounts and valuation in the context of such accounts must be laid down in order to ensure that items are disclosed consistently, and may readily be compared not only as regards the methods used in their valuation but also as regards the periods covered by the accounts;

Whereas participating interests in the capital of undertakings over which undertakings included in a consolidation exercise significant influence must be included in consolidated accounts by means of the equity method;

Whereas the notes on consolidated accounts must give details of the undertakings to be consolidated;

Whereas certain derogations originally provided for on a transitional basis in Directive 78/660/EEC may be continued subject to review at a later date,

Has adopted this directive:

SECTION I. CONDITIONS FOR THE PREPARATION OF CONSOLIDATED ACCOUNTS

Article 1.   1. A Member State shall require any undertaking governed by its national law to draw up consolidated accounts and a consolidated annual report if that undertaking (a parent undertaking):

(a) has a majority of the shareholders' or members' voting rights in another undertaking (a subsidiary undertaking); or

(b) has the right to appoint or remove a majority of the members of the administrative, management or supervisory body of another undertaking (a subsidiary undertaking) and is at the same time a shareholder in or member of that undertaking; or

(c) has the right to exercise a dominant influence over an undertaking (a subsidiary undertaking) of which it is a shareholder or member, pursuant to a contract entered into with that undertaking or to a provision in its memorandum or articles of association, where the law governing that subsidiary undertaking permits its being subject to such contracts or provisions. A Member State need not prescribe that a parent undertaking must be a shareholder in or member of its subsidiary undertaking. Those Member States the laws of which do not provide for such contracts or clauses shall not be required to apply this provision; or

(d) is a shareholder in or member of an undertaking, and:

    (aa) a majority of the members of the administrative, management or supervisory bodies of that undertaking (a subsidiary undertaking) who have held office during the financial year, during the preceding financial year and up to the time when the consolidated accounts are drawn up, have been appointed solely as a result of the exercise of its voting rights; or

    (bb) controls alone, pursuant to an agreement with other shareholders in or members of that undertaking (a subsidiary undertaking), a majority of shareholders' or members' voting rights in that undertaking. The Member States may introduce more detailed provisions concerning the form and contents of such agreements.

    The Member States shall prescribe at least the arrangements referred to in (bb) above.

They may make the application of (aa) above dependent upon the holding's representing 20% or more of the shareholders' or members' voting rights.

However, (aa) above shall not apply where another undertaking has the rights referred to in subparagraphs (a), (b) or (c) above with regard to that subsidiary undertaking.

2. Apart from the cases mentioned in paragraph 1 above and pending subsequent coordination, the Member States may require any undertaking governed by their national law to draw up consolidated accounts and a consolidated annual report if that undertaking (a parent undertaking) holds a participating interest as defined in Article 17 of Directive 78/660/EEC in another undertaking (a subsidiary undertaking), and:

(a) it actually exercises a dominant influence over it; or

(b) it and the subsidiary undertaking are managed on a unified basis by the parent undertaking.

Article 2. 1. For the purposes of Article 1 (1) (a), (b) and (d), the voting rights and the rights of appointment and removal of any other subsidiary undertaking as well as those of any person acting in his own name but on behalf of the parent undertaking or of another subsidiary undertaking must be added to those of the parent undertaking.

2. For the purposes of Article 1 (1) (a), (b) and (d), the rights mentioned in paragraph 1 above must be reduced by the rights:

(a) attaching to shares held on behalf of a person who is neither the parent undertaking nor a subsidiary thereof; or
(b) attaching to shares held by way of security, provided that the rights in question are exercised in accordance with the instructions received, or held in connection with the granting of loans as part of normal business activities, provided that the voting rights are exercised in the interests of the person providing the security.

3. For the purposes of Article 1 (1) (a) and (d), the total of the shareholders' or members' voting rights in the subsidiary undertaking must be reduced by the voting rights attaching to the shares held by that undertaking itself by a subsidiary undertaking of that undertaking or by a person acting in his own name but on behalf of those undertakings.

Article 3. 1. Without prejudice to Articles 13, 14 and 15, a parent undertaking and all of its subsidiary undertakings shall be undertakings to be consolidated regardless of where the registered offices of such subsidiary undertakings are situated.

2. For the purposes of paragraph 1 above, any subsidiary undertaking of a subsidiary undertaking shall be considered a subsidiary undertaking of the parent undertaking which is the parent of the undertakings to be consolidated.

Article 4. 1. For the purposes of this Directive, a parent undertaking and all of its subsidiary undertakings shall be undertakings to be consolidated where either the parent undertaking or one or more subsidiary undertakings is established as one of the following types of company:

(a) *in Germany:*
die Aktiengesellschaft, die Kommanditgesellschaft auf Aktien, die Gesellschaft mit beschränkter Haftung;
(b) *in Belgium:*
la société anonyme/de naamloze vennootschap, la société en commandite par actions/de commanditaire vennootschap op aandelen, la société

de personnes à responsabilité limitée/de personenvennootschap met beperkte aansprakelijkheid;

(c) *in Denmark:*
aktieselskaber, kommanditaktieselskaber, anpartsselskaber;

(d) *in France:*
la société anonyme, la société en commandite par actions, la société à responsabilité limitée;

(e) *in Greece:*
ή άνώνυμη έταιρία, ή έταιρία περιορισμένης εύθύνης, ή έτερόρρυθμη κατά μετοχές έταιρία;

(f) *in Ireland:*
public companies limited by shares or by guarantee, private companies limited by shares or by guarantee;

(g) *in Italy:*
la società per azioni, la società in accomandita per azioni, la società a responsabilità limitata;

(h) *in Luxembourg:*
la société anonyme, la société en commandite par actions, la société à responsabilité limitée;

(i) *in the Netherlands:*
de naamloze vennootschap, de besloten vennootschap met beperkte aansprakelijkheid;

(j) *in the United Kingdom:*
public companies limited by shares or by guarantee, private companies limited by shares or by guarantee;

(k) *in Spain:*
la sociedad anónima, la sociedad comanditaria por acciones, la sociedad de responsabilidad limitada;

(l) *in Portugal:*
a sociedade anonima de responsabilidade limitada, a sociedade em comandita por acçoes, a sociedade por quotas de responsabilidade limitada.

2. A Member State may, however, grant exemption from the obligation imposed in Article 1 (1) where the parent undertaking is not established as one of the types of company listed in paragraph 1 above.

Article 5. 1. A Member State may grant exemption from the obligation imposed in Article 1 (1) where the parent undertaking is a financial holding company as defined in Article 5 (3) of Directive 78/660/EEC, and:

(a) it has not intervened during the financial year, directly or indirectly, in the management of a subsidiary undertaking;

(b) it has not exercised the voting rights attaching to its participating interest in respect of the appointment of a member of a subsidiary undertaking's administrative, management or supervisory bodies during the financial year or the five preceding financial years or, where the exercise of voting rights was necessary for the operation of the administrative, management or supervisory bodies of the subsidiary undertaking, no shareholder in or member of the parent undertaking with majority voting rights or member of the administrative, management or supervisory bodies of that undertaking or of a member thereof with majority voting rights is a member of the administrative, management or supervisory bodies of the subsidiary undertaking and the members of those bodies so appointed have fulfilled their functions without any interference or influence on the part of the parent undertaking or of any of its subsidiary undertakings;

(c) it has made loans only to undertakings in which it holds participating interests. Where such loans have been made to other parties, they must have been repaid by the end of the previous financial year; and

(d) the exemption is granted by an administrative authority after fulfilment of the above conditions has been checked.

2.

(a) Where a financial holding company has been exempted, Article 43 (2) of Directive 78/660/EEC shall not apply to its annual accounts with respect to any majority holdings in subsidiary undertakings as from the date provided for in Article 49 (2).

(b) The disclosures in respect of such majority holdings provided for in point 2 of Article 43 (1) of Directive 78/660/EEC may be omitted when their nature is such that they would be seriously prejudicial to the company, to its shareholders or members or to one of its subsidiaries. A Member State may make such omissions subject to prior administrative or judicial authorization. Any such omission must be disclosed in the notes on the accounts.

Article 6. 1. Without prejudice to Articles 4 (2) and 5, a Member State may provide for an exemption from the obligation imposed in Article 1 (1) if as at the balance sheet date of a parent undertaking the undertakings to be consolidated do not together, on the basis of their latest annual accounts, exceed the limits of two of the three criteria laid down in Article 27 of Directive 78/660/EEC.

2. A Member State may require or permit that the set-off referred to in Article 19 (1) and the elimination referred to in Article 26 (1) (a) and (b) be not effected when the aforementioned limits are calculated. In that case, the limits for the balance sheet total and net turnover criteria shall be increased by 20%.

3. Article 12 of Directive 78/660/EEC shall apply to the above criteria.

4. This Article shall not apply where one of the undertakings to be consolidated is a company the securities of which have been admitted to official listing on a stock exchange established in a Member State.

5. For 10 years after the date referred to in Article 49 (2), the Member States may multiply the criteria expressed in ECU by up to 2.5 and may increase the average number of persons employed during the financial year to a maximum of 500.

Article 7. 1. Notwithstanding Articles 4 (2), 5 and 6, a Member State shall exempt from the obligation imposed in Article 1 (1) any parent undertaking governed by its national law which is also a subsidiary undertaking if its own parent undertaking is governed by the law of a Member State in the following two cases:

(a) where that parent undertaking holds all of the shares in the exempted undertaking. The shares in that undertaking held by members of its administrative, management or supervisory bodies pursuant to an obligation in law or in the memorandum or articles of association shall be ignored for this purpose; or

(b) where that parent undertaking holds 90% or more of the shares in the exempted undertaking and the remaining shareholders in or members of that undertaking have approved the exemption.

In so far as the laws of a Member State prescribe consolidation in this case at the time of the adoption of this Directive, that Member State need not apply this provision for 10 years after the date referred to in Article 49 (2).

2. Exemption shall be conditional upon compliance with all of the following conditions:

(a) the exempted undertaking and, without prejudice to Articles 13, 14 and 15, all of its subsidiary undertakings must be consolidated in the accounts of a larger body of undertakings, the parent undertaking of which is governed by the law of a Member State;

(b) (aa) the consolidated accounts referred to in (a) above and the consolidated annual report of the larger body of undertakings must be drawn up by the parent undertaking of that body and audited, according to the law of the Member State by which the parent undertaking of that larger body of undertakings is governed, in accordance with this Directive;

(bb) the consolidated accounts referred to in (a) above and the consolidated annual report referred to in (aa) above, the report by the person responsible for auditing those accounts and, where appropriate, the appendix referred to in Article 9 must be published for the exempted undertaking in the manner prescribed by the law of the Member State governing that undertaking in accordance with Article 38. That Member State may require that those documents be published in its official language and that the translation be certified;

(c) the notes on the annual accounts of the exempted undertaking must disclose:

(aa) the name and registered office of the parent undertaking that draws up the consolidated accounts referred to in (a) above; and

(bb) the exemption from the obligation to draw up consolidated accounts and a consolidated annual report.

3. A Member State need not, however, apply this Article to companies the securities of which have been admitted to official listing on a stock exchange established in a Member State.

Article 8. 1. In cases not covered by Article 7 (1), a Member State may, without prejudice to Articles 4 (2), 5 and 6, exempt from the obligation imposed in Article 1 (1) any parent undertaking governed by its national law which is also a subsidiary undertaking, the parent undertaking of which is governed by the law of a Member State, provided that all the conditions set out in Article 7 (2) are fulfilled and that the shareholders in or members of the exempted undertaking who own a minimum proportion of the sub-scribed capital of that undertaking have not requested the preparation of consolidated accounts at least six months before the end of the financial year. The Member States may fix that proportion at not more than 10% for public limited liability companies and for limited partnerships with share capital, and at not more than 20% for undertakings of other types.

2. A Member State may not make it a condition for this exemption that the parent undertaking which prepared the consolidated accounts described in Article 7 (2) (a) must also be governed by its national law.

3. A Member State may not make exemption subject to conditions concerning the preparation and auditing of the consolidated accounts referred to in Article 7 (2) (a).

Article 9. 1. A Member State may make the exemptions provided for in Articles 7 and 8 dependent upon the disclosure of additional information, in accordance with this Directive, in the consolidated accounts referred to in Article 7 (2) (a), or in an appendix thereto, if that information is required of undertakings governed by the national law of that Member State which are obliged to prepare consolidated accounts and are in the same circumstances.

2. A Member State may also make exemption dependent upon the

disclosure, in the notes on the consolidated accounts referred to in Article 7 (2) (a), or in the annual accounts of the exempted undertaking, of all or some of the following information regarding the body of undertakings, the parent undertaking of which it is exempting from the obligation to draw up consolidated accounts:

— the amount of the fixed assets,
— the net turnover,
— the profit or loss for the financial year and the amount of the capital and reserves,
— the average number of persons employed during the financial year.

Article 10.   Articles 7 to 9 shall not affect any Member State's legislation on the drawing up of consolidated accounts or consolidated annual reports in so far as those documents are required:

— for the information of employees or their representatives, or
— by an administrative or judicial authority for its own purposes.

Article 11.   1. Without prejudice to Articles 4 (2), 5 and 6, a Member State may exempt from the obligations imposed in Article 1 (1) any parent undertaking governed by its national law which is also a subsidiary undertaking of a parent undertaking not governed by the law of a Member State, if all of the following conditions are fulfilled:

(a) the exempted undertaking and, without prejudice to Articles 13, 14 and 15, all of its subsidiary undertakings must be consolidated in the accounts of a larger body of undertakings;
(b) the consolidated accounts referred to in (a) above and, where appropriate, the consolidated annual report must be drawn up in accordance with this Directive or in a manner equivalent to consolidated accounts and consolidated annual reports drawn up in accordance with this Directive;
(c) the consolidated accounts referred to in (a) above must have been · audited by one or more persons authorized to audit accounts under the national law governing the undertaking which drew them up.

2. Articles 7 (2) (b) (bb) and (c) and 8 to 10 shall apply.

3. A Member State may provide for exemptions under this Article only if it provides for the same exemptions under Articles 7 to 10.

Article 12.   1. Without prejudice to Articles 1 to 10, a Member State may require any undertaking governed by its national law to draw up consolidated accounts and a consolidated annual report if:

(a) that undertaking and one or more other undertakings with which it is not connected, as described in Article 1 (1) or (2), are managed on a unified basis pursuant to a contract concluded with that undertaking or provisions in the memorandum or articles of association of those undertakings; or

(b) the administrative, management or supervisory bodies of that undertaking and of one or more other undertakings with which it is not connected, as described in Article 1 (1) or (2), consist for the major part of the same persons in office during the financial year and until the consolidated accounts are drawn up.

2. Where paragraph 1 above is applied, undertakings related as defined in that paragraph together with all of their subsidiary undertakings shall be undertakings to be consolidated, as defined in this Directive, where one or more of those undertakings is established as one of the types of company listed in Article 4.

3. Articles 3, 4 (2), 5, 6, 13 to 28, 29 (1), (3), (4) and (5), 30 to 38 and 39 (2) shall apply to the consolidated accounts and the consolidated annual report covered by this Article, references to parent undertakings being understood to refer to parent undertakings specified in paragraph 1 above. Without prejudice to Article 19 (2), however, the items 'capital', 'share premium account', 'revaluation reserve', 'reserves', 'profit or loss brought forward', and 'profit or loss for the financial year' to be included in the consolidated accounts shall be the aggregate amounts attributable to each of the undertakings specified in paragraph 1.

Article 13. 1. An undertaking need not be included in consolidated accounts where it is not material for the purposes of Article 16 (3).

2. Where two or more undertakings satisfy the requirements of paragraph 1 above, they must nevertheless be included in consolidated accounts if, as a whole, they are material for the purposes of Article 16 (3).

3. In addition, an undertaking need not be included in consolidated accounts where:

(a) severe long-term restrictions substantially hinder:
    (aa) the parent undertaking in the exercise of its rights over the assets or management of that undertaking; or
    (bb) the exercise of unified management of that undertaking where it is in one of the relationships defined in Article 12 (1); or
(b) the information necessary for the preparation of consolidated accounts in accordance with this Directive cannot be obtained without disproportionate expense or undue delay; or
(c) the shares of that undertaking are held exclusively with a view to their subsequent resale.

Article 14. 1. Where the activities of one or more undertakings to be consolidated are so different that their inclusion in the consolidated accounts would be incompatible with the obligation imposed in Article 16 (3), such undertakings must, without prejudice to Article 33 of this Directive, be excluded from the consolidation.

2. Paragraph 1 above shall not be applicable merely by virtue of the fact that the undertakings to be consolidated are partly industrial, partly commercial, and partly provide services, or because such undertakings carry on industrial or commercial activities involving different products or provide different services.

3. Any application of paragraph 1 above and the reasons therefor must be disclosed in the notes on the accounts. Where the annual or consolidated accounts of the undertakings thus excluded from the consolidation are not published in the same Member State in accordance with Directive 68/151/EEC,[1] they must be attached to the consolidated accounts or made available to the public. In the latter case it must be possible to obtain a copy of such documents upon request. The price of such a copy must not exceed its administrative cost.

Article 15. 1. A Member State may, for the purposes of Article 16 (3), permit the omission from consolidated accounts of any parent undertaking not carrying on any industrial or commercial activity which holds shares in a subsidiary undertaking on the basis of a joint arrangement with one or more undertakings not included in the consolidated accounts.

2. The annual accounts of the parent undertaking shall be attached to the consolidated accounts.

3. Where use is made of this derogation, either Article 59 of Directive 78/660/EEC shall apply to the parent undertaking's annual accounts or the information which would have resulted from its application must be given in the notes on those accounts.

SECTION 2. THE PREPARATION OF CONSOLIDATED ACCOUNTS

Article 16. 1. Consolidated accounts shall comprise the consolidated balance sheet, the consolidated profit-and-loss account and the notes on the accounts. These documents shall constitute a composite whole.

2. Consolidated accounts shall be drawn up clearly and in accordance with this Directive.

3. Consolidated accounts shall give a true and fair view of the assets, liabilities, financial position and profit or loss of the undertakings included therein taken as a whole.

[1] OJ No L 65, 14. 3. 1968, p. 8.

4. Where the application of the provisions of this Directive would not be sufficient to give a true and fair view within the meaning of paragraph 3 above, additional information must be given.

5. Where, in exceptional cases, the application of a provision of Articles 17 to 35 and 39 is incompatible with the obligation imposed in paragraph 3 above, that provision must be departed from in order to give a true and fair view within the meaning of paragraph 3. Any such departure must be disclosed in the notes on the accounts together with an explanation of the reasons for it and a statement of its effect on the assets, liabilities, financial position and profit or loss. The Member States may define the exceptional cases in question and lay down the relevant special rules.

6. A Member State may require or permit the disclosure in the consolidated accounts of other information as well as that which must be disclosed in accordance with this Directive.

Article 17. 1. Articles 3 to 10, 13, to 26 and 28 to 30 of Directive 78/660/EEC shall apply in respect of the layout of consolidated accounts, without prejudice to the provisions of this Directive and taking account of the essential adjustments resulting from the particular characteristics of consolidated accounts as compared with annual accounts.

2. Where there are special circumstances which would entail undue expense a Member State may permit stocks to be combined in the consolidated accounts.

Article 18. The assets and liabilities of undertakings included in a consolidation shall be incorporated in full in the consolidated balance sheet.

Article 19. 1. The book values of shares in the capital of undertakings included in a consolidation shall be set off against the proportion which they represent of the capital and reserves of those undertakings:

(a) That set-off shall be effected on the basis of book values as at the date as at which such undertakings are included in the consolidations for the first time. Differences arising from such set-offs shall as far as possible be entered directly against those items in the consolidated balance sheet which have values above or below their book values.

(b) A Member State may require or permit set-offs on the basis of the values of identifiable assets and liabilities as at the date of acquisition of the shares or, in the event of acquisition in two or more stages, as at the date on which the undertaking became a subsidiary.

(c) Any difference remaining after the application of (a) or resulting from the application of (b) shall be shown as a separate item in the consolidated balance sheet with an appropriate heading. That item, the methods used and any significant changes in relation to the preceding financial year must be explained in the notes on the accounts. Where the offsetting of positive and negative differences is authorized by a Member State, a breakdown of such differences must also be given in the notes on the accounts.

2. However, paragraph 1 above shall not apply to shares in the capital of the parent undertaking held either by that undertaking itself or by another undertaking included in the consolidation. In the consolidated accounts such shares shall be treated as own shares in accordance with Directive 78/660/EEC.

Article 20. 1. A Member State may require or permit the book values of shares held in the capital of an undertaking included in the consolidation to be set off against the corresponding percentage of capital only, provided that:

(a) the shares held represent at least 90% of the nominal value or, in the absence of a nominal value, of the accounting par value of the shares of that undertaking other than shares of the kind described in Article 29 (2) (a) of Directive 77/91/EEC;[1]

(b) the proportion referred to in (a) above has been attained pursuant to an arrangement providing for the issue of shares by an undertaking included in the consolidation; and

(c) the arrangement referred to in (b) above did not include a cash payment exceeding 10% of the nominal value or, in the absence of a nominal value, of the accounting par value of the shares issued.

2. Any difference arising under paragraph 1 above shall be added to or deducted from consolidated reserves as appropriate.

3. The application of the method described in paragraph 1 above, the resulting movement in reserves and the names and registered offices of the undertakings concerned shall be disclosed in the notes on the accounts.

Article 21. The amount attributable to shares in subsidiary undertakings included in the consolidation held by persons other than the undertakings included in the consolidation shall be shown in the consolidated balance sheet as a separate item with an appropriate heading.

Article 22. The income and expenditure of undertakings included in a consolidation shall be incorporated in full in the consolidated profit-and-loss account.

[1] OJ No L 26, 31. 1. 1977, p. 1.

Article 23. The amount of any profit or loss attributable to shares in subsidiary undertakings included in the consolidation held by persons other than the undertakings included in the consolidation shall be shown in the consolidated profit-and-loss account as a separate item with an appropriate heading.

Article 24. Consolidated accounts shall be drawn up in accordance with the principles enunciated in Articles 25 to 28.

Article 25. 1. The methods of consolidation must be applied consistently from one financial year to another.

2. Derogations from the provisions of paragraph 1 above shall be permitted in exceptional cases. Any such derogations must be disclosed in the notes on the accounts and the reasons for them given together with an assessment of their effect on the assets, liabilities, financial position and profit or loss of the undertakings included in the consolidation taken as a whole.

Article 26. 1. Consolidated accounts shall show the assets, liabilities, financial positions and profits or losses of the undertakings included in a consolidation as if the latter were a single undertaking. In particular:

(a) debts and claims between the undertakings included in a consolidation shall be eliminated from the consolidated accounts;
(b) income and expenditure relating to transactions between the undertakings included in a consolidation shall be eliminated from the consolidated accounts;
(c) where profits and losses resulting from transactions between the undertakings included in a consolidation are included in the book values of assets, they shall be eliminated from the consolidated accounts. Pending subsequent coordination, however, a Member State may allow the eliminations mentioned above to be effected in proportion to the percentage of the capital held by the parent undertaking in each of the subsidiary undertakings included in the consolidation.

2. A Member State may permit derogations from the provisions of paragraph 1 (c) above where a transaction has been concluded according to normal market conditions and where the elimination of the profit or loss would entail undue expense. Any such derogations must be disclosed and where the effect on the assets, liabilities, financial position and profit or loss of the undertakings, included in the consolidation, taken as a whole, is material, that fact must be disclosed in the notes on the consolidated accounts.

3. Derogations from the provisions of paragraph 1 (a), (b) or (c) above

shall be permitted where the amounts concerned are not material for the purposes of Article 16 (3).

Article 27. 1. Consolidated accounts must be drawn up as at the same date as the annual accounts of the parent undertaking.

2. A Member State may, however, require or permit consolidated accounts to be drawn up as at another date in order to take account of the balance sheet dates of the largest number or the most important of the undertakings included in the consolidation. Where use is made of this derogation that fact shall be disclosed in the notes on the consolidated accounts together with the reasons therefor. In addition, account must be taken or disclosure made of important events concerning the assets and liabilities, the financial position or the profit or loss of an undertaking included in a consolidation which have occurred between that undertaking's balance sheet date and the consolidated balance sheet date.

3. Where an undertaking's balance sheet date precedes the consolidated balance sheet date by more than three months, that undertaking shall be consolidated on the basis of interim accounts drawn up as at the consolidated balance sheet date.

Article 28. If the composition of the undertakings included in a consolidation has changed significantly in the course of a financial year, the consolidated accounts must include information which makes the comparison of successive sets of consolidated accounts meaningful. Where such a change is a major one, a Member State may require or permit this obligation to be fulfilled by the preparation of an adjusted opening balance sheet and an adjusted profit-and-loss account.

Article 29. 1. Assets and liabilities to be included in consolidated accounts shall be valued according to uniform methods and in accordance with Articles 31 to 42 and 60 of Directive 78/660/EEC.

2.

(a) An undertaking which draws up consolidated accounts must apply the same methods of valuation as in its annual accounts. However, a Member State may require or permit the use in consolidated accounts of other methods of valuation in accordance with the abovementioned Articles of Directive 78/660/EEC.

(b) Where use is made of this derogation that fact shall be disclosed in the notes on the consolidated accounts and the reasons therefor given.

3. Where assets and liabilities to be included in consolidated accounts have been valued by undertakings included in the consolidation by methods differing from those used for the consolidation, they must be revalued in

accordance with the methods used for the consolidation, unless the results of such revaluation are not material for the purposes of Article 16 (3). Departures from this principle shall be permitted in exceptional cases. Any such departures shall be disclosed in the notes on the consolidated accounts and the reasons for them given.

4. Account shall be taken in the consolidated balance sheet and in the consolidated profit-and-loss account of any difference arising on consolidation between the tax chargeable for the financial year and for preceding financial year and for preceding financial years and the amount of tax paid or payable in respect of those years, provided that it is probable that an actual charge to tax will arise within the foreseeable future for one of the undertakings included in the consolidation.

5. Where assets to be included in consolidated accounts have been the subject of exceptional value adjustments solely for tax purposes, they shall be incorporated in the consolidated accounts only after those adjustments have been eliminated. A Member State may, however, require or permit that such assets be incorporated in the consolidated accounts without the elimination of the adjustments, provided that their amounts, together with the reasons for them, are disclosed in the notes on the consolidated accounts.

Article 30. 1. A separate item as defined in Article 19 (1) (c) which corresponds to a positive consolidation difference shall be dealt with in accordance with the rules laid down in Directive 78/660/EEC for the item 'goodwill'.

2. A Member State may permit a positive consolidation difference to be immediately and clearly deducted from reserves.

Article 31. An amount shown as a separate item, as defined in Article 19 (1) (c), which corresponds to a negative consolidation difference may be transferred to the consolidated profit-and-loss account only:

(a) where that difference corresponds to the expectation at the date of acquisition of unfavourable future results in that undertaking, or to the expectation of costs which that undertaking would incur, in so far as such an expectation materializes; or

(b) in so far as such a difference corresponds to a realized gain.

Article 32. 1. Where an undertaking included in a consolidation manages another undertaking jointly with one or more undertakings not included in that consolidation, a Member State may require or permit the inclusion of that other undertaking in the consolidated accounts in proportion to the rights in its capital held by the undertaking included in the consolidation.

2. Articles 13 to 31 shall apply *mutatis mutandis* to the proportional consolidation referred to in paragraph 1 above.

3. Where this Article is applied, Article 33 shall not apply if the undertaking proportionally consolidated is an associated undertaking as defined in Article 33.

Article 33.   1. Where an undertaking included in a consolidation exercises a significant influence over the operating and financial policy of an undertaking not included in the consolidation (an associated undertaking) in which it holds a participating interest, as defined in Article 17 of Directive 78/660/EEC, that participating interest shall be shown in the consolidated balance sheet as a separate item with an appropriate heading. An undertaking shall be presumed to exercise a significant influence over another undertaking where it has 20% or more of the shareholders' or members' voting rights in that undertaking. Article 2 shall apply.

2. When this Article is applied for the first time to a participating interest covered by paragraph 1 above, that participating interest shall be shown in the consolidated balance sheet either:

(a) at its book value calculated in accordance with the valuation rules laid down in Directive 78/660/EEC. The difference between that value and the amount corresponding to the proportion of capital and reserves represented by that participating interest shall be disclosed separately in the consolidated balance sheet or in the notes on the accounts. That difference shall be calculated as at the date as at which that method is used for the first time; or

(b) at an amount corresponding to the proportion of the associated undertaking's capital and reserves represented by that participating interest. The difference between that amount and the book value calculated in accordance with the valuation rules laid down in Directive 78/660/EEC shall be disclosed separately in the consolidated balance sheet or in the notes on the accounts. That difference shall be calculated as at the date as at which that method is used for the first time.

(c) A Member State may prescribe the application of one or other of (a) and (b) above. The consolidated balance sheet or the notes on the accounts must indicate whether (a) or (b) has been used.

(d) In addition, for the purposes of (a) and (b) above, a Member State may require or permit the calculation of the difference as at the date of acquisition of the shares or, where they were acquired in two or more stages, as at the date on which the undertaking became an associated undertaking.

3. Where an associated undertaking's assets or liabilities have been valued by methods other than those used for consolidation in accordance

with Article 29 (2), they may, for the purpose of calculating the difference referred to in paragraph 2 (a) or (b) above, be revalued by the methods used for consolidation. Where such revaluation has not been carried out that fact must be disclosed in the notes on the accounts. A Member State may require such revaluation.

4. The book value referred to in paragraph 2 (a) above, or the amount corresponding to the proportion of the associated undertaking's capital and reserves referred to in paragraph 2 (b) above, shall be increased or reduced by the amount of any variation which has taken place during the financial year in the proportion of the associated undertaking's capital and reserves represented by that participating interest; it shall be reduced by the amount of the dividends relating to that participating interest.

5. In so far as the positive difference referred to in paragraph 2 (a) or (b) above cannot be related to any category of assets or liabilities it shall be dealt with in accordance with Articles 30 and 39 (3).

6. The proportion of the profit or loss of the associated undertakings attributable to such participating interests shall be shown in the consolidated profit-and-loss account as a separate item under an appropriate heading.

7. The eliminations referred to in Article 26 (1) (c) shall be effected in so far as the facts are known or can be ascertained. Article 26 (2) and (3) shall apply.

8. Where an associated undertaking draws up consolidated accounts, the foregoing provisions shall apply to the capital and reserves shown in such consolidated accounts.

9. This Article need not be applied where the participating interest in the capital of the associated undertaking is not material for the purposes of Article 16 (3).

Article 34. In addition to the information required under other provisions of this Directive, the notes on the accounts must set out information in respect of the following matters at least:

1. The valuation methods applied to the various items in the consolidated accounts, and the methods employed in calculating the value adjustments. For items included in the consolidated accounts which are or were originally expressed in foreign currency the bases of conversion used to express them in the currency in which the consolidated accounts are drawn up must be disclosed.

2.

(a) The names and registered offices of the undertakings included in the consolidation; the proportion of the capital held in undertakings included in the consolidation, other than the parent undertaking, by the undertakings included in the consolidation or by persons acting in their own names but on behalf of those undertakings; which of the conditions referred to in Articles 1 and 12 (1) following application of Article 2 has formed the basis on which the consolidation has been carried out. The latter disclosure may, however, be omitted where consolidation has been carried out on the basis of Article 1 (1) (a) and where the proportion of the capital and the proportion of the voting rights held are the same.

(b) The same information must be given in respect of undertakings excluded from a consolidation pursuant to Articles 13 and 14 and, without prejudice to Article 14 (3), an explanation must be given for the exclusion of the undertakings referred to in Article 13.

3.

(a) The names and registered offices of undertakings associated with an undertaking included in the consolidation as described in Article 33 (1) and the proportion of their capital held by undertakings included in the consolidation or by persons acting in their own names but on behalf of those undertakings.

(b) The same information must be given in respect of the associated undertakings referred to in Article 33 (9), together with the reasons for applying that provision.

4. The names and registered offices of undertakings proportionally consolidated pursuant to Article 32, the factors on which joint management is based, and the proportion of their capital held by the undertakings included in the consolidation or by persons acting in their own names but on behalf of those undertakings.

5. The name and registered office of each of the undertakings, other than those referred to in paragraphs 2, 3 and 4 above, in which undertakings included in the consolidation and those excluded pursuant to Article 14, either themselves or through persons acting in their own names but on behalf of those undertakings, hold at least a percentage of the capital which the Member States cannot fix at more than 20%, showing the proportion of the capital held, the amount of the capital and reserves, and the profit or loss for the latest financial year of the undertaking concerned for which accounts have been adopted. This information may be omitted where, for the purposes of Article 16 (3), it is of negligible importance only. The information concerning capital and reserves and the profit or loss may also be omitted where the undertaking concerned does not publish its balance sheet and where less than 50% of its capital is held (directly or indirectly) by the abovementioned undertakings.

6. The total amount shown as owed in the consolidated balance sheet and becoming due and payable after more than five years, as well as the total amount shown as owed in the consolidated balance sheet and covered by

valuable security furnished by undertakings included in the consolidation, with an indication of the nature and form of the security.

7. The total amount of any financial commitments that are not included in the consolidated balance sheet, in so far as this information is of assistance in assessing the financial position of the undertakings included in the consolidation taken as a whole. Any commitments concerning pensions and affiliated undertakings which are not included in the consolidation must be disclosed separately.

8. The consolidated net turnover as defined in Article 28 of Directive 78/660/EEC, broken down by categories of activity and into geographical markets in so far as, taking account of the manner in which the sale of products and the provision of services falling within the ordinary activities of the undertakings included in the consolidation taken as a whole are organized, these categories and markets differ substantially from one another.

9.

(a) The average number of persons employed during the financial year by undertakings included in the consolidation broken down by categories and, if they are not disclosed separately in the consolidated profit-and-loss account, the staff costs relating to the financial year.

(b) The average number of persons employed during the financial year by undertakings to which Article 32 has been applied shall be disclosed separately.

10. The extent to which the calculation of the consolidated profit or loss for the financial year has been affected by a valuation of the items which, by way of derogation from the principles enunciated in Articles 31 and 34 to 42 of Directive 78/660/EEC and in Article 29 (5) of this Directive, was made in the financial year in question or in an earlier financial year with a view to obtaining tax relief. Where the influence of such a valuation on the future tax charges of the undertakings included in the consolidation taken as a whole is material, details must be disclosed.

11. The difference between the tax charged to the consolidated profit-and-loss account for the financial year and to those for earlier financial years and the amount of tax payable in respect of those years, provided that this difference is material for the purposes of future taxation. This amount may also be disclosed in the balance sheet as a cumulative amount under a separate item with an appropriate heading.

12. The amount of the emoluments granted in respect of the financial year to the members of the administrative, managerial and supervisory bodies of the parent undertaking by reason of their responsibilities in the parent undertaking and its subsidiary undertakings, and any commitments arising or entered into under the same conditions in respect of retirement pensions for former members of those bodies, with an indication of the total

for each category. A Member State may require that emoluments granted by reason of responsibilities assumed in undertakings linked as described in Article 32 or 33 shall also be included with the information specified in the first sentence.

13. The amount of advances and credits granted to the members of the administrative, managerial and supervisory bodies of the parent undertaking by that undertaking or by one of its subsidiary undertakings, with indications of the interest rates, main conditions and any amounts repaid, as well as commitments entered into on their behalf by way of guarantee of any kind with an indication of the total for each category. A Member State may require that advances and credits granted by undertakings linked as described in Article 32 or 33 shall also be included with the information specified in the first sentence.

Article 35. 1. A Member State may allow the disclosures prescribed in Article 34 (2), (3), (4) and (5):

(a) to take the form of a statement deposited in accordance with Article 3 (1) and (2) of Directive 68/151/EEC; this must be disclosed in the notes on the accounts;

(b) to be omitted when their nature is such that they would be seriously prejudicial to any of the undertakings affected by these provisions. A Member State may make such omissions subject to prior administrative or judicial authorization. Any such omission must be disclosed in the notes on the accounts.

2. Paragraph 1 (b) shall also apply to the information prescribed in Article 34 (8).

SECTION 3. THE CONSOLIDATED ANNUAL REPORT

Article 36. 1. The consolidated annual report must include at least a fair review of the development of business and the position of the undertakings included in the consolidation taken as a whole.

2. In respect of those undertakings, the report shall also give an indication of:

(a) any important events that have occurred since the end of the financial year;

(b) the likely future development of those undertakings taken as a whole;

(c) the activities of those undertakings taken as a whole in the field of research and development;

(d) the number and nominal value or, in the absence of a nominal value, the accounting par value of all of the parent undertaking's shares held by that undertaking itself, by subsidiary undertakings of that undertaking or by a person acting in his own name but on behalf of those undertakings. A Member State may require or permit the disclosure of these particulars in the notes on the accounts.

SECTION 4. THE AUDITING OF CONSOLIDATED ACCOUNTS

Article 37. 1. An undertaking which draws up consolidated accounts must have them audited by one or more persons authorized to audit accounts under the laws of the Member State which govern that undertaking.

2. The person or persons responsible for auditing the consolidated accounts must also verify that the consolidated annual report is consistent with the consolidated accounts for the same financial year.

SECTION 5. THE PUBLICATION OF CONSOLIDATED ACCOUNTS

Article 38. 1. Consolidated accounts, duly approved, and the consolidated annual report, together with the opinion submitted by the person responsible for auditing the consolidated accounts, shall be published for the undertaking which drew up the consolidated accounts as laid down by the laws of the Member State which govern it in accordance with Article 3 of Directive 68/151/EEC.

2. The second subparagraph of Article 47 (1) of Directive 78/660/EEC shall apply with respect to the consolidated annual report.

3. The following shall be substituted for the second subparagraph of Article 47 (1) of Directive 78/660/EEC: 'It must be possible to obtain a copy of all or part of any such report upon request. The price of such a copy must not exceed its administrative cost'.

4. However, where the undertaking which drew up the consolidated accounts is not established as one of the types of company listed in Article 4 and is not required by its national law to publish the documents referred to in paragraph 1 in the same manner as prescribed in Article 3 of Directive 68/151/EEC, it must at least make them available to the public at its head office. It must be possible to obtain a copy of such documents upon request. The price of such a copy must not exceed its administrative cost.

5. Articles 48 and 49 of Directive 78/660/EEC shall apply.

6. The Member States shall provide for appropriate sanctions for failure to comply with the publication obligations imposed in this Article.

SECTION 6. TRANSITIONAL AND FINAL PROVISIONS

Article 39. 1. When, for the first time, consolidated accounts are drawn up in accordance with this Directive for a body of undertakings which was already connected, as described in Article 1 (1), before application of the provisions referred to in Article 49 (1), a Member State may require or permit that, for the purposes of Article 19 (1), account be taken of the book value of a holding and the proportion of the capital and reserves that it represents as at a date before or the same as that of the first consolidation.

2. Paragraph 1 above shall apply *mutatis mutandis* to the valuation for the purposes of Article 33 (2) of a holding, or of the proportion of capital and reserves that it represents, in the capital of an undertaking associated with an undertaking included in the consolidation, and to the proportional consolidation referred to in Article 32.

3. Where the separate item defined in Article 19 (1) corresponds to a positive consolidation difference which arose before the date of the first consolidated accounts drawn up in accordance with this Directive, a Member State may:

(a) for the purposes of Article 30 (1), permit the calculation of the limited period of more than five years provided for in Article 37 (2) of Directive 78/660/EEC as from the date of the first consolidated accounts drawn up in accordance with this Directive; and

(b) for the purposes of Article 30 (2), permit the deduction to be made from reserves as at the date of the first consolidated accounts drawn up in accordance with this Directive.

Article 40.   1. Until expiry of the deadline imposed for the application in national law of the Directives supplementing Directive 78/660/EEC as regards the harmonization of the rules governing the annual accounts of banks and other financial institutions and insurance undertakings, a Member State may derogate from the provisions of this Directive concerning the layout of consolidated accounts, the methods of valuing the items included in those accounts and the information to be given in the notes on the accounts:

(a) with regard to any undertaking to be consolidated which is a bank, another financial institution or an insurance undertaking;

(b) where the undertakings to be consolidated comprise principally banks, financial institutions or insurance undertakings.

They may also derogate from Article 6, but only in so far as the limits and criteria to be applied to the above undertakings are concerned.

2. In so far as a Member State has not required all undertakings which are banks, other financial institutions or insurance undertakings to draw up consolidated accounts before implementation of the provisions referred to in Article 49 (1), it may, until its national law implements one of the Directives mentioned in paragraph 1 above, but not in respect of financial years ending after 1993:

(a) suspend the application of the obligation imposed in Article 1 (1) with respect to any of the above undertakings which is a parent undertaking. That fact must be disclosed in the annual accounts of the parent undertaking and the information prescribed in point 2 of Article 43 (1) of Directive 78/660/EEC must be given for all subsidiary undertakings;

(b) where consolidated accounts are drawn up and without prejudice to Article 33, permit the omission from the consolidation of any of the above undertakings which is a subsidiary undertaking. The information prescribed in Article 34 (2) must be given in the notes on the accounts in respect of any such subsidiary undertaking.

3. In the cases referred to in paragraph 2 (b) above, the annual or consolidated accounts of the subsidiary undertaking must, in so far as their publication is compulsory, be attached to the consolidated accounts or, in the absence of consolidated accounts, to the annual accounts of the parent undertaking or be made available to the public. In the latter case it must be possible to obtain a copy of such documents upon request. The price of such a copy must not exceed its administrative cost.

Article 41. 1. Undertakings which are connected as described in Article 1 (1) (a), (b) and (d) (bb), and those other undertakings which are similarly connected with one of the aforementioned undertakings, shall be affiliated undertakings for the purposes of this Directive and of Directive 78/660/EEC.

2. Where a Member State prescribes the preparation of consolidated accounts pursuant to Article 1 (1) (c), (d) (aa) or (2) or Article 12 (1), the undertakings which are connected as described in those Articles and those other undertakings which are connected similarly, or are connected as described in paragraph 1 above to one of the aforementioned undertakings, shall be affiliated undertakings as defined in paragraph 1.

3. Even where a Member State does not prescribe the preparation of consolidated accounts pursuant to Article 1 (1) (c), (d) (aa) or (2) or Article 12 (1), it may apply paragraph 2 of this Article.

4. Articles 2 and 3 (2) shall apply.

5. When a Member State applies Article 4 (2), it may exclude from the application of paragraph 1 above affiliated undertakings which are parent undertakings and which by virtue of their legal form are not required by that Member State to draw up consolidated accounts in accordance with the provisions of this Directive, as well as parent undertakings with a similar legal form.

Article 42. The following shall be substituted for Article 56 of Directive 78/660/EEC:

Article 56. 1. The obligation to show in annual accounts the items prescribed by

Articles 9, 10 and 23 to 26 which relate to affiliated undertakings, as defined by Article 41 of Directive 83/349/EEC, and the obligation to provide information concerning these undertakings in accordance with Articles 13 (2), and 14 and point 7 of Article 43 (1) shall enter into force on the date fixed in Article 49 (2) of that Directive.

2. The notes on the accounts must also disclose:

(a) the name and registered office of the undertaking which draws up the consolidated accounts of the largest body of undertakings of which the company forms part as a subsidiary undertaking;

(b) the name and registered office of the undertaking which draws up the consolidated accounts of the smallest body of undertakings of which the company forms part as a subsidiary undertaking and which is also included in the body of undertakings referred to in (a) above;

(c) the place where copies of the consolidated accounts referred to in (a) and (b) above may be obtained provided that they are available.

Article 43.   The following shall be substituted for Article 57 of Directive 78/660/EEC:

Article 57.   Notwithstanding the provisions of Directives 68/151/EEC and 77/91/EEC, a Member State need not apply the provisions of this Directive concerning the content, auditing and publication of annual accounts to companies governed by their national laws which are subsidiary undertakings, as defined in Directive 83/349/EEC, where the following conditions are fulfilled:

(a) the parent undertaking must be subject to the laws of a Member State;

(b) all shareholders or members of the subsidiary undertaking must have declared their agreement to the exemption from such obligation; this declaration must be made in respect of every financial year;

(c) the parent undertaking must have declared that it guarantees the commitments entered into by the subsidiary undertaking;

(d) the declarations referred to in (b) and (c) must be published by the subsidiary undertaking as laid down by the laws of the Member State in accordance with Article 3 of Directive 68/151/EEC;

(e) the subsidiary undertaking must be included in the consolidated accounts drawn up by the parent undertaking in accordance with Directive 83/349/EEC;

(f) the above exemption must be disclosed in the notes on the consolidated accounts drawn up by the parent undertaking;

(g) the consolidated accounts referred to in (e), the consolidated annual report, and the report by the person responsible for auditing those accounts must be published for the subsidiary undertaking as laid down by the laws of the Member State in accordance with Article 3 of Directive 68/151/EEC.

Article 44.   The following shall be substituted for Article 58 of Directive 78/660/EEC:

Article 58.   A Member State need not apply the provisions of this Directive concerning the auditing and publication of the profit-and-loss account to companies governed by their national laws which are parent undertakings for the purposes of Directive 83/349/EEC where the following conditions are fulfilled:

(a) the parent undertaking must draw up consolidated accounts in accordance with Directive 83/349/EEC and be included in the consolidated accounts;
(b) the above exemption must be disclosed in the notes on the annual accounts of the parent undertaking;
(c) the above exemption must be disclosed in the notes on the consolidated accounts drawn up by the parent undertaking;
(d) the profit or loss of the parent company, determined in accordance with this Directive, must be shown in the balance sheet of the parent company.

Article 45. The following shall be substituted for Article 59 of Directive 78/660/EEC:

Article 59. 1. A Member State may require or permit that participating interests, as defined in Article 17, in the capital of undertakings over the operating and financial policies of which significant influence is exercised, be shown in the balance sheet in accordance with paragraphs 2 to 9 below, as sub-items of the items 'shares in affiliated undertakings' or 'participating interests', as the case may be. An undertaking shall be presumed to exercise a significant influence over another undertaking where it has 20% or more of the shareholders' or members' voting rights in that undertaking. Article 2 of Directive 83/349/EEC shall apply.

2. When this Article is first applied to a participating interest covered by paragraph 1, it shall be shown in the balance sheet either:

(a) at its book value calculated in accordance with Articles 31 to 42. The difference between that value and the amount corresponding to the proportion of capital and reserves represented by the participating interest shall be disclosed separately in the balance sheet or in the notes on the accounts. That difference shall be calculated as at the date as at which the method is applied for the first time; or
(b) at the amount corresponding to the proportion of the capital and reserves represented by the participating interest. The difference between that amount and the book value calculated in accordance with Articles 31 to 42 shall be disclosed separately in the balance sheet or in the notes on the accounts. That difference shall be calculated as at the date as at which the method is applied for the first time.
(c) A Member State may prescribe the application of one or other of the above paragraphs. The balance sheet or the notes on the accounts must indicate whether (a) or (b) above has been used.
(d) In addition, when applying (a) and (b) above, a Member State may require or permit calculation of the difference as at the date of acquisition of the participating interest referred to in paragraph 1 or, where the acquisition took place in two or more stages, as at the date as at which the holding became a participating interest within the meaning of paragraph 1 above.

3. Where the assets or liabilities of an undertaking in which a participating interest within the meaning of paragraph 1 above is held have been valued by methods other

than those used by the company drawing up the annual accounts, they may, for the purpose of calculating the difference referred to in paragraph 2 (a) or (b) above, be revalued by the methods used by the company drawing up the annual accounts. Disclosure must be made in the notes on the accounts where such revaluation has not been carried out. A Member State may require such revaluation.

4. The book value referred to in paragraph 2 (a) above, or the amount corresponding to the proportion of capital and reserves referred to in paragraph 2 (b) above, shall be increased or reduced by the amount of the variation which has taken place during the financial year in the proportion of capital and reserves represented by that participating interest; it shall be reduced by the amount of the dividends relating to the participating interest.

5. In so far as a positive difference covered by paragraph 2 (a) or (b) above cannot be related to any category of asset or liability, it shall be dealt with in accordance with the rules applicable to the item 'goodwill'.

6.

(a) The proportion of the profit or loss attributable to participating interests within the meaning of paragraph 1 above shall be shown in the profit-and-loss account as a separate item with an appropriate heading.

(b) Where that amount exceeds the amount of dividends already received or the payment of which can be claimed, the amount of the difference must be placed in a reserve which cannot be distributed to shareholders.

(c) A Member State may require or permit that the proportion of the profit or loss attributable to the participating interests referred to in paragraph 1 above be shown in the profit-and-loss account only to the extent of the amount corresponding to dividends already received or the payment of which can be claimed.

7. The eliminations referred to in Article 26 (1) (c) of Directive 83/349/EEC shall be effected in so far as the facts are known or can be ascertained. Article 26 (2) and (3) of that Directive shall apply.

8. Where an undertaking in which a participating interest within the meaning of paragraph 1 above is held draws up consolidated accounts, the foregoing paragraphs shall apply to the capital and reserves shown in such consolidated accounts.

9. This Article need not be applied where a participating interest as defined in paragraph 1 is not material for the purposes of Article 2 (3).

Article 46.   The following shall be substituted for Article 61 of Directive 78/660/EEC:

Article 61.   A Member State need not apply the provisions of point 2 of Article 43 (1) of this Directive concerning the amount of capital and reserves and profits and losses of the undertakings concerned to companies governed by their national laws which are parent undertakings for the purposes of Directive 83/349/EEC:

(a) where the undertakings concerned are included in consolidated accounts of a larger body of undertakings as referred to in Article 7 (2) of Directive 83/349/EEC; or

(b) where the holdings in the undertakings concerned have been dealt with by the parent undertaking in its annual accounts in accordance with Article 59, or in the consolidated accounts drawn up by that parent undertaking in accordance with Article 33 of Directive 83/349/EEC.

Article 47.   The Contact Committee set up pursuant to Article 52 of Directive 78/660/EEC shall also:

(a) facilitate, without prejudice to Articles 169 and 170 of the Treaty, harmonized application of this Directive through regular meetings dealing, in particular, with practical problems arising in connection with its application;
(b) advise the Commission, if necessary, on additions or amendments to this Directive.

Article 48.   This Directive shall not affect laws in the Member States requiring that consolidated accounts in which undertakings not falling within their jurisdiction are included be filed in a register in which branches of such undertakings are listed.

Article 49.   1. The Member States shall bring into force the laws, regulations and administrative provisions necessary for them to comply with this Directive before 1 January 1988. They shall forthwith inform the Commission thereof.

2. A Member State may provide that the provisions referred to in paragraph 1 above shall first apply to consolidated accounts for financial years beginning on 1 January 1990 or during the calendar year 1990.

3. The Member States shall ensure that they communicate to the Commission the texts of the main provisions of national law which they adopt in the field covered by this Directive.

Article 50.   1. Five years after the date referred to in Article 49 (2), the Council, acting on a proposal from the Commission, shall examine and if need be revise Articles 1 (1) (d) (second subparagraph), 4 (2), 5, 6, 7 (1), 12, 43 and 44 in the light of the experience acquired in applying this Directive, the aims of this Directive and the economic and monetary situation at the time.

2. Paragraph 1 above shall not affect Article 53 (2) of Directive 78/660/EEC.

Article 51.   This Directive is addressed to the Member States.
Done at Luxembourg, 13 June 1983.

For the Council, The President, H. Tietmeyer

Eighth Council Directive

of 10 April 1984 based on Article 54 (3) (g) of the Treaty
on the approval of persons responsible for carrying out
the statutory audits of accounting documents

(84/253/EEC)

The Council of the European Communities,

Having regard to the Treaty establishing the European Economic Community, and in particular Article 54 (3) (g) thereof,

Having regard to the proposal from the Commission,[1]

Having regard to the opinion of the European Parliament,[2]

Having regard to the opinion of the Economic and Social Committee,[3]

Whereas, under Directive 78/660/EEC,[4] the annual accounts of certain types of company must be audited by one or more persons entitled to carry out such audits from which only the companies mentioned in Article 11 of that Directive may be exempted;

Whereas the aforementioned Directive has been supplemented by Directive 83/349/EEC[5] on consolidated accounts;

Whereas the qualifications of persons entitled to carry out the statutory audits of accounting documents should be harmonized; whereas it should be ensured that such persons are independent and of good repute;

Whereas the high level of theoretical knowledge required for the statutory auditing of accounting documents and the ability to apply that knowledge in practice must be ensured by means of an examination of professional competence;

Whereas the Member States should be given the power to approve persons who, while not fulfilling all the conditions imposed concerning theoretical training, nevertheless have engaged in professional activities for a long time, affording them sufficient experience in the fields of finance, law and accountancy and have passed the examination of professional competence;

Whereas the Member States should also be authorized to adopt transitional provisions for the benefit of professional persons;

Whereas the Member States will be able to approve both natural persons and firms of auditors which may be legal persons or other types of company, firms or partnership;

---

[1] OJ No C 112, 13. 5. 1978, p. 6; OJ No C 317, 18. 12. 1975, p. 6.
[2] OJ No C 140, 5. 6. 1979, p. 154.   [3] OJ No C 171, 9. 7. 1979, p. 30.
[4] OJ No L 222, 14. 8. 1978, p. 11.   [5] OJ No L 193, 18.7, 1983, p. 1.

Whereas natural persons who carry out the statutory audits of accounting documents on behalf of such firms of auditors must fulfill the conditions of this Directive;

Whereas a Member State will be able to approve persons who have obtained qualifications outside that State which are equivalent to those required by this Directive;

Whereas a Member State which, when this Directive is adopted, recognizes categories of natural persons who fulfil the conditions imposed in this Directive, but whose level of examination of professional competence is below university, final examination level, should be allowed to continue, under certain conditions and until subsequent coordination, to grant such persons special approval for the purpose of carrying out the statutory audits of the accounting documents of companies and bodies of undertakings, of limited size, when such Member State has not made use of the possibilities for exemption afforded by Community Directives in respect of the preparation of consolidated accounts;

Whereas this Directive does not cover either the right of establishment or the freedom to provide services with regard to persons responsible for carrying out the statutory audits of accounting documents;

Whereas recognition of the approval given to nationals of other Member States for the purpose of carrying out such audits will be specifically regulated by Directives on the taking up and pursuit of activities in the fields of finance, economics and accountancy, as well as on the freedom to provide services in those fields,

Has adopted this directive:

SECTION I. SCOPE

Article 1. 1. The coordination measures prescribed in this Directive shall apply to the laws, regulations and administrative provisions of the Member States concerning persons responsible for:

(a) carrying out statutory audits of the annual accounts of companies and firms and verifying that the annual reports are consistent with those annual accounts in so far as such audits and such verification are required by Community law;

(b) carrying out statutory audits of the consolidated accounts of bodies of undertakings and verifying that the consolidated annual reports are consistent with those consolidated accounts in so far as such audits and such verification are required by Community law.

2. The persons referred to in paragraph 1 may, depending on the legislation of each Member State, be natural or legal persons or other types of company, firm or partnership (firms of auditors as defined in this Directive).

SECTION II. RULES ON APPROVAL

Article 2.   1. Statutory audits of the documents referred to in Article 1 (1) shall be carried out only by approved persons. The authorities of the Member States may approve only:

(a) natural persons who satisfy at least the conditions laid down in Articles 3 to 19;

(b) firms of auditors which satisfy at least the following conditions:

    (i) the natural persons to carry out statutory audits of the documents referred to in Article 1 on behalf of firms of auditors must satisfy at least the conditions imposed in Articles 3 to 19; the Member States may provide that such natural persons must also be approved;

    (ii) a majority of the voting rights must be held by natural persons or firms of auditors who satisfy at least the conditions imposed in Articles 3 to 19 with the exception of Article 11 (1) (b); the Member States may provide that such natural persons or firms of auditors must also be approved. However, those Member States which do not impose such majority at the time of the adoption of this Directive need not impose it provided that all the shares in a firm of auditors are registered and can be transferred only with the agreement of the firm of auditors and/or, where the Member State so provides, with the approval of the competent authority;

    (iii) a majority of the members of the administrative or management body of a firm of auditors must be natural persons or firms of auditors who satisfy at least the conditions imposed in Articles 3 to 19; the Member States may provide that such natural persons or firms of auditors must also be approved. Where such body has no more than two members, one of those members must satisfy at least those conditions.

Without prejudice to Article 14 (2), the approval of a firm of auditors must be withdrawn when any of the conditions imposed in (b) is no longer fulfilled. The Member States may, however, provide for a period of grace of not more than two years for the purpose of meeting the requirements imposed in (b) (ii) and (iii).

2. For the purposes of this Directive, the authorities of the Member States may be professional associations provided that they are authorized by national law to grant approval as defined in this Directive.

Article 3.   The authorities of a Member State shall grant approval only to persons of good repute who are not carrying on any activity which is incompatible, under the law of that Member State, with the statutory auditing of the documents referred to in Article 1 (1).

Article 4. A natural person may be approved to carry out statutory audits of the documents referred to in Article 1 (1) only after having attained university entrance level, then completed a course of theoretical instruction, undergone practical training and passed an examination of professional competence of university, final examination level organized or recognized by the State.

Article 5. The examination of professional competence referred to in Article 4 must guarantee the necessary level of theoretical knowledge of subjects relevant to the statutory auditing of the documents referred to in Article 1 (1) and the ability to apply such knowledge in practice.

Part at least of that examination must be written.

Article 6. The text of theoretical knowledge included in the examination must cover the following subjects in particular:

(a) — auditing,
   — analysis and critical assessment of annual accounts,
   — general accounting,
   — consolidated accounts,
   — cost and management accounting,
   — internal audit,
   — standards relating to the preparation of annual and consolidated accounts and to methods of valuing balance sheet items and of computing profits and losses,
   — legal and professional standards relating to the statutory auditing of accounting documents and to those carrying out such audits;
(b) in so far as they are relevant to auditing:
   — company law,
   — the law of insolvency and similar procedures,
   — tax law,
   — civil and commercial law,
   — social-security law and law of employment,
   — information and computer systems,
   — business, general and financial economics,
   — mathematics and statistics,
   — basic principles of the financial management of undertakings.

Article 7. 1. By way of derogation from Articles 5 and 6, a Member State may provide that a person who has passed a university or equivalent examination or holds a university degree or equivalent qualification in one or more of the subjects referred to in Article 6 may be exempted from the test of theoretical knowledge in the subjects covered by that examination or degree.

2. By way of derogation from Article 5, a Member State may provide that a holder of a university degree or equivalent qualification in one or more of the subjects referred to in Article 6 may be exempted from the test of the ability to apply in practice his theoretical knowledge of such subjects when he has received practical training in them attested by an examination or diploma recognized by the State.

Article 8.   1. In order to ensure the ability to apply theoretical knowledge in practice, a test of which is included in the examination, a trainee must complete a minimum of three years' practical training in *inter alia* the auditing of annual accounts, consolidated accounts or similar financial statements. At least two-thirds of such practical training must be completed under a person approved under the law of the Member State in accordance with this Directive; the Member State may, however, permit practical training to be carried out under a person approved by the law of another Member State in accordance with this Directive.

2. Member States shall ensure that all training is carried out under persons providing adequate guarantees regarding training.

Article 9.   Member States may approve persons to carry out statutory audits of the documents referred to in Article 1 (1) even if they do not fulfil the conditions imposed in Article 4, if they can show either:

(a) that they have, for 15 years, engaged in professional activities which have enabled them to acquire sufficient experience in the fields of finance, law and accountancy and have passed the examination of professional competence referred to in Article 4, or
(b) that they have, for seven years, engaged in professional activities in those fields and have, in addition, undergone the practical training referred to in Article 8 and passed the examination of professional competence referred to in Article 4.

Article 10.   1. Member States may deduct periods of theoretical instruction in the fields referred to in Article 6 from the years of professional activity referred to in Article 9, provided that such instruction is attested by an examination recognized by the State. Such instruction must last not less than one year, nor may it reduce the period of professional activity by more than four years.

2. The period of professional activity as well as the practical training must not be shorter than the programme of theoretical instruction and the practical training required by Article 4.

Article 11.   1. The authorities of a Member State may approve persons who have obtained all or part of their qualifications in another State provided they fulfil the following two conditions:

(a) the competent authorities must consider their qualifications equivalent to those required under the law of that Member State in accordance with this Directive; and

(b) they must have furnished proof of the legal knowledge required in that Member State for purposes of the statutory auditing of the documents referred to in Article 1 (1). The authorities of that Member State need not, however, require such proof where they consider legal knowledge obtained in another State sufficient.

2. Article 3 shall apply.

Article 12. 1. A Member State may consider to be approved, in accordance with this Directive, those professional persons who were approved by individual acts of that Member State's competent authorities before the application of the provisions referred to in Article 30 (2).

2. The admission of a natural person to a professional association recognized by the State where, according to the law of that State, such admission confers on the members of that association the right to carry out statutory audits of the documents referred to in Article 1 (1), may be considered as approval by individual act for the purposes of paragraph 1 of this Article.

Article 13. Until the application of the provisions referred to in Article 30 (2), a Member State may consider approved, in accordance with this Directive, those professional persons who have not been approved by individual acts of the competent authorities but who have nevertheless the same qualifications in that Member State as persons approved by individual acts who on the date of approval are carrying out statutory audits of the documents referred to in Article 1 (1) on behalf of such approved persons.

Article 14. 1. A Member State may consider to be approved in accordance with this Directive those firms of auditors which have been approved by individual acts of that Member State's competent authorities before the application of the provisions referred to in Article 30 (2).

2. The conditions imposed in Article 2 (1) (b) (ii) and (iii) must be complied with no later than the end of a period which may not be fixed at more than five years from the date of application of the provisions referred to in Article 30 (2).

3. Those natural persons who, until the application of the provisions referred to in Article 30 (2), carried out statutory audits of the documents referred to in Article 1 (1) in the name of a firm of auditors may, after that date, be authorized to continue to do so even if they do not fulfil all the conditions imposed by this Directive.

Article 15. Until one year after the application of the provisions referred to in Article 30 (2), those professional persons who have not been approved by individual acts of the competent authorities but who are nevertheless qualified in a Member State to carry out statutory audits of the documents referred to in Article 1 (1) and have in fact carried on such activities until that date may be approved by that Member State in accordance with this Directive.

Article 16. For one year after the application of the provisions referred to in Article 30 (2), Member States may apply transitional measures in respect of professional persons who, after that date, maintain the right to audit the annual accounting documents of certain types of company or firm not subject to statutory audit but who will no longer be able to carry out such audits upon the introduction of new statutory audits unless special measures are enacted for their benefit.

Article 17. Article 3 shall apply to Articles 15 and 16.

Article 18. 1. For six years after the application of the provisions referred to in Article 30 (2), Member States may apply transitional measures in respect of persons already undergoing professional or practical training when those provisions are applied who, on completion of their training, would not fulfil the conditions imposed by this Directive and would therefore be unable to carry out statutory audits of the documents referred to in Article 1 (1) for which they had been trained.
2. Article 3 shall apply.

Article 19. None of the professional persons referred to in Articles 15 and 16 or of those persons referred to in Article 18 may be approved by way of derogation from Article 4 unless the competent authorities consider that they are fit to carry out statutory audits of the documents referred to in Article 1 (1) and have qualifications equivalent to those of persons approved under Article 4.

Article 20. A Member State which does not make use of the possibility provided for in Article 51 (2) of Directive 78/660/EEC and in which, at the time of the adoption of this Directive, several categories of natural persons may, under national legislation, carry out statutory audits of the documents referred to in Article 1 (1) (a) of this Directive, may, until subsequent coordination of the statutory auditing of accounting documents, specially approve, for the purpose of carrying out statutory audits of the documents referred to in Article 1 (1) (a) in the case of a company which does not exceed the limits of two of the three criteria established in Article 27 of Directive 78/660/EEC, natural persons acting in their own names who:

(a) fulfil the conditions imposed in Articles 3 to 19 of this Directive save that the level of the examination of professional competence may be lower than that required in Article 4 of this Directive; and

(b) have already carried out the statutory audit of the company in question before it exceeded the limits of two of the three criteria established in Article 11 of Directive 78/660/EEC.

However, if a company forms part of a body of undertakings to be consolidated which exceeds the limits of two of the three criteria established in Article 27 of Directive 78/660/EEC, such persons may not carry out the statutory audit of the documents referred to in Article 1 (1) (a) of this Directive in the case of that company.

Article 21. A Member State which does not make use of the possibility provided for in Article 6 (1) of Directive 83/349/EEC and in which, when this Directive is adopted, several categories of natural persons may, under national legislation, carry out statutory audits of the documents referred to in Article 1 (1) (b) of this Directive may, until subsequent coordination of the statutory auditing of accounting documents, specially approve, for the purpose of carrying out statutory audits of the documents referred to in Article 1 (1) (b), a person approved pursuant to Article 20 of this Directive if on the parent undertaking's balance sheet date, the body of undertakings to be consolidated does not, on the basis of those undertakings' latest annual accounts, exceed the limits of two of the three criteria established in Article 27 of Directive 78/660/EEC, provided that he is empowered to carry out the statutory audit, of the documents referred to in Article 1 (1) (a) of this Directive, of all the undertakings included in the consolidation.

Article 22. A Member State which makes use of Article 20 may allow the practical training of the persons concerned as referred to in Article 8 to be completed under a person who has been approved under the law of that Member State to carry out the statutory audits referred to in Article 20.

SECTION III. PROFESSIONAL INTEGRITY AND INDEPENDENCE

Article 23. Member States shall prescribe that persons approved for the statutory auditing of the documents referred to in Article 1 (1) shall carry out such audits with professional integrity.

Article 24. Member States shall prescribe that such persons shall not carry out statutory audits which they have required if such persons are not independent in accordance with the law of the Member State which requires the audit.

Article 25.   Articles 23 and 24 shall also apply to natural persons who satisfy the conditions imposed in Articles 3 to 19 and carry out the statutory audit of the documents referred to in Article 1 (1) on behalf of a firm of auditors.

Article 26.   Member States shall ensure that approved persons are liable to appropriate sanctions when they do not carry out audits in accordance with Articles 23, 24 and 25.

Article 27.   Member States shall ensure at least that the members and shareholders of approved firms of auditors and the members of the administrative, management and supervisory bodies of such firms who do not personally satisfy the conditions laid down in Articles 3 to 19 in a particular Member State do not intervene in the execution of audits in any way which jeopardizes the independence of the natural persons auditing the documents referred to in Article 1 (1) on behalf of such firms of auditors.

SECTION IV. PUBLICITY

Article 28.   1. Member States shall ensure that the names and addresses of all natural persons and firms of auditors approved by them to carry out statutory audits of the documents referred to in Article 1 (1) are made available to the public.

2. In addition, the following must be made available to the public in respect of each approved firm of auditors:

(a) the names and addresses of the natural persons referred to in Article 2 (1) (b) (i); and
(b) the names and addresses of the members or shareholders of the firm of auditors;
(c) the names and addresses of the members of the administrative or management body of the firm of auditors.

3. Where a natural person is permitted to carry out statutory audits of the documents referred to in Article 1 (1) in the case of a company according to the conditions referred to in Articles 20, 21 and 22, paragraph 1 of this Article shall apply. The category of company or firm or the bodies of undertakings in respect of which such an audit is permitted must, however, be indicated.

SECTION V. FINAL PROVISIONS

Article 29.   The Contact Committee set up by Article 52 of Directive 78/660/EEC shall also:

(a) facilitate, without prejudice to Articles 169 and 170 of the Treaty, harmonized application of this Directive through regular meetings dealing, in particular, with practical problems arising in connection with its application;

(b) advise the Commission, if necessary, on additions or amendments to this Directive.

Article 30. 1. Member States shall bring into force before 1 January 1988 the laws, regulations and administrative provisions necessary for them to comply with this Directive. They shall forthwith inform the Commission thereof.

2. Member States may provide that the provisions referred to in paragraph 1 shall not apply until 1 January 1990.

3. Member States shall ensure that they communicate to the Commission the texts of the main provisions of national law which they adopt in the field covered by this Directive.

4. Member States shall also ensure that they communicate, to the Commission, lists of the examinations organized or recognized pursuant to Article 4.

Article 31. This Directive is addressed to the Member States.

Done at Brussels, 10 April 1984.

For the Council, The President, C. Cheysson

Eleventh Council Directive

of 21 December 1989 concerning disclosure requirements
in respect of branches opened in a Member State
by certain types of company governed by the law of
another State

(89/666/EEC)

The Council of the European Communities,

Having regard to the Treaty establishing the European Economic Community, and in particular Article 54 thereof,

Having regard to the proposal from the Commission,[1]

In co-operation with the European Parliament,[2]

Having regard to the opinion of the Economic and Social Committee,[3]

Whereas in order to facilitate the exercise of freedom of establishment in respect of companies covered by Article 58 of the Treaty, Article 54 (3) (g) and the general programme on the elimination of restrictions on the freedom of establishment require co-ordination of the safeguards required of companies and firms in the Member States for the protection of the interests of members and others;

Whereas hitherto this co-ordination has been effected in respect of disclosure by the adoption of the First Directive 68/151/EEC[4] covering companies with share capital, as last amended by the 1985 Act of Accession; whereas it was continued in this field of accounting by the Fourth Directive 78/660/EEC[5] on the annual accounts of certain types of companies, as last amended by the 1985 Act of Accession, the Seventh Directive 83/349/EEC[6] on consolidated accounts, as amended by the 1985 Act of Accession, and the Eighth Directive 84/253/EEC[7] on the persons responsible for carrying out statutory audits of accounting documents;

Whereas these Directives apply to companies as such but do not cover their branches; whereas the opening of a branch, like the creation of a subsidiary, is one of the possibilities currently open to companies in the exercise of their right of establishment in another Member State;

Whereas in respect of branches the lack of co-ordination, in particular concerning disclosure, gives rise to some disparities, in the protection of shareholders and third parties, between companies which operate in other

---

[1] OJ No C 105, 21. 4. 1988, p. 6.

[2] OJ No C 345, 21. 12. 1987, p. 76 and OJ No C 256, 9. 10. 1989, p. 27

[3] OJ No C 319, 30. 11. 1987, p. 61.   [4] OJ No L 65, 14. 3. 1968, p. 8

[5] OJ No L 222, 14. 8. 1978, p. 11.   [6] OJ No L 193, 18. 7. 1983, p. 1.

[7] OJ No L 126, 12. 5. 1984, p. 20.

Member States by opening branches and those which operate there by creating subsidiaries;

Whereas in this field the differences in the laws of the Member States may interfere with the exercise of the right of establishment; whereas it is therefore necessary to eliminate such differences in order to safeguard, *inter alia*, the exercise of that right;

Whereas to ensure the protection of persons who deal with companies through the intermediary of branches, measures in respect of disclosure are required in the Member State in which a branch is situated; whereas, in certain respects, the economic and social influence of a branch may be comparable to that of a subsidiary company, so that there is public interest in disclosure of the company at the branch; whereas to effect such disclosure it is necessary to make use of the procedure already instituted for companies with share capital within the Community;

Whereas such disclosure relates to a range of important documents and particulars and amendments thereto;

Whereas such disclosure, with the exception of the powers of representation, the name and legal form and the winding-up of the company and the insolvency proceedings to which it is subject, may be confined to information concerning a branch itself together with a reference to the register of the Company of which that branch is part, since under existing Community rules all information covering the company as such is available in that register;

Whereas national provisions in respect of the disclosure of accounting documents relating to a branch can no longer be justified following the co-ordination of national law in respect of the drawing up, audit and disclosure of companies' accounting documents; whereas it is accordingly sufficient to disclose, in the register of the branch, the accounting documents as audited and disclosed by the company;

Whereas letters and order forms used by a branch must give at least the same information as letters and order forms used by the company, and state the register in which the branch is entered;

Whereas to ensure that the purposes of this Directive are fully realised and to avoid any discrimination on the basis of a company's country of origin, this Directive must also cover branches opened by companies governed by the law of non-member countries and set up in legal forms comparable to companies to which Directive 68/151/EEC applies; whereas for these branches it is necessary to apply certain provisions different from those that apply to the branches of companies governed by the law of other Member States since the Directives referred to above do not apply to companies from non-member countries;

Whereas this Directive in no way affects the disclosure requirements for branches under other provisions of, for example, employment law on workers' rights to information and tax law, or for statistical purposes;

Has adopted this directive:

Article 1. 1. Documents and particulars relating to a branch opened in a Member State by a company which is governed by the law of another Member State and to which Directive 68/151/EEC applies shall be disclosed pursuant to the law of the Member State of the branch, in accordance with Article 3 of that Directive.

2. Where disclosure requirements in respect of the branch differ from those in respect of the company, the branch's disclosure requirements shall take precedence with regard to transactions carried out with the branch.

Article 2. 1. The compulsory disclosure provided for in Article 1 shall cover the following documents and particulars only:

(a) the address of the branch;
(b) the activities of the branch;
(c) the register in which the company file mentioned in Article 3 of Council Directive 68/151/EEC is kept together with the registration number in that register;
(d) the name and legal form of the company and the name of the branch if that is different from the name of the company;
(e) the appointment, termination of office and particulars of the persons who are authorised to represent the company in dealings with third parties and in legal proceedings;
  — as a company organ constituted pursuant to law or as members of any such organ, in accordance with the disclosure by the company as provided for in Article 2 (1) (d) of Directive 68/151/EEC,
  — as permanent representatives of the company for the activities of the branch, with an indication of the extent of their powers;
(f) the winding-up of the company, the appointment of liquidators, particulars concerning them and their powers and the termination of the liquidation in accordance with disclosure by the company as provided for in Article 2 (1) (h), (j) and (k) of Directive 68/151/EEC,
  — insolvency proceedings, arrangements, compositions, or any analogous proceedings to which the company is subject;
(g) the accounting documents in accordance with Article 3;
(h) the closure of the branch.

2. The Member State in which the branch has been opened may provide for the disclosure, as referred to in Article 1, of

(a) the signature of the persons referred to in pargaraph 1 (e) and (f) of this Article;

(b) the instruments of constitution and the memorandum and articles of association if they are contained in a separate instrument in accordance with Article 2 (1) (a), (b) and (c) of Directive 68/151/EEC, together with amendments to those documents;

(c) an attestation from the register referred to in paragraph 1 (c) of this Article relating to the existence of the Company;

(d) an indication of the securities on the company's property situated in that Member State, provided such disclosure relates to the validity of those securities.

Article 3.   The compulsory disclosure provided for by Article 2 (1) (g) shall be limited to the accounting documents of the company as drawn up, audited and disclosed pursuant to the law of the Member State by which the company is governed in accordance with Directives 78/660/EEC, 83/349/EEC and 84/253/EEC.

Article 4.   The Member State in which the branch has been opened may stipulate that the documents referred to in Article 2 (2) (b) and Article 3 must be published in another official language of the Community and that the translation of such documents must be certified.

Article 5.   Where a company has opened more than one branch in a Member State, the disclosure referred to in Article 2 (2) (b) and Article 3 may be made in the register of the branch of the company's choice.

In this case, compulsory disclosure by the other branches shall cover the particulars of the branch register of which disclosure was made, together with the number of that branch in that register.

SECTION II. BRANCHES OF COMPANIES FROM THIRD COUNTRIES

Article 7.   1. Documents and particulars concerning a branch opened in a Member State by a company which is not governed by the law of a Member State but which is of a legal form comparable with the types of company to which Directive 68/151/EEC applies shall be disclosed in accordance with the law of the Member State of the branch as laid down in Article 3 of that Directive.

2. Article 1 (2) shall apply.

Article 8.   The compulsory disclosure provided for in Article 7 shall cover at least the following documents and particulars:

(a) the address of the branch;

(b) the activities of the branch;

(c) the law of the State by which the company is governed;

(d) where that law so provides, the register in which the company is entered and the registration number of the company in that register;

(e) the instruments of constitution, and memorandum and articles of association if they are contained in a separate instrument, with all the amendments to these documents;

(f) the legal form of the company, its principal place of business and its object and, at least annually, the amount of subscribed capital if these particulars are not given in the documents referred to in subparagraph (e);

(g) the name of the company and the name of the branch if that is different from the name of the company;

(h) the appointment, termination of office and particulars of the persons who are authorised to represent the company in dealings with third parties and in legal proceedings:

  — as a company organ constituted pursuant to law or as members of any such organ,

  — as permanent representatives of the company for the activities of the branch.

The extent of the powers of the persons authorised to represent the company must be stated, together with whether they may do so alone or act jointly;

(i) — the winding-up of the company and the appointment of liquidators, particulars concerning them and their powers and the termination of the liquidation;

  — insolvency proceedings, arrangements, compositions or any analogous proceedings to which the company is subject;

(j) the accounting documents in accordance with Article 7;

(k) the closure of the branch.

Article 9.   1. The compulsory disclosure provided for by Article 8 (1) (j) shall apply to the accounting documents of the company as drawn up, audited and disclosed pursuant to the law of the State which governs the company. Where they are not drawn up in accordance with or in a manner equivalent to Directives 78/660/EEC and 83/349/EEC, Member States may require that accounting documents relating to the activities of the branch be drawn up and disclosed.

2. Articles 4 and 5 shall apply.

Article 10.   The Member States shall prescribe that letters and order forms used by a branch state the register in which the file in respect of the branch is kept together with the number of the branch in that register. Where the law of the State by which the company is governed requires entry in a register, the register in which the company is entered, and the registration number of the company in that register must also be stated.

SECTION III. INDICATION OF BRANCHES IN THE COMPANY'S ANNUAL REPORT

Article 11. The following subparagraph is added to Article 46 (2) of Directive 78/660/EEC:

'(e) the existence of branches of the company'.

SECTION IV. TRANSITIONAL AND FINAL PROVISIONS

Article 12. The Member States shall provide for appropriate penalties in the event of failure to disclose the matters set out in Articles 1, 2, 3, 7, 8 and 9 and of omission from letters and order forms of the compulsory particulars provided for in Articles 6 and 10.

Article 13. Each Member State shall determine who shall carry out the disclosure formalities provided for in this Directive.

Article 14. 1. Articles 3 and 9 shall not apply to branches opened by credit institutions and financial institutions covered by Directive 89/117/EEC.[8]

2. Pending subsequent co-ordination, the Member States need not apply Articles 3 and 9 to branches opened by insurance companies.

Article 15. Article 54 of Directive 78/660/EEC and Article 48 of Directive 83/349/EEC shall be deleted.

Article 16. 1. Member States shall adopt the laws, regulations and administrative provisions necessary to comply with this Directive not later than 1 January 1992. They shall forthwith inform the Commission thereof.

2. Member States shall stipulate that the provisions referred to in paragraph 1 shall apply from 1 January 1993 and, with regard to accounting documents, shall apply for the first time to annual accounts for the financial year beginning on 1 January 1993 or during 1993.

3. Member States shall communicate to the Commission the texts of the provisions of national law which they adopt in the field covered by this Directive.

[8] OJ No L 44, 16. 2. 1989, p. 40.

Article 17. The Contact Committee set up pursuant to Article 52 of Directive 78/660/EEC shall also:

(a) facilitate, without prejudice to Articles 169 and 170 of the Treaty, the harmonised application of this Directive, through regular meetings dealing, in particular, with practical problems arising in connection with its application;

(b) advise the Commission, if necessary, on any additions or amendments to this Directive.

Article 18. This Directive is addressed to the Member States.
 Done at Brussels, 21 December 1989.

For the Council, The President, E. Cresson

Twelfth Council Company Law Directive

of 21 December 1989 on single-member private limited-liability companies

(89/667/EEC)

The Council of the European Communites,

Having regard to the Treaty establishing the European Economic Community,

Having regard to the porposal from the Commission,[1]

In cooperation with the European Parliament,[2]

Having regard to the opinion of the Economic and Social Committee,[3]

Whereas certain safeguards which, for the protection of the interests of members and others, are required by Member States of companies and firms within the meaning of the second paragraph of Article 58 of the Treaty should be coordinated with a view to making such safeguards equivalent throughout the Community;

Whereas, in this field, Directives 68/151/EEC[4] and 78/660/EEC,[5] as last amended by the Act of Accession of Spain and Portugal, and Directive 83/349/EEC,[6] as amended by the Act of Accession of Spain and Portugal, on disclosure, the validity of commitments, nullity, annual accounts and consolidated accounts, apply to all share capital companies; whereas Directives 77/91/EEC[7] and 78/855/EEC,[8] as last amended by the Act of Accession of Spain and Portugal, and Directive 82/891/EEC[9] on formation and capital, mergers and divisions apply only to public limited-liability companies;

Whereas the small and medium-sized enterprises (SME) action programme[10] was approved by the Council in its Resolution of 3 November 1986;

Whereas reforms in the legislation of certain Member States in the last few years, permitting single-member private limited-liability companies, have created divergences between the laws of the Member States;

Whereas it is important to provide a legal instrument allowing the limitation of liability of the individual entrepreneur throughout the Community, without prejudice to the laws of the Member States which, in

[1] OJ No C 173, 2. 7. 1988, p. 10.
[2] OJ No C 96, 17. 4. 1989, p. 92 and OJ No C 291, 20. 11. 1989, p. 53.
[3] OJ No C 318, 12. 12. 1988, p. 9.　　　[4] OJ No L 65, 14. 3. 1968, p. 8.
[5] OJ No L 222, 14. 8. 1978, p. 11.　　　[6] OJ No L 193, 18. 7. 1983, p. 1.
[7] OJ No L 26, 30. 1. 1977, p. 1.　　　[8] OJ No L 295, 20. 10. 1978, p. 36.
[9] OJ No L 378, 31. 12. 1982, p. 47.　　　[10] OJ No C 287, 14. 11. 1986, p. 1.

exceptional circumstances, require that entrepreneur to be liable for the obligations of his undertaking;

Whereas a private limited-liability company may be a single-member company from the time of its formation, or may become one because its shares have come to be held by a single shareholder; whereas, pending the coordination of national provisions on the laws relating to groups, Member States may lay down certain special provisions and penalties for cases where a natural person is the sole member of several companies or where a single-member company or any other legal person is the sole member of a company; whereas the sole aim of this provision is to take account of the differences which currently exist in certain national laws; whereas, for that purpose, Member States may in specific cases lay down restrictions on the use of single-member companies or remove the limits on the liabilities of sole members; whereas Member States are free to lay down rules to cover the risks that single member companies may present as a consequence of having single members, particularly to ensure that the subscribed capital is paid;

Whereas the fact that all the shares have come to be held by a single shareholder and the identity of the single member must be disclosed by an entry in a register accessible to the public;

Whereas decisions taken by the sole member in his capacity as general meeting must be recorded in writing;

Whereas contracts between a sole member and his company as represented by him must likewise be recorded in writing, insofar as such contracts do not relate to current operations concluded under normal conditions,

Has adopted this directive:

Article 1. The coordination measures prescribed by this Directive shall apply to the laws, regulations and administrative provisions of the Member States relating to the following types of company:

— *in Germany:*
Gesellschaft mit beschränkter Haftung,
— *in Belgium:*
Société privée à responsabilité limitée/de besloten venootschap met beperkte aansprakelijkheid,
— *in Denmark:*
Anpartsselskaber,
— *in Spain:*
Sociedad de responsabilidad limitada,
— *in France:*
Société à responsabilité limitée,
— *in Greece:*
Εταιρεία περιορισμένης ευθύνης,

— *in Ireland:*
Private company limited by shares or by guarantee,
— *in Italy:*
Società a responsabilità limitata,
— *in Luxembourg:*
Société à responsabilité limitée,
— *in the Netherlands:*
Besloten vennootschap met beperkte aansprakelijkheid,
— *in Portugal:*
Sociedade por quotas,
— *in the United Kingdom:*
Private company limited by shares or by guarantee.

Article 2. 1. A company may have a sole member when it is formed and also when all its shares come to be held by a single person (single-member company).

2. Member States may, pending coordination of national laws relating to groups, lay down special provisions or sanctions for cases where:

(a) a natural person is the sole member of several companies;
(b) a single-member company or any other legal person is the sole member of a company.

Article 3. Where a company becomes a single-member company because all its shares come to be held by a single person, that fact, together with the identity of the sole member, must either be recorded in the file or entered in the register within the meaning of Article 3 (1) and (2) of Directive 68/151/EEC or be entered in a register kept by the company and accessible to the public.

Article 4. 1. The sole member shall excrcise the powers of the general meeting of the company.

2. Decisions taken by the sole member in the field referred to in paragraph 1 shall be recorded in minutes or drawn up in writing.

Article 5. 1. Contracts between the sole member and his company as represented by him shall be recorded in minutes or drawn up in writing.

2. Member States need not apply paragraph 1 to current operations concluded under normal conditions.

Article 6. Where a Member State allows single-member companies as defined by Article 2 (1) in the case of public limited companies as well, this Directive shall apply.

Article 7.   A Member State need not allow the formation of single-member companies where its legislation provides that an individual entrepreneur may set up an undertaking the liability of which is limited to a sum devoted to a stated activity, on condition that safeguards are laid down for such undertakings which are equivalent to those imposed by this Director or by any other Community provisions applicable to the companies referred to in Article 1.

Article 8.   1. Member States shall bring into force the laws, regulations and administrative provisions necessary to comply with this Directive by 1 January 1992. They shall inform the Commission thereof.

2. Member States may provide that, in the case of companies already in existence on 1 January 1992, this Directive shall not apply until 1 January 1993.

3. Member States shall communicate to the Commission the texts of the main provisions of national law which they adopt in the field covered by this Directive.

Article 9.   This Directive is addressed to the Member States.
    Done at Brussels, 21 December 1989.

For the Council, The President, E. Cresson

D

Financial Markets

Council Directive

of 20 December 1985 on the coordination of laws,
regulations and administrative provisions relating to
undertakings for collective investment in transferable
securities (UCITS)

(85/611/EEC)

The Council of the European Communities,

Having regard to the Treaty establishing the European Economic Community, and in particular Article 57 (2) thereof,

Having regard to the proposal from the Commission,[1]

Having regard to the opinion of the European Parliament,[2]

Having regard to the opinion of the Economic and Social Committee,[3]

Whereas the laws of the Member States relating to collective investment undertakings differ appreciably from one state to another, particularly as regards the obligations and controls which are imposed on those undertakings; whereas those differences distort the conditions of competition between those undertakings and do not ensure equivalent protection for unit-holders;

Whereas national laws governing collective investment undertakings should be coordinated with a view to approximating the conditions of competition between those undertakings at Community level, while at the same time entering more effective and more uniform protection for unit-holders; whereas such coordination will make it easier for a collective investment undertaking situated in one Member State to market its units in other Member States;

Whereas the attainment of these objectives will facilitate the removal of the restrictions on the free circulation of the units of collective investment undertakings in the Community, and such coordination will help to bring about a European capital market;

Whereas, having regard to these objectives, it is desirable that common basic rules be established for the authorization, supervision, structure and activities of collective investment undertakings situated in the Member States and the information they must publish;

Whereas the application of these common rules is a sufficient guarantee to permit collective investment undertakings situated in Member States, subject to the applicable provisions relating to capital movements, to market

[1] OJ No C 171, 26. 7. 1976, p. 1.   [2] OJ No C 57, 7. 3. 1977, p. 31.
[3] OJ No C 75, 26. 2. 1977, p. 10.

their units in other Member States without those Member States' being able to subject those undertakings or their units to any provision whatsoever other than provisions which, in those states, do not fall within the field covered by this Directive; whereas, nevertheless, if a collective investment undertaking situated in one Member State markets its units in a different Member State it must take all necessary steps to ensure that unit-holders in that other Member State can exercise their financial rights there with ease and are provided with the necessary information,

Whereas the coordination of the laws of the Member States should be confined initially to collective investment undertakings other than of the closed-ended type which promote the sale of their units to the public in the Community and the sole object of which is investment in transferable securities (which are essentially transferable securities officially listed on stock exchanges or similar regulated markets); whereas regulation of the collective investment undertakings not covered by the Directive poses a variety of problems which must be dealt with by means of other provisions, and such undertakings will accordingly be the subject of coordination at a later stage; whereas pending such coordination any Member State may, *inter alia*, prescribe those categories of undertakings for collective investment in transferable securities (UCITS) excluded from this Directive's scope on account of their investment and borrowing policies and lay down those specific rules to which such UCITS are subject in carrying on their business within its territory;

Whereas the free marketing of the units issued by UCITS authorized to invest up to 100% of their assets in transferable securities issued by the same body (State, local authority, etc.) may not have the direct or indirect effect of disturbing the functioning of the capital market or the financing of the Member States or of creating economic situations similar to those which Article 68 (3) of the Treaty seeks to prevent;

Whereas account should be taken of the special situations of the Hellenic Republic's and Portuguese Republic's financial markets by allowing those countries an additional period in which to implement this Directive,

Has adopted this directive.

SECTION I. GENERAL PROVISIONS AND SCOPE

Article 1.   1. The Member States shall apply this Directive to undertakings for collective investment in transferable securities (hereinafter referred to as UCITS) situated within their territories.

2. For the purposes of this Directive, and subject to Article 2, UCITS shall be undertakings:

— the sole object of which is the collective investment in transferable

securities of capital raised from the public and which operate on the principle of risk-spreading, and
— the units of which are, at the request of holders, re-purchased or redeemed, directly or indirectly, out of those undertakings' assets. Action taken by a UCITS to ensure that the stock exchange value of its units does not significantly vary from their net asset value shall be regarded as equivalent to such re-purchase or redemption.

3. Such undertakings may be constituted according to law, either under the law of contract (as common funds managed by management companies) or trust law (as unit trusts) or under statute (as investment companies).

For the purposes of this Directive 'common funds' shall also include unit trusts.

4. Investment companies the assets of which are invested through the intermediary of subsidiary companies mainly otherwise than in transferable securities shall not, however, be subject to this Directive.

5. The Member States shall prohibit UCITS which are subject to this Directive from transforming themselves into collective investment undertakings which are not covered by this Directive.

6. Subject to the provisions governing capital movements and to Articles 44, 45 and 52 (2) no Member State may apply any other provisions whatsoever in the field covered by this Directive to UCITS situated in another Member State or to the units issued by such UCITS, where they market their units within its territory.

7. Without prejudice to paragraph 6, a Member State may apply to UCITS situated within its territory requirements which are stricter than or additional to those laid down in Article 4 *et seq.* of this Directive, provided that they are of general application and do not conflict with the provisions of this Directive.

Article 2. 1. The following shall not be UCITS subject to this Directive:
— UCITS of the closed-ended type;
— UCITS which raise capital without promoting the sale of their units to the public within the Community or any part of it;
— UCITS the units of which, under the fund rules or the investment company's instruments of incorporation, may be sold only to the public in non-member countries;
— categories of UCITS prescribed by the regulations of the Member States in which such UCITS are situated for which the rules laid down in Section V and Article 36 are inappropriate in view of their investment and borrowing policies.

2. Five years after the implementation of this Directive the Commission shall submit to the Council a report on the implementation of paragraph 1

and, in particular, of its fourth indent. If necessary, it shall propose suitable measures to extend the scope.

Article 3.   For the purposes of this Directive, a UCITS shall be deemed to be situated in the Member State in which the investment company or the management company of the unit trust has its registered office; the Member States must require that the head office be situated in the same Member State as the registered office.

SECTION II. AUTHORIZATION OF UCITS

Article 4.   1.   No UCITS shall carry on activities as such unless it has been authorized by the competent authorities of the Member State in which it is situated, hereinafter referred to as 'the competent authorities'.

Such authorization shall be valid for all Member States.

2.   A unit trust shall be authorized only if the competent authorities have approved the management company, the fund rules and the choice of depositary. An investment company shall be authorized only if the competent authorities have approved both its instruments of incorporation and the choice of depositary.

3.   The competent authorities may not authorize a UCITS if the directors of the management company, of the investment company or of the depositary are not of sufficiently good repute or lack the experience required for the performance of their duties. To that end, the names of the directors of the management company, of the investment company and of the depositary and of every person succeeding them in office must be communicated forthwith to the competent authorities.

'Directors' shall mean those persons who, under the law or the instruments of incorporation, represent the management company, the investment company or the depositary, or who effectively determine the policy of the management company, the investment company or the depositary.

4.   Neither the management company nor the depositary may be replaced, nor may the fund rules or the investment company's instruments of incorporation be amended, without the approval of the competent authorities.

SECTION III. OBLIGATIONS REGARDING THE STRUCTURE OF UNIT TRUSTS

Article 5.   A management company must have sufficient financial resources at its disposal to enable it to conduct its business effectively and meet its liabilities.

Article 6.   No management company may engage in activities other than the management of unit trusts and of investment companies.

Article 7.   1. A unit trust's assets must be entrusted to a depositary for safe-keeping.

2. A depositary's liability as referred to in Article 9 shall not be affected by the fact that it has entrusted to a third party all or some of the assets in its safe-keeping.

3. A depositary must, moreover:

(a) ensure that the sale, issue, re-purchase, redemption and cancellation of units effected on behalf of a unit trust or by a management company are carried out in accordance with the law and the fund rules;

(b) ensure that the value of units is calculated in accordance with the law and the fund rules;

(c) carry out the instructions of the management company, unless they conflict with the law or the fund rules;

(d) ensure that in transactions involving a unit trust's assets any consideration is remitted to it within the usual time limits;

(e) ensure that a unit trust's income is applied in accordance with the law and the fund rules.

Article 8.   1. A depositary must either have its registered office in the same Member State as that of the management company or be established in that Member State if its registered office is in another Member State.

2. A depositary must be an institution which is subject to public control. It must also furnish sufficient financial and professional guarantees to be able effectively to pursue its business as depositary and meet the commitments inherent in that function.

3. The Member States shall determine which of the categories of institutions referred to in paragraph 2 shall be eligible to be depositaries.

Article 9.   A depositary shall, in accordance with the national law of the State in which the management company's registered office is situated, be liable to the management company and the unit-holders for any loss suffered by them as a result of its unjustifiable failure to perform its obligations or its improper performance of them. Liability to unit-holders may be invoked either directly or indirectly through the management company, depending on the legal nature of the relationship between the depositary, the management company and the unit-holders.

Article 10.   1. No single company shall act as both management company and depositary.

2. In the context of their respective roles the management company and

the depositary must act independently and solely in the interest of the unit-holders.

Article 11.   The law or the fund rules shall lay down the conditions for the replacement of the management company and the depositary and rules to ensure the protection of unit-holders in the event of such replacement.

SECTION IV. OBLIGATIONS REGARDING THE STRUCTURE OF
INVESTMENT COMPANIES AND THEIR DEPOSITARIES

Article 12.   The Member States shall determine the legal form which an investment company must take. It must have sufficient paid-up capital to enable it to conduct its business effectively and meet its liabilities.

Article 13.   No investment company may engage in activities other than those referred to in Article 1 (2).

Article 14.   1. An investment company's assets must be entrusted to a depositary for safe-keeping.
   2. A depositary's liability as referred to in Article 16 shall not be affected by the fact that it has entrusted to a third party all or some of the assets in its safe-keeping.
   3. A depositary must, moreover:
(a) ensure that the sale, issue, re-purchase, redemption and cancellation of units effected by or on behalf of a company are carried out in accordance with the law and with the company's instruments of incorporation;
(b) ensure that in transactions involving a company's assets any consideration is remitted to it within the usual time limits;
(c) ensure that a company's income is applied in accordance with the law and its instruments of incorporation.

   4. A Member State may decide that investment companies situated within its territory which market their units exclusively through one or more stock exchanges on which their units are admitted to official listing shall not be required to have depositaries within the meaning of this Directive.
   Articles 34, 37 and 38 shall not apply to such companies. However, the rules for the valuation of such companies' assets must be stated in law or in their instruments of incorporation.
   5. A Member State may decide that investment companies situated within its territory which market at least 80% of their units through one or more stock exchanges designated in their instruments of incorporation shall not be required to have depositaries within the meaning of this Directive provided that their units are admitted to official listing on the stock exchanges of those Member States within the territories of which the units are

marketed, and that any transactions which such a company may effect outwith stock exchanges are effected at stock exchange prices only. A company's instruments of incorporation must specify the stock exchange in the country of marketing the prices on which shall determine the prices at which that company will effect any transactions outwith stock exchanges in that country.

A Member State shall avail itself of the option provided for in the preceding subparagraph only if it considers that unit-holders have protection equivalent to that of unit-holders in UCITS which have depositaries within the meaning of this Directive.

In particular, such companies and the companies referred to in paragraph 4, must:

(a) in the absence of provision in law, state in their instruments of incorporation the methods of calculation of the net asset values of their units;

(b) intervene on the market to prevent the stock exchange values of their units from deviating by more than 5% from their net asset values;

(c) establish the net asset values of their units, communicate them to the competent authorities at least twice a week and publish them twice a month.

At least twice a month, an independent auditor must ensure that the calculation of the value of units is effected in accordance with the law and the company's instruments of incorporation. On such occasions, the auditor must make sure that the company's assets are invested in accordance with the rules laid down by law and the company's instruments of incorporation.

6. The Member States shall inform the Comission of the identities of the companies benefiting from the derogations provided for in paragraphs 4 and 5.

The Commission shall report to the Contact Committee on the application of paragraphs 4 and 5 within five years of the implementation of this Directive. After obtaining the Contact Committee's opinion, the Commission shall, if need be, propose appropriate measures.

Article 15. 1. A depositary must either have its registered office in the same Member State as that of the investment company or be established in that Member State if its registered office is in another Member State.

2. A depositary must be an institution which is subject to public control. It must also furnish sufficient financial and professional guarantees to be able effectively to pursue its business as depositary and meet the commitments inherent in that function.

3. The Member States shall determine which of the categories of institutions referred to in paragraph 2 shall be eligible to be depositaries.

Article 16. A depositary shall, in accordance with the national law of the State in which the investment company's registered office is situated, be liable to the investment company and the unit-holders for any loss suffered by them as a result of its unjustifiable failure to perform its obligations, or its improper performance of them.

Article 17. 1. No single company shall act as both investment company and depositary.

2. In carrying out its role as depositary, the depositary must act solely in the interests of the unit-holders.

Article 18. The law or the investment company's instruments of incorporation shall lay down the conditions for the replacement of the depositary and rules to ensure the protection of unit-holders in the event of such replacement.

SECTION V. OBLIGATIONS CONCERNING THE INVESTMENT
POLICIES OF UCITS

Article 19. 1. The investments of a unit trust or of an investment company must consist solely of:

(a) transferable securities admitted to official listing on a stock exchange in a Member State and/or;

(b) transferable securities dealt with on another regulated market in a Member State which operates regularly and is recognized and open to the public and/or;

(c) transferable securities admitted to official listing on a stock exchange in a non-member State or dealt in on another regulated market in a non-member State which operates regularly and is recognized and open to the public provided that the choice of stock exchange or market has been approved by the component authorities or is provided for in law or the fund rules or the investment company's instruments of incorporation and/or;

(d) recently issued transferable securities, provided that:

— the terms of issue include an undertaking that application will be made for admission to official listing on a stock exchange or to another regulated market which operates regularly and is recognized and open to the public, provided that the choice of stock exchange or market has been approved by the competent authorities or is provided for in law or the fund rules or the investment company's instruments of incorporation;

— such admission is secured within a year of issue.

2. However:

(a) a UCITS may invest no more than 10% of its assets in transferable securities other than those referred to in paragraph 1;

(b) a Member State may provide that a UCITS may invest no more than 10% of its assets in debt instruments which, for purposes of this Directive, shall be treated, because of their characteristics, as equivalent to transferable securities and which are, *inter alia*, transferable, liquid and have a value which can be accurately determined at any time or at least with the frequency stipulated in Article 34;

(c) an investment company may acquire movable and immovable property which is essential for the direct pursuit of its business;

(d) a UCITS may not acquire either precious metals or certificates representing them.

3. The total of the investments referred to in paragraph 2 (a) and (b) may not under any circumstances amount to more than 10% of the assets of a UCITS.

4. Unit trusts and investment companies may hold ancillary liquid assets.

Article 20. 1. The Member States shall send to the Commission:

(a) no later than date of implementation of this Directive, lists of the debt instruments which, in accordance with Article 19 (2) (b), they plan to treat as equivalent to transferable securities, stating the characteristics of those instruments and the reasons for so doing;

(b) details of any amendments which they contemplate making to the lists of instruments referred to in (a) or any further instruments which they contemplate treating as equivalent to transferable securities, together with their reasons for so doing.

2. The Commission shall immediately forward that information to the other Member States together with any comments which it considers appropriate. Such communications may be the subject of exchanges of views within the Contract Committee in accordance with the procedure laid down in Article 53 (4).

Article 21. 1. The Member States may authorize UCITS to employ techniques and instruments relating to transferable securities under the conditions and within the limits which they lay down provided that such techniques and instruments are used for the purpose of efficient portfolio management.

2. The Member States may also authorize UCITS to employ techniques and instruments intended to provide protection against exchange risks in the context of the management of their assets and liabilities.

Article 22. 1. A UCITS may invest no more than 5% of its assets in transferable securities issued by the same body.

2. The Member States may raise the limit laid down in paragraph 1 to a maximum of 10%. However, the total value of the transferable securities held by a UCITS in the issuing bodies in each of which it invests more than 5% of its assets must not then exceed 40% of the value of its assets.

3. The Member States may raise the limit laid down in paragraph 1 to a maximum of 35% if the transferable securities are issued or guaranteed by a Member State, by its local authorities, by a non-member State or by public international bodies of which one or more Member States are members.

Article 23. 1. By way of derogation from Article 22 and without prejudice to Article 68 (3) of the Treaty, the Member States may authorize UCITS to invest in accordance with the principle of risk-spreading up to 100% of their assets in different transferable securities issued or guaranteed by any Member State, its local authorities, a non-member State or public international bodies of which one or more Member States are members.

The competent authorities shall grant such a derogation only if they consider that unit-holders in the UCITS have protection equivalent to that of unit-holders in UCITS complying with the limits laid down in Article 22.

Such a UCITS must hold securities from at least six different issues, but securities from any one issue may not account for more than 30% of its total assets.

2. The UCITS referred to in paragraph 1 must make express mention in the fund rules or in the investment company's instruments of incorporation of the States, local authorities or public international bodies issuing or guaranteeing securities in which they intend to invest more than 35% of their assets; such fund rules or instruments of incorporation must be approved by the competent authorities.

3. In addition each such UCITS referred to in paragraph 1 must include a prominent statement in its prospectus and any promotional literature drawing attention to such authorization and indicating the States, local authorities and/or public international bodies in the securities of which it intends to invest or has invested more than 35% of its assets.

Article 24. 1. A UCITS may not acquire the units of other collective investment undertakings of the open-ended type unless they are collective investment undertakings within the meaning of the first and second indents of Article 1 (2).

2. A UCITS may invest no more than 5% of its assets in the units of such collective investment undertakings.

3. Investment in the units of a unit trust managed by the same management company or by any other company with which the management

company is linked by common management or control, or by a substantial direct or indirect holding, shall be permitted only in the case of a trust which, in accordance with its rules, has specialized in investment in a specific geographical area or economic sector, and provided that such investment is authorized by the competent authorities. Authorization shall be granted only if the trust has announced its intention of making use of that option and that option has been expressly stated in its rules.

A management company may not charge any fees or costs on account of transactions relating to a unit trust's units where some of a unit trust's assets are invested in the units of another unit trust managed by the same management company or by any other company with which the management company is linked by common management or control, or by a substantial direct or indirect holding.

4. Paragraph 3 shall also apply where an investment company acquires units in another investment company to which it is linked within the meaning of paragraph 3.

Paragraph 3 shall also apply when an investment company acquires units of a unit trust to which it is linked, or where a unit trust acquires units of an investment company to which it is linked.

Article 25. 1. An investment company or a management company acting in connection with all of the unit trusts which it manages and which fall within the scope of this Directive may not acquire any shares carrying voting rights which would enable it to exercise significant influence over the management of an issuing body.

Pending further coordination, the Member States shall take account of existing rules defining the principle stated in the first subparagraph under other Member States' legislation.

2. Moreover, an investment company or unit trust may acquire no more than:

— 10% of the non-voting shares of any single issuing body;
— 10% of the debt securities of any single issuing body;
— 10% of the units of any single collective investment undertaking within the meaning of the first and second indents of Article 1 (2).

The limits laid down in the second and third indents may be disregarded at the time of acquisition if at that time the gross amount of the debt securities or the net amount of the securities in issue cannot be calculated.

3. A Member State may waive application of paragraphs 1 and 2 as regards:

(a) transferable securities issued or guaranteed by a Member State or its local authorities;
(b) transferable securities issued or guaranteed by a non-member State;

(c) transferable securities issued by public international bodies of which one or more Member States are members;

(d) shares held by a UCITS in the capital of a company incorporated in a non-member State investing its assets mainly in the securities of issuing bodies having their registered offices in that State, where under the legislation of that State such a holding represents the only way in which the UCITS can invest in the securities of issuing bodies of that State. This derogation, however, shall apply only if in its investment policy the company from the non-member State complies with the limits laid down in Articles 22, 24 and 25 (1) and (2). Where the limits set in Articles 22 and 24 are exceeded Article 26 shall apply *mutatis mutandis*;

(e) shares held by an investment company in the capital of subsidiary companies carrying on the business of management, advice or marketing exclusively on its behalf.

Article 26.   1. UCITS need not comply with the limits laid down in this Section when exercising subscription rights attaching to transferable securities which form part of their assets.

While ensuring observance of the principle of risk-spreading, the Member States may allow recently authorized UCITS to derogate from Articles 22 and 23 for six months following the date of their authorization.

2. If the limits referred to in paragraph 1 are exceeded for reasons beyond the control of a UCITS or as a result of the exercise of subscription rights, that UCITS must adopt as a priority objective for its sales transactions the remedying of that situation, taking due account of the interest of its unit-holders.

SECTION VI. OBLIGATIONS CONCERNING INFORMATION TO BE SUPPLIED TO UNIT-HOLDERS

A. Publication of a prospectus and periodical reports

Article 27.   1. An investment company and, for each of the trusts it manages, a management company must publish:

— a prospectus,
— an annual report for each financial year, and
— a half-yearly report covering the first six months of the financial year.

2. The annual and half-yearly reports must be published within the following time limits, with effect from the ends of the periods to which they relate:

— four months in the case of the annual report.
— two months in the case of the half-yearly report.

Article 28. 1. A prospectus must include the information necessary for investors to be able to make an informed judgement of the investment proposed to them. It shall contain at least the information provided for in Schedule A annexed to this Directive, insofar as that information does not already appear in the documents annexed to the prospectus in accordance with Article 29 (1).

2. The annual report must include a balance-sheet or a statement of assets and liabilities, a detailed income and expenditure account for the financial year, a report on the activities of the financial year and the other information provided for in Schedule B annexed to this Directive, as well as any significant information which will enable investors to make an informed judgement on the development of the activities of the UCITS and its results.

3. The half-yearly report must include at least the information provided for in Chapters I to IV of Schedule B annexed to this Directive; where a UCITS has paid or proposes to pay an interim dividend, the figures must indicate the results after tax for the half-year concerned and the interim dividend paid or proposed.

Article 29. 1. The fund rules or an investment company's instruments of incorporation shall form an integral part of the prospectus and must be annexed thereto.

2. The documents referred to in paragraph 1 need not, however, be annexed to the prospectus provided that the unit-holder is informed that on request he or she will be sent those documents or be apprised of the place where, in each Member State in which the units are placed on the market, he or she may consult them.

Article 30. The essential elements of the prospectus must be kept up to date.

Article 31. The accounting information given in the annual report must be audited by one or more persons empowered by law to audit accounts in accordance with Council Directive 84/253/EEC of 10 April 1984 based on Article 54 (3) (g) of the EEC Treaty on the approval of persons responsible for carrying out the statutory audits of accounting documents.[1] The auditor's report, including any qualifications, shall be reproduced in full in the annual report.

Article 32. A UCITS must send its prospectus and any amendments thereto, as well as its annual and half-yearly reports, to the competent authorities.

[1] OJ No L 126, 12. 5. 1984, p. 20.

Article 33. 1. The prospectus, the latest annual report and any subsequent half-yearly report published must be offered to subscribers free of charge before the conclusion of a contract.

2. In addition, the annual and half-yearly reports must be available to the public at the places specified in the prospectus.

3. The annual and half-yearly reports shall be supplied to unit-holders free of charge on request.

B. Publication of other information

Article 34. A UCITS must make public in an appropriate manner the issue, sale, re-purchase or redemption price of its units each time it issues, sells, re-purchases or redeems them, and at least twice a month. The competent authorities may, however, permit a UCITS to reduce the frequency to once a month on condition that such a derogation does not prejudice the interests of the unit-holders.

Article 35. All publicity comprising an invitation to purchase the units of a UCITS must indicate that a prospectus exists and the places where it may be obtained by the public.

SECTION VII. THE GENERAL OBLIGATIONS OF UCITS

Article 36. 1. Neither:

— an investment company, nor
— a management company or depositary acting on behalf of a unit trust,
may borrow.

However, a UCITS may acquire foreign currency by means of a 'back-to-back' loan.

2. By way of derogation from paragraph 1, a Member State may authorize a UCITS to borrow:

(a) up to 10%

— of its assets, in the case of an investment company, or
— of the value of the fund, in the case of a unit trust,

provided that the borrowing is on a temporary basis;

(b) up to 10% of its assets, in the case of an investment company, provided that the borrowing is to make possible the acquisition of immovable property essential for the direct pursuit of its business; in this case the borrowing and that referred to in subparagraph (a) may not in any case in total exceed 15% of the borrower's assets.

Article 37. 1. A UCITS must re-purchase or redeem its units at the request of any unit-holder.

2. By way of derogation from paragraph 1:

(a) a UCITS may, in the cases and according to the procedures provided for by law, the fund rules or the investment company's instruments of incorporation, temporarily suspend the re-purchase or redemption of its units. Suspension may be provided for only in exceptional cases where circumstances so require, and suspension is justified having regard to the interests of the unit-holders;

(b) the Member States may allow the competent authorities to require the suspension of the re-purchase or redemption of units in the interest of the unit-holders or of the public.

3. In the cases mentioned in paragraph 2 (a), a UCITS must without delay communicate its decision to the competent authorities and to the authorities of all Member States in which it markets its units.

Article 38. The rules for the valuation of assets and the rules for calculating the sale or issue price and the re-purchase or redemption price of the units of a UCITS must be laid down in the law, in the fund rules or in the investment company's instruments of incorporation.

Article 39. The distribution or reinvestment of the income of a unit trust or of an investment company shall be effected in accordance with the law and with the fund rules or the investment company's instruments of incorporation.

Article 40. A UCITS unit may not be issued unless the equivalent of the net issue price is paid into the assets of the UCITS within the usual time limits. This provision shall not preclude the distribution of bonus units.

Article 41. 1. Without prejudice to the application of Articles 19 and 21, neither:

— an investment company, nor
— a management company or depositary acting on behalf of a unit trust

may grant loans or act as a guarantor on behalf of third parties.

2. Paragraph 1 shall not prevent such undertakings from acquiring transferable securities which are not fully paid.

Article 42. Neither:

— an investment company, nor
— a management company or depository acting on behalf of a unit trust

may carry out uncovered sales of transferable securities.

Article 43.   The law or the fund rules must prescribe the remuneration and the expenditure which a management company is empowered to charge to a unit trust and the method of calculation of such remuneration.

The law or an investment company's instruments of incorporation must prescribe the nature of the cost to be borne by the company.

SECTION VIII. SPECIAL PROVISIONS APPLICABLE TO UCITS WHICH MARKET THEIR UNITS IN MEMBER STATES OTHER THAN THOSE IN WHICH THEY ARE SITUATED

Article 44.   1. A UCITS which markets its units in another Member State must comply with the laws, regulations and administrative provisions in force in that State which do not fall within the field governed by this Directive.

2. Any UCITS may advertise its units in the Member State in which they are marketed. It must comply with the provisions governing advertising in that State.

3. The provisions referred to in paragraphs 1 and 2 must be applied without discrimination.

Article 45.   In the case referred to in Article 44, the UCITS must, *inter alia*, in accordance with the laws, regulations and administrative provisions in force in the Member State of marketing, take the measures necessary to ensure that facilities are available in that State for making payments to unit-holders, re-purchasing or redeeming units and making available the information which UCITS are obliged to provide.

Article 46.   If a UCITS proposes to market its units in a Member State other than that in which it is situated, it must first inform the competent authorities and the authorities of that other Member State accordingly. It must simultaneously send the latter authorities:

— an attestation by the competent authorities to the effect that it fulfils the conditions imposed by this Directive,
— its fund rules or its instruments of incorporation,
— its prospectus,
— where appropriate, its latest annual report and any subsequent half-yearly report and
— details of the arrangements made for the marketing of its units in that other Member State.

A UCITS may begin to market its units in that other Member State two months after such communication unless the authorities of the Member State concerned establish, in a reasoned decision taken before the expiry of that period of two months, that the arrangements made for the marketing of units do not comply with the provisions referred to in Articles 44 (1) and 45.

Article 47.   If a UCITS markets its units in a Member State other than that in which it is situated, it must distribute in that other Member State, in at least one of that other Member State's official languages, the documents and information which must be published in the Member State in which it is situated, in accordance with the same procedures as those provided for in the latter State.

Article 48.   For the purpose of carrying on its activities, a UCITS may use the same generic name (such as investment company or unit trust) in the Community as it uses in the Member State in which it is situated. In the event of any danger of confusion, the host Member State may, for the purpose of clarification, require that the name be accompanied by certain explanatory particulars.

SECTION IX. PROVISIONS CONCERNING THE AUTHORITIES
RESPONSIBLE FOR AUTHORIZATION AND SUPERVISION

Article 49.   1. The Member States shall designate the authorities which are to carry out the duties provided for in this Directive. They shall inform the Commission thereof, indicating any division of duties.

2. The authorities referred to in paragraph 1 must be public authorities or bodies appointed by public authorities.

3. The authorities of the State in which a UCITS is situated shall be competent to supervise that UCITS. However, the authorities of the State in which a UCITS markets its units in accordance with Article 44 shall be competent to supervise compliance with Section VIII.

4. The authorities concerned must be granted all the powers necessary to carry out their task.

Article 50.   1. The authorities of the Member States referred to in Article 49 shall collaborate closely in order to carry out their task and must for that purpose alone communicate to each other all information required.

2. The Member States shall provide that all persons employed or formerly employed by the authorities referred to in Article 49 shall be bound by professional secrecy. This means that any confidential information received in the course of their duties may not be divulged to any person or authority except by virtue of provisions laid down by law.

3. Paragraph 2 shall not, however, preclude communications between the authorities of the various Member States referred to in Article 49, as provided for in this Directive. Information thus exchanged shall be covered

by the obligation of professional secrecy on persons employed or formerly employed by the authorities receiving the information.

4. Without prejudice to cases covered by criminal law, an authority of the type referred to in Article 49 receiving such information may use it only for the performance of its duties or in the context of administrative appeals or legal proceedings relating to such performance.

Article 51. 1. The authorities referred to in Article 49 must give reasons for any decision to refuse authorization, and any negative decision taken in implementation of the general measures adopted in application of this Directive, and communicate them to applicants.

2. The Member States shall provide that decisions taken in respect of a UCITS pursuant to laws, regulations and administrative provisions adopted in accordance with this Directive are subject to the right to apply to the courts; the same shall apply if no decision is taken within six months of its submission on an authorization application made by a UCITS which includes all the information required under the provisions in force.

Article 52. 1. Only the authorities of the Member State in which a UCITS is situated shall have the power to take action against it if it infringes any law, regulation or administrative provision or any regulation laid down in the fund rules or in the investment company's instruments of incorporation.

2. Nevertheless, the authorities of the Member State in which the units of a UCITS are marketed may take action against it if it infringes the provisions referred to in Section VIII.

3. Any decision to withdraw authorization, or any other serious measure taken against a UCITS, or any suspension of re-purchase or redemption imposed upon it, must be communicated without delay by the authorities of the Member State in which the UCITS in question is situated to the authorities of the other Member States in which its units are marketed.

SECTION X. CONTACT COMMITTEE

Article 53. 1. A Contact Committee, hereinafter referred to as 'the Committee', shall be set up alongside the Commission. Its function shall be:

(a) to facilitate, without prejudice to Articles 169 and 170 of the Treaty, the harmonized implementation of this Directive through regular consultations on any practical problems arising from its application and on which exchanges of views are deemed useful;
(b) to facilitate consultation between Member States either on more rigorous or additional requirements which they may adopt in accordance with Article 1 (7), or on the provisions which they may adopt in accordance with Articles 44 and 45;

(c) to advise the Commission, if necessary, on additions or amendments to be made to this Directive.

2. It shall not be the function of the Committee to appraise the merits of decisions taken in individual cases by the authorities referred to in Article 49.

3. The Committee shall be composed of persons appointed by the Member States and of representatives of the Commission. The Chairman shall be a representative of the Commission. Secretarial services shall be provided by the Commission.

4. Meetings of the Committee shall be convened by its chairman, either on his own initiative or at the request of a Member State delegation. The Committee shall draw up its rules of procedure.

SECTION XI. TRANSITIONAL PROVISIONS, DEROGATIONS AND FINAL PROVISIONS

Article 54. Solely for the purpose of Danish UCITS, *pantebreve* issued in Denmark shall be treated as equivalent to the transferable securities referred to in Article 19 (1) (b).

Article 55. By way of derogation from Articles 7 (1) and 14 (1), the competent authorities may authorize those UCITS which, on the date of adoption of this Directive, had two or more depositaries in accordance with their national law to maintain that number of depositaries if those authorities have guarantees that the functions to be performed under Articles 7 (3) and 14 (3) will be performed in practice.

Article 56. 1. By way of derogation from Article 6, the Member States may authorize management companies to issue bearer certificates representing the registered securities of other companies.

2. The Member States may authorize those management companies which, on the date of adoption of this Directive, also carry on activities other than those provided for in Article 6 to continue those other activities for five years after that date.

Article 57. 1. The Member States shall bring into force no later than 1 October 1989 the measures necessary for them to comply with this Directive. They shall forthwith inform the Commission thereof.

2. The Member States may grant UCITS existing on the date of implementation of this Directive a period of not more than 12 months from that date in order to comply with the new national legislation.

3. The Hellenic Republic and the Portuguese Republic shall be authorized to postpone the implementation of this Directive until 1 April 1992 at the latest.

One year before that date the Commission shall report to the Council on progress in implementing the Directive and on any difficulties which the Hellenic Republic or the Portuguese Republic may encounter in implementing the Directive by the date referred to in the first subparagraph.

The Commission shall, if necessary, propose that the Council extend the postponement by up to four years.

Article 58.   The Member States shall ensure that the Commission is informed of the texts of the main laws, regulations and administrative provisions which they adopt in the field covered by this Directive.

Article 59.   This Directive is addressed to the Member States.
Done at Brussels, 20 December 1985.

For the Council, The President, R. Krieps

ANNEX

SCHEDULE A

1. Information concerning the unit trust	1. Information concerning the management company	1. Information concerning the investment company
1.1 Name	1.1. Name or style, form in law, registered office and head office if different from the registered office.	1.1. Name or style, form in law, registered office and head office if different from the registered office.
1.2 Date of establishment of the unit trust. Indication of duration, if limited.	1.2. Date of incorporation of the company. Indication of duration if limited.	1.2 Date of the incorporation of the company. Indication of duration, if limited.
	1.3. If the company manages other unit trusts, indication of those other trusts.	
1.4. Statement of the place where the fund rules, if they are not annexed, and periodic reports may be obtained.		1.4. Statement of the place where the instruments of incorporation, if they are not annexed, and periodical reports may be obtained.
1.5. Brief indications relevant to unit-holders of the tax system applicable to the unit trust. Details of whether deductions are made at source from the income and capital gains paid by the trust		1.5. Brief indications relevant to unit-holders of the tax system applicable to the company. Details of whether deductions are made at source from the income and capital gains paid by the

1. Information concerning the unit trust	1. Information concerning the management company	1. Information concerning the investment company
to unit-holders.		company to unit-holders.
1.6. Accounting and distribution dates		1.6. Accounting and distribution dates.
1.7. Names of the persons responsible for auditing the accounting information referred to in Article 31.		1.7. Names of the persons responsible for auditing the accounting information referred to in Article 31.
	1.8. Names and positions in the company of the members of the administrative, management and supervisory bodies. Details of their main activities outside the company where these are of significance with respect to that company.	1.8. Names and positions in the company of the members of the administrative, management and supervisory bodies. Details of their main activities outside the company where these are of significance with respect to that company.
	1.9. Amount of the subscribed capital with an indication of the capital paid-up	1.9. Capital
1.10. Details of the types and main characteristics of the units and in particular: — the nature of the right (real, personal or other) represented by the unit, — original securities or certificates providing evidence of title; entry in a register or in an account, — characteristics of the units: registered or bearer. Indication of any denominations which may be provided for, — indication of unit-holders' voting rights if these exist, — circumstances in which winding-up of the unit trust can		1.10 Details of the types and main characteristics of the units and in particular: — original securities or certificates providing evidence of title; entry in a register or in an account, — characteristics of the units: registered or bearer. Indication of any denominations which may be provided for, — indication of unit-holders' voting rights, — circumstances in which winding-up of the investment company can be decided on and winding-up procedure, in particular as regards the rights of unit-

I. Information concerning the unit trust *(continued)*	I. Information concerning the management company *(continued)*	I. Information concerning the investment company *(continued)*
be decided on and winding-up procedure, in particular as regards the rights of unit-holders.		holders.
1.11. Where applicable, indication of stock exchanges or markets where the units are listed or dealt in.		1.11. Where applicable, indication of stock exchanges or markets where the units are listed or dealt in.
1.12. Procedures and conditions of issue and sale of units.		1.12. Procedures and conditions of issue and sale of units.
1.13. Procedures and conditions for re-purchase or redemption of units, and circumstances in which re-purchase or redemption may be suspended.		1.13. Procedures and conditions for re-purchase or redemption of units, and circumstances in which re-purchase or redemption may be suspended.
1.14. Description of rules for determining and applying income.		1.14. Description of rules for determining and applying income.
1.15. Description of the unit trust's investment objectives, including its financial objectives (e.g. capital growth or income), investment policy (e.g. specialization in geographical or industrial sectors), any limitations on that investment policy and an indication of any techniques and instruments or borrowing powers which may be used in the management of the unit trust.		1.15. Description of the company's investment objectives, including its financial objectives (e.g. capital growth or income), investment policy (e.g. specialization in geographical or industrial sectors), any limitations on that investment policy and an indication of any techniques and instruments or borrowing powers which may be used in the management of the company.
1.16. Rules for the valuation of assets.		1.16. Rules for the valuation of assets.
1.17. Determination of the sale or issue price and the re-purchase or redemption price of units, in particular: — the method and frequency of the calculation of those		1.17. Determination of the sale or issue price and the re-purchase or redemption price of units, in particular: — the method and frequency of the calculation of those

I. Information concerning the unit trust	I. Information concerning the management company	I. Information concerning the investment company
prices, — information concerning the charges relating to the sale or issue and the re-purchase or redemption of units, — the means, places and frequency of the publication of those prices.		prices, — information concerning the charges relating to the sale or issue and the re-purchase or redemption of units, — the means, places and frequency of the publication of those prices.[1]
1.18. Information concerning the manner, amount and calculation of remuneration payable by the unit trust to the management company, the depositary or third parties, and reimbursement of costs by the unit trust to the management company, to the depositary or to third parties.		1.18. Information concerning the manner, amount and calculation of remuneration paid by the company to its directors, and members of the administrative, management and supervisory bodies, to the depositary, or to third parties, and reimbursement of costs by the company to its directors, to the depositary or to third parties.

2. Information concerning the depositary:

2.1. Name or style, form in law, registered office and head office if different from the registered office;

2.2. Main activity.

3. Information concerning the advisory firms or external investment advisers who give advice under contract which is paid for out of the assets of the UCITS:

3.1. Name or style of the firm or name of the adviser;

3.2. Material provisions of the contract with the management company or the investment company which may be relevant to the unit-holders, excluding those relating to renumeration;

3.3. Other significant activities.

4. Information concerning the arrangements for making payments to unit-holders, re-purchasing or redeeming units and making available information concerning the UCITS. Such information must in any case be given in the Member State in which the UCITS is situated. In addition, where units are marketed in another Member State, such information shall be given in respect of that Member State in the prospectus published there.

---

[1] Investment companies within the meaning of Article 14 (5) of the Directive shall also indicate:
— the method and frequency of calculation of the net asset value of units,
— the means, place and frequency of the publication of that value,
— the stock exchange in the country of marketing the price on which determines the price of transactions effected outwith stock exchanges in that country.

SCHEDULE B

Information to be Included in the Periodic Reports

I. Statement of assets and liabilities

— transferable securities,
— debt instruments of the type referred to in Article 19 (2) (b),
— bank balances,
— other assets,
— total assets,
— liabilities,
— net asset value.

II. Number of units in circulation

III. Net asset value per unit

IV. Portfolio, distinguishing between:

(a) transferable securities admitted to official stock exchange listing;
(b) transferable securities dealt in on another regulated market;
(c) recently issued transferable securities of the type referred to in Article 19 (1) (d);
(d) other transferable securities of the type referred to in Article 19 (2) (a);
(e) debt instruments treated as equivalent in accordance with Article 19 (2) (b);

and analyzed in accordance with the most appropriate criteria in the light of the investment policy of the UCITS (e.g. in accordance with economic, geographical or currency criteria) as a percentage of net assets; for each of the above investments the proportion it represents of the total assets of the UCITS should be stated.

Statement of changes in the composition of the portfolio during the reference period.

V. Statement of the developments concerning the assets of the UCITS during the reference period including the following:

— income from investments,
— other income,
— management charges,
— depositary's charges,
— other charges and taxes,

— net income,
— distributions and income reinvested,
— changes in capital account,
— appreciation or depreciation of investments,
— any other changes affecting the assets and liabilities of the UCITS.

VI. A comparative table covering the last three financial years and including, for each financial year, at the end of the financial year:

— the total net asset value,
— the net asset value per unit.

VII. Details, by category of transaction within the meaning of Article 21 carried out by the UCITS during the reference period, of the resulting amount of commitments.

Council Recommendation

of 20 December 1985 concerning the second
subparagraph of Article 25 (1) of Directive 85/611/EEC

(85/612/EEC)

The Council of the European Communities,
  1. Hereby recommends
that each time the concept of 'significant influence' for the purposes of Article 25 (1) of Directive 85/611/EEC is represented in another Member State's legislation by a numerical limit, the Member State's competent authorities should ensure, if so requested by that other Member State, that such limits are observed by investment and management companies situated within its territory when they acquire shares carrying voting rights issued by a company established within the territory of a Member State where such limits apply. With a view to implementing this recommendation, the Member States in which such limits apply when that Directive is published should communicate them to the Commission, which in turn will inform the other Member States; the same applies to any subsequent relaxation of those limits.
  2. Hereby invites
the competent authorities to collaborate closely with each other, in accordance with Article 50 of that Directive, to implement this recommendation.
  Done at Brussels, 20 December 1985.

For the Council, The President, R. Krieps

Council Directive

of 22 March 1988 amending, as regards the investment policies of certain UCITS, Directive 85/611/EEC on the coordination of laws, regulations and administrative provisions relating to undertakings for collective investments in transferable securities (UCITS)

(88/220/EEC)

The Council of the European Communities,

Having regard to the Treaty establishing the European Economic Community, and in particular the third sentence of Article 57 (2) thereof,

Having regard to the proposal from the Commission,[1]

In cooperation with the European Parliament,[2]

Having regard to the opinion of the Economic and Social Committee,[3]

Whereas Article 22 (1) and (2) of Directive 85/611/EEC[4] limits the investment of UCITS assets in transferable securities from the same issuer to 5%, a limit which may, if required, be increased to 10%;

Whereas that limit poses special problems for UCITS established in Denmark in cases where they wish to invest an appreciable proportion of their assets on the domestic bond market, since that market is dominated by mortgage credit bonds and the number of institutions issuing such bonds is very small;

Whereas those mortgage credit bonds are subject in Denmark to special rules and supervision designed to protect holders and are treated under Danish legislation as equivalent to bonds issued or guaranteed by the State;

Whereas Article 22 (3) of Directive 85/611/EEC derogates from paragraphs 1 and 2 of that Article in the case of bonds issued or guaranteed by a Member State and authorizes UCITS to invest in particular up to 35% of their assets in such bonds;

Whereas a similar derogation, but of a more limited extent is justified with regard to private sector bonds which, even in the absence of a State guarantee, nevertheless offer special guarantees to the investor under the specific rules applicable thereto; whereas it is necessary therefore to extend such a derogation to the totality of such bonds which fulfil jointly fixed criteria, while leaving it to the Member States to draw up the list of bonds to which they intend, where appropriate, to grant a derogation, and providing

---

[1] OJ No C 155, 21. 6. 1986, p. 4.

[2] Opinion published in OJ No C 125, 11. 5. 1987, p. 162 and Decision of 10 February 1988 (not yet published in the Official Journal).

[3] OJ No C 333, 29. 12. 1986, p. 10.   [4] OJ No L 375, 31. 12. 1985, p. 3.

for a procedure for informing the other Member States identical to that provided for in Article 20 of Directive 85/611/EEC,

Has adopted this directive:

Article 1. In Article 22 of Directive 85/611/EEC, the following paragraphs shall be added:

4. Member States may raise the limit laid down in paragraph 1 to a maximum of 25% in the case of certain bonds when these are issued by a credit institution which has its registered office in a Member State and is subject by law to special public supervision designed to protect bond-holders. In particular, sums deriving from the issue of these bonds must be invested in conformity with the law in assets which, during the whole period of validity of the bonds, are capable of covering claims attaching to the bonds and which, in the event of failure of the issuer, would be used on a priority basis for the reimbursement of the principal and payment of the accrued interest.

When a UCITS invests more than 5% of its assets in the bonds referred to in the first subparagraph and issued by one issuer, the total value of these investments may not exceed 80% of the value of the assets of the UCITS.

As laid down in Article 20 (1), Member States shall send the Commission a list of the aforementioned categories of bonds together with the categories of issuers authorized, in accordance with the laws and supervisory arrangements mentioned in the first subparagraph, to issue bonds complying with the criteria set out above. A notice specifying the status of the guarantees offered shall be attached to these lists. The procedure laid down in Article 20 (2) shall apply.

5. The transferable securities referred to in paragraphs 3 and 4 shall not be taken into account for the purpose of applying the limit of 40% referred to in paragraph 2.

The limits provided for in paragraphs 1, 2, 3 and 4 may not be combined, and thus investments in transferable securities issued by the same body carried out in accordance with paragraphs 1, 2, 3 and 4 shall under no circumstances exceed in total 35% of the assets of an UCITS.

Article 2. The Member States shall bring into force the measures necessary to comply with this Directive by the same dates as those provided for in Directive 85/611/EEC. They shall forthwith inform the Commission thereof.

Article 3. This Directive is addressed to the Member States.

Done at Brussels, 22 March 1988.

For the Council, The President, M. Bangemann

Council Directive

of 5 March 1979 coordinating the conditions for the
admission of securities to official stock exchange listing

(79/279/EEC)

The Council of the European Communities,

Having regard to the Treaty establishing the European Economic
Community, and in particular Articles 54 (3) (g) and 100 thereof,

Having regard to the proposal from the Commission,[1]

Having regard to the opinion of the European Parliament,[2]

Having regard to the opinion of the Economic and Social Committee,[3]

Whereas the coordination of the conditions for the admission of securities
to official listing on stock exchanges situated or operating in the Member
States is likely to provide equivalent protection for investors at Community
level, because of the more uniform guarantees offered to investors in the
various Member States; whereas it will facilitate both the admission to
official stock exchange listing, in each such State, of securities from other
Member States and the listing of any given security on a number of stock
exchanges in the Community; whereas it will accordingly make for greater
interpenetration of national securities markets and therefore contribute to
the prospect of establishing a European capital market;

Whereas such coordination must therefore apply to securities, independently of the legal status of their issuers, and must therefore also apply to
securities issued by non-member States or their regional or local authorities
or international public bodies; whereas this Directive therefore covers
entities not covered by the second paragraph of Article 58 of the Treaty and
goes beyond the scope of Article 54 (3) (g) while directly affecting the
establishment and functioning of the common market within the meaning of
Article 100;

Whereas there should be the possibility of a right to apply to the courts
against decisions by the competent national authorities in respect of the
application of this Directive, although such right to apply must not be
allowed to restrict the discretion of these authorities;

Whereas, initially, this coordination should be sufficiently flexible to
enable account to be taken of present differences in the structures of
securities markets in the Member States and to enable the Member States to
take account of any specific situations with which they may be confronted;

[1] OJ No C 56, 10. 3. 1976, p. 3.   [2] OJ No C 238, 11. 10. 1976, p. 38.
[3] OJ No C 204, 30. 8. 1976, p. 5.

Whereas, for this reason, coordination should first be limited to the establishment of minimum conditions for the admission of securities to official listing on stock exchanges situated or operating in the Member States, without however giving issuers any right to listing;

Whereas, this partial coordination of the conditions for admission to official listing constitutes a first step towards subsequent closer alignment of the rules of Member States in this field,

Has adopted this directive:

SECTION I. GENERAL PROVISIONS

Article 1. 1. This Directive concerns securities which are admitted to official listing or are the subject of an application for admission to official listing on a stock exchange situated or operating within a Member State.

2. Member States may decide not to apply this Directive to:

— units issued by collective investment undertakings other than the closed-up type,

— securities issued by a Member State or its regional or local authorities.

Article 2. For the purposes of applying this Directive:

(a) collective investment undertakings other than the closed-end type shall mean unit trusts and investment companies:

— the object of which is the collective investment of capital provided by the public, and which operate on the principle of risk spreading, and

— the units of which are, at the request of holders, repurchased or redeemed, directly or indirectly, out of the assets of these undertakings. Action taken by such undertakings to ensure that the stock exchange value of its units does not significantly vary from their net asset value shall be regarded as equivalent to such repurchase or redemption;

(b) units shall mean securities issued by collective investment undertakings as representing the rights of participants in the assets of such undertakings;

(c) European unit of account shall mean the unit of account as defined in Article 10 of the Financial Regulation of 21 December 1977 applicable to the general budget of the European Communities.[1]

Article 3. Member States shall ensure that:

— securities may not be admitted to official listing on any stock exchange situated or operating within their territory unless the conditions laid down by this Directive are satisfied, and that

[1] OJ No L 356, 31. 12. 1977, p. 1.

— issuers of securities admitted to such official listing, whether admission takes place before or after the date on which this Directive is implemented, are subject to the obligations provided for by this Directive.

Article 4. 1. The admission of securities to official listing shall be subject to the conditions set out in Schedules A and B to this Directive, relating to shares and debt securities respectively.

2. The issues of securities admitted to official listing must fulfil the obligations set out in Schedules C and D to this Directive, relating to shares and debt securities respectively.

3. Certificates representing shares may be admitted to official listing only if the issuer of the shares represented fulfils the conditions set out in I (1) to I (3) of Schedule A and the obligations set out in Schedule C and if the certificates fulfil the conditions set out in II (1) to II (6) of Schedule A.

Article 5. 1. Subject to the prohibitions provided for in Article 6 and in Schedules A and B, the Member States may make the admission of securities to official listing subject to more stringent conditions than those set out in Schedules A and B or to additional conditions, provided that these more stringent and additional conditions apply generally for all issuers or for individual classes of issuer and that they have been published before application for admission of such securities is made.

2. Member States may make the issuers of securities admitted to official listing subject to more stringent obligations than those set out in Schedules C and D or to additional obligations, provided that these more stringent and additional obligations apply generally for all issuers or for individual classes of issuer.

3. Member States may, under the same conditions as those laid down in Article 7, authorize derogations from the additional or more stringent conditions and obligations referred to in paragraphs 1 and 2 hereof.

4. Member States may, in accordance with the applicable national rules require issuers of securities admitted to official listing to inform the public on a regular basis of their financial position and the general course of their business.

Article 6. Member States may not make the admission to official listing of securities issued by companies or other legal persons which are nationals of another Member State subject to the condition that the securities must already have been admitted to official listing on a stock exchange situated or operating in one of the Member States.

Article 7. Any derogations from the conditions for the admission of securities to official listing which may be authorized in accordance with

Schedules A and B must apply generally for all issuers where the circumstances justifying them are similar.

Article 8. Member States may decide not to apply the conditions set out in Schedule B and the obligations set out in A (4) (a) and (c) of Schedule D in respect of applications for admission to official listing of debt securities issued by companies and other legal persons which are nationals of a Member State and which are set up by, governed by or managed pursuant to a special law where repayments and interest payments in respect of those securities are guaranteed by a Member State or one of its federal states.

SECTION II. AUTHORITIES COMPETENT TO ADMIT SECURITIES TO OFFICIAL LISTING

Article 9. 1. Member States shall designate the national authority or authorities competent to decide on the admission of securities to official listing on a stock exchange situated or operating within their territories and shall ensure that this Directive is applied. They shall inform the Commission accordingly, indicating, if appropriate, how duties have been allocated.

2. Member States shall ensure that the competent authorities have such powers as may be necessary for the exercise of their duties.

3. Without prejudice to the other powers conferred upon them, the competent authorities may reject an application for the admission of a security to official listing if, in their opinion, the issuer's situation is such that admission would be detrimental to investors' interests.

Article 10. By way of derogation from Article 5, Member States may, solely in the interests of protecting the investors, give the competent authorities power to make the admission of a security to official listing subject to any special condition which the competent authorities consider appropriate and of which they have explicitly informed the applicant.

Article 11. The competent authorities may refuse to admit to official listing a security already officially listed in another Member State where the issuer fails to comply with the obligations resulting from admission in that Member State.

Article 12. Without prejudice to any other action or penalties which they may contemplate in the event of failure on the part of the issuer to comply with the obligations resulting from admission to official listing, the competent authorities may make public the fact that an issuer is failing to comply with those obligations.

Article 13. 1. An issuer whose securities are admitted to official listing shall provide the competent authorities with all the information which the latter consider appropriate in order to protect investors or ensure the smooth operation of the market.

2. Where protection of investors or the smooth operation of the market so requires, an issuer may be required by the competent authorities to publish such information in such a form and within such time limits as they consider appropriate. Should the issuer fail to comply with such requirements, the competent authorities may themselves publish such information after having heard the issuer.

Article 14. 1. The competent authorities may decide to suspend the listing of a security where the smooth operation of the market is, or may be, temporarily jeopardized or where protection of investors so requires.

2. The competent authorities may decide that the listing of the security be discontinued where they are satisfied that, owing to special circumstances, normal regular dealings in a security are no longer possible.

Article 15. 1. Member States shall ensure decisions of the competent authorities refusing the admission of a security to official listing or discontinuing such a listing shall be subject to the right to apply to the courts.

2. An applicant shall be notified of a decision regarding his application for admission to official listing within six months of receipt of the application or, should the competent authority require any further information within that period, within six months of the applicant's supplying such information.

3. Failure to give a decision within the time limit specified in paragraph 2 shall be deemed a rejection of the application. Such rejection shall give rise to the right to apply to the courts provided for in paragraph 1.

Article 16. Where an application for admission to official listing relates to certificates representing shares, the application shall be considered only if the competent authorities are of the opinion that the issuer of the certificates is offering adequate safeguards for the protection of investors.

SECTION III. PUBLICATION OF THE INFORMATION TO BE MADE
AVAILABLE TO THE PUBLIC

Article 17. 1. The information which issuers of a security admitted to official listing in a Member State are required to make available to the public in accordance with the requirements of Schedules C and D shall be published in one or more newspapers distributed throughout the Member State or distributed widely therein or shall be made available to the public either in writing in places indicated by announcements to be published in one or more newspapers distributed throughout the Member State or widely distributed therein or by other equivalent means approved by the competent authorities. The issuers must simultaneously send such information to the competent authorities.

2. The information referred to in paragraph 1 shall be published in the official language or languages, or in one of the official languages or in another language provided that in the Member State in question the official language or languages or such other language is or are customary in the sphere of finance and accepted by the competent authorities.

SECTION IV. COOPERATION BETWEEN MEMBER STATES

Article 18.   1. The competent authorities shall cooperate wherever necessary for the purpose of carrying out their duties and shall exchange any information required for that purpose.

2. Where applications are to be made simultaneously or within short intervals of one another for admission of the same securities to official listing on stock exchanges situated or operating in more than one Member State, or where an application for admission is made in respect of a security already listed on a stock exchange in another Member State, the competent authorities shall communicate with each other and make such arrangements as may be necessary to expedite the procedure and simplify as far as possible the formalities and any additional conditions required for admission of the security concerned.

3. In order to facilitate the work of the competent authorities, any application for the admission of a security to official listing on a stock exchange situated or operating in a Member State must state whether a similar application is being or has been made in another Member State, or will be made in the near future.

Article 19.   1. Member States shall provide that all persons employed or formerly employed by the competent authorities shall be bound by professional secrecy. This means that any confidential information received in the course of their duties may not be divulged to any person or authority except by virtue of provisions laid down by law.

2. Paragraph 1 shall not, however, preclude the competent authorities of the various Member States from exchanging information as provided for in this Directive. Information thus exchanged shall be covered by the obligation of professional secrecy to which the persons employed or formerly employed by the competent authorities receiving the information are subject.

SECTION V. CONTACT COMMITTEE

Article 20.   1. A Contact Committee (hereinafter called 'the Committee') shall be set up alongside the Commission. Its function shall be:

(a) without prejudice to Articles 169 and 170 of the EEC Treaty to facilitate the harmonized implementation of this Directive through regular consultations on any practical problems arising from its application and on which exchanges of view are deemed useful;

(b) to facilitate the establishment of a concerted attitude between the Member States on the more stringent or additional conditions and obligations which, pursuant to Article 5 of this Directive, they may lay down at national level;

(c) to advise the Commission, if necessary, on any supplements or amendments to be made to this Directive or on any adjustments to be made in accordance with Article 21.

2. It shall not be the function of the Committee to appraise the merits of decisions taken by the competent authorities in individual cases.

3. The Committee shall be composed of persons appointed by the Member States and of representatives of the Commission. The chairman shall be a representative of the Commission. Secretarial services shall be provided by the Commission.

4. Meetings of the Committee shall be convened by its chairman, either on his own initiative or at the request of one Member State delegation. The Committee shall draw up its rules of procedure.

Article 21.   1. For the purpose of adjusting, in the light of the requirements of the economic situation, the minimum amount of the foreseeable market capitalization laid down in the first paragraph of I (2) of Schedule A, the Commission shall submit to the Committee a draft of the measures to be taken. The Committee shall deliver its opinion within the period laid down by its chairman. Its decisions shall require 41 votes in favour, the votes of the Member States being weighted as provided for in Article 148 (2) of the Treaty.

2. When the Committee has delivered an opinion in favour of the draft of the measures envisaged by the Commission the latter shall adopt them.

Where the opinion of the Committee is not in accordance with the draft of the measures envisaged by the Commission or where the Committee has not delivered an opinion within the required period, the Commission shall without delay lay before the Council, which shall act by qualified majority, a proposal concerning the measures to be taken.

Where the Council fails to act on the proposal within three months of its receipt, the measures proposed shall be adopted by the Commission.

SECTION VI. FINAL PROVISIONS

Article 22. 1. Member States shall take the measures necessary to comply with this Directive within two years of its notification. They shall forthwith inform the Commission thereof.

This period shall be extended by one year in the case of Member States simultaneously introducing this Directive and the proposed Council Directive on the particulars to be published when securities issued by companies within the meaning of the second paragraph of Article 58 of the Treaty are admitted to official stock exchange listing.

2. As from the notification of this Directive, the Member States shall communicate to the Commission the texts of the main laws, regulations and administrative provisions which they adopt in the field covered by this Directive.

Article 23. This Directive is addressed to the Member States.

Done at Brussels, 5 March 1979.

For the Council, The President, J. François-Poncet

ANNEX

SCHEDULE A

Conditions for the Admission of Shares to Official Listing on a Stock Exchange

I. Conditions relating to companies for the shares of which admission to official listing is sought

1. *Legal position of the company*

The legal position of the company must be in conformity with the laws and regulations to which it is subject, as regards both its formation and its operation under its statutes.

2. *Minimum size of the company*

The foreseeable market capitalization of the shares for which admission to official listing is sought or, if this cannot be assessed, the company's capital and reserves, including profit or loss, from the last financial year, must be at least one million European units of account.

However, Member States may provide for admission to official listing, even when this condition is not fulfilled, provided that the competent authorities are satisfied that there will be an adequate market for the shares concerned.

A higher foreseeable market capitalization or higher capital and reserves may be required by a Member State for admission to official listing only if another regulated, regularly operating, recognized open market exists in that State and the requirements for it are equal to or less than those referred to in the first paragraph.

The condition set out in the first paragraph shall not be applicable for the admission to official listing of a further block of shares of the same class as those already admitted.

The equivalent in national currency of one million European units of account shall initially be that applicable on the date on which the Directive is adopted.

If, as a result of adjustment of the equivalent of the European unit of account in national currency, the market capitalization expressed in national currency remains for a period of one year at least 10% more or less than the value of one million European units of account the Member State must, within the 12 months following the expiry of that period, adjust its laws, regulations or administrative provisions to comply with the first paragraph.

3. *A company's period of existence*

A company must have published or filed its annual accounts in accordance with national law for the three financial years preceding the application for official listing. By way of exception, the competent authorities may derogate from this condition where such derogation is desirable in the interests of the company or of investors and where the competent authorities are satisfied that investors have the necessary information available to be able to arrive at an informed judgment on the company and the shares for which admission to official listing is sought.

II. Conditions relating to the shares for which admission to official listing is sought

1. *Legal position of the shares*

The legal position of the shares must be in conformity with the laws and regulations to which they are subject.

2. *Negotiability of the shares*

The shares must be freely negotiable.

The competent authorities may treat shares which are not fully paid up as freely negotiable, if arrangements have been made to ensure that the negotiability of such shares is not restricted and that dealing is made open and proper by providing the public with all appropriate information.

The competent authorities may, in the case of the admission to official listing of shares which may be acquired only subject to approval, derogate from the first paragraph only if the use of the approval clause does not disturb the market.

3. *Public issue preceding admission to official listing*

Where public issue precedes admission to official listing, the first listing may be made only after the end of the period during which subscription applications may be submitted.

4. *Distribution of shares*

A sufficient number of shares must be distributed to the public in one or more Member States not later than the time of admission.

This condition shall not apply where shares are to be distributed to the public through the stock exchange. In that event, admission to official listing may be granted only if the competent authorities are satisfied that a sufficient number of shares will be distributed through the stock exchange within a short period.

Where admission to official listing is sought for a further block of shares of the same class, the competent authorities may assess whether a sufficient number of shares has been distributed to the public in relation to all the shares issued and not only in relation to this further block.

However, by way of derogation from the first paragraph, if the shares are admitted to official listing in one or more non-Member States, the competent authorities may provide for their admission to official listing if a sufficient number of shares is distributed to the public in the non-member State or States where they are listed.

A sufficient number of shares shall be deemed to have been distributed either when the shares in respect of which application for admission has been made are in the hands of the public to the extent of a least 25% of the subscribed capital represented by the class of shares concerned or when, in view of the large number of shares of the same class and the extent of their distribution to the public, the market will operate properly with a lower percentage.

5. *Listing of shares of the same class*

The application for admission to official listing must cover all the shares of the same class already issued.

However, Member States may provide that this condition shall not apply to applications for admission not covering all the shares of the same class already issued where the shares of that class for which admission is not sought belong to blocks serving to maintain control of the company or are not negotiable for a certain time under agreements, provided that the public is informed of such situations and that there is no danger of such situations prejudicing the interests of the holders of the shares for which admission to official listing is sought.

6. *Physical form of shares*

For the admission to official listing of shares issued by companies which are nationals of another Member State and which shares have a physical form it is necessary and sufficient that their physical form comply with the standards laid down in that other Member State. Where the physical form does not conform to the standards in force in the Member State in which admission to official listing is applied for, the competent authorities of that State shall make that fact known to the public.

The physical form of shares issued by companies which are nationals of a non-member State must afford sufficient safeguard for the protection of the investors.

7. *Shares issued by companies from a non-member State*

If the shares issued by a company which is a national of a non-member State are not listed in either the country of origin or in the country in which the major proportion of the shares is held, they may not be admitted to official listing unless the competent authorities are satisfied that the absence of a listing in the country of origin or in the country in which the major proportion is held is not due to the need to protect investors.

SCHEDULE B

Conditions for the Admission of Debt Securities to Official Listing on a Stock Exchange

A. ADMISSION TO OFFICIAL LISTING OF DEBT SECURITIES ISSUED BY AN UNDERTAKING

I. Conditions relating to undertakings for the debt securities of which admission to official listing is sought

Legal position of the undertaking

The legal position of the undertaking must be in conformity with the laws and regulations to which it is subject, as regards both its formation and its operation under its statutes.

II. Conditions relating to the debt securities for which admission to official listing is sought

1. *Legal position of the debt securities*

The legal position of the debt securities must be in conformity with the laws and regulations to which they are subject.

2. *Negotiability of the debt securities*

The debt securities must be freely negotiable.

The competent authorities may treat debt securities which are not fully paid up as freely negotiable if arrangements have been made to ensure that the negotiability of these debt securities is not restricted and that dealing is made open and proper by providing the public with all appropriate information.

3. *Public issue preceding admission to official listing*

Where public issue precedes admission to official listing, the first listing may be made only after the end of the period during which subscription applications may be submitted. This provision shall not apply in the case of tap issues of debt securities when the closing date for subscription is not fixed.

4. *Listing of debt securities ranking* pari passu

The application for admission to official listing must cover all debt securities ranking *pari passu*.

5. *Physical form of debt securities*

For the admission to official listing of debt securities issued by undertakings which are nationals of another Member State and which debt securities have a physical form, it is necessary and sufficient that their physical form comply with the standards laid down in that other Member State. Where the physical form does not conform to the standards in force in the Member State in which admission to official listing is applied for, the competent authorities of that State shall make that fact known to the public.

However, the physical form of debt securities issued in a single Member State must conform to the standards in force in that State.

The physical form of debt securities issued by undertakings which are nationals of a non-member State must afford sufficient safeguard for the protection of the investors.

III. Other conditions

1. *Minimum amount of the loan*

The amount of the loan may not be less than 200 000 European units of account. This provision shall not be applicable in the case of tap issues where the amount of the loan is not fixed.

Member States may, however, provide for admission to official listing even when this condition is not fulfilled, where the competent authorities are satisfied that there will be a sufficient market for the debt securities concerned.

The equivalent in national currency of 200 000 European units of account shall initially be that applicable on the date on which this Directive is adopted.

If as a result of adjustment of the equivalent of the European unit of account in national currency the minimum amount of the loan expressed in national currency remains, for a period of one year, at least 10% less than the value of 200000 European units of account the Member State must, within the 12 months following the expiry of that period, amend its laws, regulations and administrative provisions to comply with the first paragraph.

2. *Convertible or exchangeable debentures, and debentures with warrants*

Convertible or exchangeable debentures and debentures with warrants may be admitted to official listing only if the related shares are already listed on the same stock exchange or on another regulated, regularly operating, recognized open market or are so admitted simultaneously.

However, Member States may, by way of derogation from the first paragraph, provide for the admission to official listing of convertible or exchangeable debentures or debentures with warrants, if the competent authorities are satisfied that holders have at their disposal all the information necessary to form an opinion concerning the value of the shares to which these debt securities relate.

B. ADMISSION TO OFFICIAL LISTING OF DEBT SECURITIES ISSUED BY A STATE, ITS REGIONAL OR LOCAL AUTHORITIES OR A PUBLIC INTERNATIONAL BODY

1. *Negotiability of the debt securities*

The debt securities must be freely negotiable.

2. *Public issue preceding admission to official listing*

Where public issue precedes admission to official listing, the first listing may be made only after the end of the period during which subscription applications may be submitted. This provision shall not apply where the closing date for subscription is not fixed.

3. *Listing of debt securities ranking* pari passu

The application for admission to official listing must cover all the securities ranking *pari passu*.

4. *Physical form of debt securities*

For the admission to official listing of debt securities which are issued by a Member State or its regional or local authorities in a physical form, it is necessary and sufficient that such physical form comply with the standards in force in that Member State. Where the physical form does not comply with the standards in force in the Member State where admission to official listing is applied for, the competent authorities of that State shall bring this situation to the attention of the public.

The physical form of debt securities issued by non-member States or their regional or local authorities or by public international bodies must afford sufficient safeguard for the protection of the investors.

SCHEDULE C

Obligations of Companies Whose Shares are admitted to Official Listing on a Stock Exchange

1. *Listing of newly issued shares of the same class*

Without prejudice to the second paragraph of II (5) of Schedule A, in the case of a new public issue of shares of the same class as those already officially listed, the company shall be required, where the new shares are not automatically admitted, to apply for their admission to the same listing, either not more than a year after their issue or when they become freely negotiable.

2. *Treatment of shareholders*

(a) The company shall ensure equal treatment for all shareholders who are in the same position.

(b) The company must ensure, at least in each Member State in which its shares are listed, that all the necessary facilities and information are available to enable shareholders to exercise their rights. In particular, it must:

— inform shareholders of the holding of meetings and enable them to exercise their right to vote,

— publish notices or distribute circulars concerning the allocation and payment of dividends, the issue of new shares including allotment, subscription, renunciation and conversion arrangements,

— designate as its agent a financial institution through which shareholders may exercise their financial rights, unless the company itself provides financial services.

3. *Amendment of the instrument of incorporation or the statutes*

(a) A company planning an amendment to its instrument of incorporation or its statutes must communicate a draft thereof to the competent authorities of the Member States in which its shares are listed.

(b) That draft must be communicated to the competent authorities no later than the calling of the general meeting which is to decide on the proposed amendment.

4. *Annual accounts and annual report*

(a) The company must make available to the public, as soon as possible, its most recent annual accounts and its last annual report.

(b) If the company prepares both annual own and annual consolidated accounts, it must make them available to the public. In that event the competent authorities may authorize the company only to make available to the public either the own or the consolidated accounts, provided that the accounts which are not made available to the public do not contain any significant additional information.

(c) If the annual accounts and reports do not comply with the provisions of Council Directives concerning companies' accounts and if they do not give a true and fair view of the company's assets and liabilities, financial position and profit or loss, more detailed and/or additional information must be provided.

5. *Additional information*

(a) The company must inform the public as soon as possible of any major new developments in its sphere of activity which are not public knowledge and which may, by virtue of their effect on its assets and liabilities or financial position or on the general course of its business, lead to substantial movements in the prices of its shares.

The competent authorities may, however, exempt the company from this requirement, if the disclosure of particular information is such as to prejudice the legitimate interests of the company.

(b) The company must inform the public without delay of any changes in the rights attaching to the various classes of shares.

(c) The company must inform the public of any changes in the structure (shareholders and breakdown of holdings) of the major holdings in its capital as compared with information previously published on that subject as soon as such changes come to its notice.

6. *Equivalence of information*

(a) A company whose shares are officially listed on stock exchanges situated or operating in different Member States must ensure that equivalent information is made availabe to the market at each of these exchanges.

(b) A company whose shares are officially listed on stock exchanges situated or operating in one or more Member States and in one or more non-member States must make available to the markets of the Member State or States in which its shares are listed information which is at least equivalent to that which it makes available to the markets of the non-member State or States in question, if such information may be of importance for the evaluation of the shares.

SCHEDULE D

Obligations of Issuers Whose Debt Securities are Admitted to Official Listing on a Stock Exchange

A. DEBT SECURITIES ISSUED BY AN UNDERTAKING

1. *Treatment of holders of debt securities*

(a) The undertaking must ensure that all holders of debt securities ranking *pari passu* are given equal treatment in respect of all the rights attaching to those debt securities.

Provided they are made in accordance with national law, this condition shall not prevent offers of early repayment of certain debt securities being made to holders by an undertaking in derogation from the conditions of issue and in particular in accordance with social priorities.

(b) The undertaking must ensure that at least in each Member State where its debt securities are officially listed all the facilities and information necessary to enable holders to exercise their rights are available. In particular, it must:

— publish notices or distribute circulars concerning the holding of meetings of holders of debt securities, the payment of interest, the exercise of any conversion, exchange, subscription or renunciation rights, and repayment,

— designate as its agent a financial institution through which holders of debt securities may exercise their financial rights, unless the undertaking itself provides financial services.

2. *Amendment of the instrument of incorporation or the statutes*

(a) An undertaking planning an amendment to its instrument of incorporation or its statutes affecting the rights of holders of debt securities must forward a draft thereof to the competent authorities of the Member States in which its debt securities are listed.

(b) That draft must be communicated to the competent authorities no later than the calling of the meeting of the body which is to decide on the proposed amendment.

3. *Annual accounts and annual report*

(a) The undertaking must make available to the public as soon as possible its most recent annual accounts and its last annual report the publication of which is required by national law.

(b) If the undertaking prepares both annual own and annual consolidated accounts, it must make them available to the public. In that event, however, the competent authority may authorize the undertaking only to make available to the public either the own accounts or the consolidated accounts, provided that the accounts which are not made available do not contain any significant additional information.

(c) If the accounts and reports do not comply with the provisions of Council Directives concerning undertakings' accounts and if they do not give a true and fair view of the undertaking's assets and liabilities, financial position and results, more detailed and/or additional information must be provided.

4. *Additional information*

(a) The undertaking must inform the public as soon as possible of any major new developments in its sphere of activity which are not public knowledge and which may significantly affect its ability to meet its commitments.

The competent authorities may, however, exempt the undertaking from this obligation at its request if the disclosure of particular information would be such as to prejudice the legitimate interests of the undertaking.

(b) The undertaking must inform the public without delay of any change in the rights of holders of debt securities resulting in particular from a change in loan terms or in interest rates.

(c) The undertaking must inform the public without delay of new loan issues and in particular of any guarantee or security in respect thereof.

(d) Where the debt securities officially listed are convertible or exchangeable debentures, or debentures with warrants, the undertaking must inform the public without delay of any changes in the rights attaching to the various classes of shares to which they relate.

5. *Equivalence of information*

(a) An undertaking the debt securities of which are officially listed on stock exchanges situated or operating in different Member States must ensure that equivalent information is made available to the market at each of these exchanges.

(b) An undertaking the debt securities of which are officially listed on stock exchanges situated or operating in one or more Member States and in one or more non-member States must make available to the markets of the Member State or Member States in which its debt securities are listed information which is at least equivalent to that which it makes available to the markets of the non-member State or States in question, if such information may be of importance for the evaluation of the debt securities.

B. DEBT SECURITIES ISSUED BY A STATE OR ITS
REGIONAL OR LOCAL AUTHORITIES OR BY A PUBLIC
INTERNATIONAL BODY

1. *Treatment of holders of debt securities*

(a) States, their regional or local authorities and public international bodies must ensure that all holders of debt securities ranking *pari passu* are given equal treatment in respect of all the rights attaching to those debt securities.

Provided they are made in accordance with national law, this condition shall not prevent offers of early repayment of certain debt securities being made to holders by an issuer in derogation from the conditions of issue and in particular in accordance with social priorities.

(b) States, their regional or local authorities and public international bodies must ensure that at least in each Member State in which their debt securities are officially listed all the facilities and information necessary to enable holders of debt securities to exercise their rights are available. In particular, they must:

— publish notices or distribute circulars concerning the holding of meetings of holders of debt securities, the payment of interest and redemption,

— designate as their agents financial institutions through which holders of debt securities may exercise their financial rights.

2. *Equivalence of information*

(a) States, their regional or local authorities and public international bodies the debt securities of which are officially listed on stock exchanges situated or operating in different Member States must ensure that equivalent information is made available to the market at each of these exchanges.

(b) States, their regional or local authorities and public international bodies the debt securities of which are officially listed on stock exchanges situated or operating in one or more Member States and in one or more non-member States must make available to the markets of the Member State or Member States in which their debt securities are listed information which is at least equivalent to that which they make available to the markets of the non-member State or States in question, if such information may be of importance for the evaluation of the debt securities.

Council Directive

of 17 March 1980 coordinating the requirements for the
drawing up, scrutiny and distribution of the listing
particulars to be published for the admission of securities
to official stock exchange listing

(80/390/EEC)

The Council of the European Communities,

Having regard to the Treaty establishing the European Economic
Community, and in particular Articles 54 (3) (g) and 100 thereof,

Having regard to the proposal from the Commission,[1]

Having regard to the opinion of the European Parliament,[2]

Having regard to the opinion of the Economic and Social Committee,[3]

Whereas the market in which undertakings operate has been enlarged to
embrace the whole Community and this enlargement involves a corresponding increase in their financial requirements and extension of the capital
markets on which they must call to satisfy them; whereas admission to
official listing on stock exchanges of Member States of securities issued by
undertakings constitutes an important means of access to these capital
markets; whereas furthermore exchange restrictions on the purchase of
securities traded on the stock exchanges of another Member State have been
eliminated as part of the liberalization of capital movements;

Whereas safeguards for the protection of the interests of actual and
potential investors are required in most Member States of undertakings
offering their securities to the public, either at the time of their offer or of
their admission to official stock exchange listing; whereas such safeguards
require the provision of information which is sufficient and as objective as
possible concerning the financial circumstances of the issuer and particulars
of the securities for which admission to official listing is requested; whereas
the form under which this information is required usually consists of the
publication of listing particulars;

Whereas the safeguards required differ from Member State to Member
State, both as regards the contents and the layout of the listing particulars
and the efficacy, methods and timing of the check on the information given
therein; whereas the effect of these differences is not only to make it more
difficult for undertakings to obtain admission of securities to official listing
on stock exchanges of several Member States but also to hinder the

---

[1] OJ No C 131, 13. 12. 1972, p. 61.   [2] OJ No C 11, 7. 2. 1974, p. 24.
[3] OJ No C 125, 16. 10. 1974, p. 1.

acquisition by investors residing in one Member State of securities listed on stock exchanges of other Member States and thus to inhibit the financing of the undertakings and investment throughout the Community;

Whereas these differences should be eliminated by coordinating the rules and regulations without necessarily making them completely uniform, in order to achieve an adequate degree of equivalence in the safeguards required in each Member State to ensure the provision of information which is sufficient and as objective as possible for actual or potential security holders; whereas at the same time, taking into account the present degree of liberalization of capital movements in the Community and the fact that a mechanism for checking at the time the securities are offered does not yet exist in all Member States, it would appear sufficient at present to limit the coordination to the admission of securities to official stock exchange listing;

Whereas such coordination must apply to securities independently of the legal status of the issuing undertaking, and accordingly, in so far as this Directive applies to entities to which no reference is made in the second paragraph of Article 58 of the Treaty and goes beyond the scope of Article 54 (3) (g), it must be based also on Article 100,

Has adopted this directive:

SECTION I. GENERAL PROVISIONS

Article 1. 1. This Directive shall apply to securities which are the subject of an application for admission to official listing on a stock exchange situated or operating within a Member State.

2. This Directive shall not apply to:

— units issued by collective investment undertakings other than the closed-end type,

— securities issued by a State or by its regional or local authorities.

Article 2. For purposes of applying this Directive:

(a) 'collective investment undertakings other than the closed-end type' shall mean unit trusts and investment companies:

— the object of which is the collective investment of capital provided by the public, and which operate on the principle of risk spreading, and

— the units of which are, at the holders' request, repurchased or redeemed, directly or indirectly, out of the assets of these undertakings. Action taken by such undertakings to ensure that the stock exchange value of its units does not significantly vary from their net asset value shall be regarded as equivalent to such repurchase or redemption;

(b) 'units of a collective investment undertaking' shall mean securities issued by a collective investment undertaking as representing the rights of participants in the assets of such an undertaking;

(c) 'issuers' shall mean companies and other legal persons and any under-taking whose securities are the subject of an application for admission to official listing on a stock exchange;

(d) 'net turnover' shall comprise the amounts derived from the sale of products and the provision of services falling within the undertaking's ordinary activities, after deduction of sales rebates and of value added tax and other taxes directly linked to the turnover;

(e) 'credit institution' shall mean an undertaking whose business is to receive deposits or other repayable funds from the public and to grant credits for its own account;

(f) 'participating interest' shall mean rights in the capital of other undertak-ings, whether or not represented by certificates, which, by creating a durable link with those undertakings, are intended to contribute to the activities of the undertaking which holds these rights;

(g) 'annual accounts' shall comprise the balance sheet, the profit and loss account and the notes on the accounts. These documents shall constitute a composite whole.

Article 3.   Member States shall ensure that the admission of securities to official listing on a stock exchange situated or operating within their terri-tories is conditional upon the publication of an information sheet, herein-after referred to as listing particulars.

Article 4.   1. The listing particulars shall contain the information which, according to the particular nature of the issuer and of the securities for the admission of which application is being made, is necessary to enable investors and their investment advisers to make an informed assessment of the assets and liabilities, financial position, profits and losses, and prospects of the issuer and of the rights attaching to such securities.

2. Member States shall ensure that the obligation referred to in para-graph 1 is incumbent upon the persons responsible for the listing particulars as provided for in heading 1.1 of Schedules A and B annexed hereto.

Article 5.   1. Without prejudice to the obligation referred to in Article 4, Member States shall ensure that, subject to the possibilities for exemptions provided for in Articles 6 and 7, listing particulars contain, in as easily analysable and comprehensible a form as possible, at least the items of information provided for in Schedules A, B or C, depending on whether shares, debt securities or certificates representing shares are involved.

2. In the specific cases covered by Articles 8 to 17 the listing particulars are to be drawn up in accordance with the specifications given in those

Articles, subject to the possibilities for exemptions provided for in Articles 6 and 7.

3. Where certain headings in Schedules A, B and C appear inappropriate to the issuer's sphere of activity or legal form, listing particulars giving equivalent information shall be drawn up by adapting these headings.

Article 6.   Member States may allow the authorities responsible for checking the listing particulars within the meaning of this Directive (hereinafter referred to as 'the competent authorities') to provide for partial or complete exemption from the obligations to publish listing particulars in the following cases:

1. where the securities for which admission to official listing is applied for are:

(a) securities which have been the subject of a public issue;
(b) securities issued in connection with a takeover offer;
(c) securities issued in connection with a merger involving the acquisition of another company or the formation of a new company, the division of a company, the transfer of all or part of an undertaking's assets and liabilities or as consideration for the transfer of assets other than cash;

and where, not more than 12 months before the admission of the securities to official listing, a document, regarded by the competent authorities as containing information equivalent to that of the listing particulars provided for by this Directive, has been published in the same Member State. Particulars shall also be published of any material changes which have occurred since such document was prepared. The document must be made available to the public at the registered office of the issuer and at the offices of the financial organizations retained to act as the latter's paying agents, and any particulars of material changes shall be published in accordance with Articles 20 (1) and 21 (1).

2. where the securities for which admission to official listing is applied for are:

(a) shares allotted free of charge to holders of shares already listed on the same stock exchange; or
(b) shares resulting from the conversion of convertible debt securities or shares created after an exchange for exchangeable debt securities, if shares of the company whose shares are offered by way of conversion or exchange are already listed on the same stock exchange; or
(c) shares resulting from the exercise of the rights conferred by warrants, if shares of the company whose shares are offered to holders of the warrants are already listed on the same stock exchange; or
(d) shares issued in substitution for shares already listed on the same stock

exchange if the issuing of such new shares does not involve any increase in the company's issued share capital;

and, where appropriate, the information provided for in Chapter 2 of Schedule A is published in accordance with Article 20 (1) and 21 (1).

3. where the securities for which admission to official listing is applied for are:

(a) shares of which either the number or the estimated market value or the nominal value or, in the absence of a nominal value, the accounting par value, amounts to less than 10% of the number or of the corresponding value of shares of the same class already listed on the same stock exchange; or

(b) debt securities issued by companies and other legal persons which are nationals of a Member State and which:

— in carrying on their business, benefit from State monopolies, and
— are set up or governed by a special law or pursuant to such a law or whose borrowings are unconditionally and irrevocably guaranteed by a Member State or one of a Member State's federated States; or

(c) debt securities issued by legal persons, other than companies, which are nationals of a Member State, and

— were set up by special law, and
— whose activities are governed by that law and consist solely in:

(i) raising funds under state control through the issue of debt securities, and
(ii) financing production by means of the resources which they have raised and resources provided by a Member State, and

— the debt securities of which are, for the purposes of admission to official listing, considered by national law as debt securities issued or guaranteed by the State; or

(d) shares allotted to employees, if shares of the same class have already been admitted to official listing on the same stock exchange; shares which differ from each other solely as to the date of first entitlement to dividends shall not be considered as being of different classes; or

(e) securities already admitted to official listing on another stock exchange in the same Member State; or

(f) shares issued in consideration for the partial or total renunciation by the management of a limited partnership with a share capital of its statutory rights over the profits, if shares of the same class have already been admitted to official listing on the same stock exchange; shares which differ from each other solely as to the date of first entitlement to dividends shall not be considered as being of different classes; or

(g) supplementary certificates representing shares issued in exchange for the original securities, where the issuing of such new certificates has not brought about any increase in the company's issued capital, and provided that certificates representing such shares are already listed on the same stock exchange, and where:

— in the case of (a), the issuer has complied with the stock exchange publicity requirements imposed by the national authorities and has produced annual accounts and annual and interim reports which these authorities have considered adequate.
— in the case of (e), listing particulars complying with this Directive have already been published, and
— in all the cases referred to in points (a) to (g), information concerning the number and type of securities to be admitted to official listing and the circumstances in which such securities have been issued has been published in accordance with Articles 20 (1) and 21 (1).

Article 7. The competent authorities may authorize omission from the listing particulars of certain information provided for by this Directive if they consider that:

(a) such information is of minor importance only and is not such as will influence assessment of the assets and liabilities, financial position, profits and losses and prospects of the issuer; or
(b) disclosure of such information would be contrary to the public interest or seriously detrimental to, the issuer, provided that, in the latter case, such omission would not be likely to mislead the public with regard to facts and circumstances, knowledge of which is essential for the assessment of the securities in question.

SECTION II. CONTENTS OF THE LISTING PARTICULARS IN CERTAIN SPECIFIC CASES

Article 8. 1. Where the application for admission to official listing relates to shares offered to shareholders of the issuer on a pre-emptive basis and shares of the latter are already listed on the same stock exchange, the competent authorities may provide that the listing particulars shall contain only the information provided for by Schedule A:

— in chapter 1,
— in chapter 2,
— in chapter 3, headings 3.1.0, 3.1.5, 3.2.0, 3.2.1, 3.2.6, 3.2.7, 3.2.8, and 3.2.9,
— in chapter 4, headings 4.2, 4.4, 4.5, 4.7.1, and 4.7.2,
— in chapter 5, headings 5.1.4, 5.1.5, and 5.5,

— in chapter 6, headings 6.1, 6.2.0, 6.2.1, 6.2.2, 6.2.3, and
— in chapter 7.

Where the shares referred to in the first subparagraph are represented by certificates, the listing particulars shall contain, at least, subject to Article 16 (2) and (3), in addition to the information mentioned in that subparagraph, that provided for in schedule C:

— in chapter 1, headings 1.1, 1.3, 1.4, 1.6 and 1.8, and
— in chapter 2.

2. Where the application for admission to official listing relates to convertible debt securities, exchangeable debt securities or debt securities with warrants which are offered on a pre-emptive basis to the shareholders of the issuer and where the latter's shares are already listed on the same stock exchange, the competent authorities may provide that the listing particulars shall contain only:

— information concerning the nature of the shares offered by way of conversion, exchange or subscription and the rights attaching thereto,
— the information provided for in Schedule A and mentioned above in the first subparagraph of paragraph 1, except for that provided for in Chapter 2 of that Schedule,
— the information provided for in Chapter 2 of Schedule B, and
— the conditions of and procedures for conversion, exchange and subscription and the situations in which they may be amended.

3. When published in accordance with Article 20, listing particulars as referred to in paragraphs 1 and 2 shall be accompanied by the annual accounts for the latest financial year.

4. Where the issuer prepares both own and consolidated annual accounts, both sets of accounts shall accompany the listing particulars. However, the competent authorities may allow the issuer to attach to the listing particulars either the own or the consolidated accounts alone, provided that the accounts not attached to the listing particulars furnish no material additional information.

Article 9.   1. Where the application for admission to official listing relates to debt securities which are neither convertible, exchangeable, nor accompanied by warrants and are issued by an undertaking which has securities already listed on the same stock exchange, the competent authorities may provide that the listing particulars shall contain only the information provided for by Schedule B:

— in chapter 1,
— in chapter 2,
— in chapter 3, headings 3.1.0, 3.1.5, 3.2.0 and 3.2.2,

— in chapter 4, heading 4.3,
— in chapter 5, headings 5.1.2, 5.1.3, 5.1.4 and 5.4,
— in chapter 6, and
— in chapter 7.

2. When published in accordance with Article 20, listing particulars as referred to in paragraph 1 shall be accompanied by the annual accounts for the latest financial year.

3. Where the issuer prepares both own and consolidated annual accounts, both sets of accounts must accompany the listing particulars. However, the competent authorities may allow the issuer to attach to the listing particulars either the own or the consolidated accounts alone, provided that the accounts not attached to the listing particulars furnish no material additional information.

Article 10. Where the application for admission to official listing relates to debt securities nearly all of which, because of their nature, are normally bought and traded in by a limited number of investors who are particularly knowledgeable in investment matters, the competent authorities may allow the omission from the listing particulars of certain information provided for by Schedule B or allow its inclusion in summary form, on condition that such information is not material from the point of view of the investors concerned.

Article 11. 1. For the admission of securities, issued by financial institutions, to official listing, the listing particulars must contain:

— at least the information specified in Chapters 1, 2, 3, 5 and 6 of Schedules A or B, according to whether the issue is of shares or debt securities, and
— information adapted, in accordance with the rules laid down for that purpose by national law or by the competent authorities, to the particular nature of the issuer of the securities in question and at least equivalent to that specified in Chapters 4 and 7 of Schedules A or B.

2. Member States shall determine the financial institutions to be covered by this Article.

3. The arrangements laid down by this Article may be extended to:

— collective investment undertakings whose units are not excluded from the scope of this Directive by the first indent of Article 1 (2).
— finance companies engaging in no activity other than raising capital to make it available to their parent company or to undertakings affiliated to that company, and
— companies holding portfolios of securities, licences or patents and engaging in no activity other than the management of such portfolios.

Article 12. Where the application for admission to official listing concerns debt securities issued in a continuous or repeated manner by credit institutions which regularly publish their annual accounts and which, within the Community, are set up or governed by a special law, or pursuant to such a law, or are subject to public supervision designed to protect savings, the Member States may provide that the listing particulars shall containly only:

— the information provided for in heading 1.1 and Chapter 2 of Schedule B, and

— information concerning any events of importance for the assessment of the securities in question which have occurred since the end of the financial year in respect of which the last annual accounts were published. Such accounts must be made available to the public at the issuer's offices or at those of the financial organizations retained to act as the latter's paying agents.

Article 13. 1. For the admission to official listing of debt securities guaranteed by a legal person, listing particulars must include:

— with respect to the issuer, the information provided for in Schedule B, and

— with respect to the guarantor, the information provided for in heading 1.3 and Chapters 3 to 7 of that Schedule.

Where the issuer or guarantor is a financial institution, the part of the listing particulars relating to that financial institution shall be drawn up in accordance with Article 11, without prejudice to the first subparagraph of this paragraph.

2. When the issuer of the guaranteed debt securities is a finance company within the meaning of Article 11 (3), the listing particulars must include:

— with respect to the issuer, the information provided for in Chapters 1, 2 and 3 and in headings 5.1.0 to 5.1.5 and 6.1 of Schedule B, and

— with respect to the guarantor, that provided for in heading 1.3 and Chapters 3 to 7 of that Schedule.

3. Where there is more than one guarantor, the information specified shall be required of each one; however, the competent authorities may allow abridgement of this information with a view to achieving greater comprehensibility of the listing particulars.

4. The guarantee contract must, in the cases referred to in paragraphs 1, 2 and 3, be made available for inspection by the public at the offices of the issuer and at those of the financial organizations retained to act as the latter's paying agents. Copies of the contract shall be provided to any person concerned on request.

Article 14. 1. Where the application for admission to official listing relates to convertible debt securities, exchangeable debt securities or debt securities with warrants, the listing particulars must include:

— information concerning the nature of the shares offered by way of conversion, exchange or subscription, and the rights attaching thereto,
— the information provided for in heading 1.3 and Chapters 3 to 7 of Schedule A,
— the information provided for in Chapter 2 of Schedule B, and
— the conditions of and procedures for conversion, exchange or subscription and details of the situations in which they may be amended.

2. When the issuer of the convertible debt securities, the exchangeable debt securities or the debt securities with warrants is not the issuer of the shares, listing particulars must include:

— information concerning the nature of the shares offered by way of conversion, exchange or subscription and the rights attaching thereto, and
— in respect of the issuer of the securities, the information provided for in Schedule B,
— in respect of the issuer of the shares, that provided for in heading 1.3 and Chapters 3 to 7 of Schedule A, and
— the conditions of and procedures for conversion, exchange or subscription and details of the situations in which they may be amended.

However, where the issuer of the debt securities is a finance company within the meaning of Article 11 (3), listing particulars need contain, in relation to that company, only the information provided for in Chapters 1, 2 and 3 and headings 5.1.0 to 5.1.5 and 6.1 of Schedule B.

Article 15. 1. Where the application for admission to official listing relates to securities issued in connection with a merger involving the acquisition of another company or the formation of a new company, the division of a company, the transfer of all or part of an undertaking's assets and liabilities, a takeover offer or as consideration for the transfer of assets other than cash, the documents describing the terms and conditions of such operations, as well as, where appropriate, any opening balance sheet, whether or not pro forma, if the issuer has not yet prepared its annual accounts, must, without prejudice to the requirement to publish the listing particulars, be made available for inspection by the public at the offices of the issuer of the securities and at those of the financial organizations retained to act as the latter's paying agents.

2. Where the transaction referred to in paragraph 1 took place more than two years previously, the competent authorities may dispense with the requirement imposed in that paragraph.

Article 16.   1. When the application for admission to official listing relates to certificates representing shares, the listing particulars must contain the information, as regards certificates, provided for in Schedule C and the information, as regards the shares represented, provided for in Schedule A.

2. However, the competent authorities may relieve the issuer of the certificates of the requirement to publish details of its own financial position, when the issuer is:

— a credit institution which is a national of a Member State and is set up or governed by a special law or pursuant to such law or is subject to public supervision designed to protect savings, or

— a subsidiary 95% or more of which is owned by a credit institution within the meaning of the preceding indent, the commitments of which towards the holders of certificates are unconditionally guaranteed by that credit institution and which is subject, *de jure* or *de facto*, to the same supervision, or

— an 'Administratiekantoor' in the Netherlands governed, for the safe custody of the original securities, by special regulations laid down by the competent authorities.

3. In the case of certificates issued by a securities transfer organization or by an auxiliary institution set up by such organization, the competent authorities may dispense with the publication of the information provided for in Chapter 1 of Schedule C.

Article 17.   1. Where debt securities for which admission to official listing is applied for benefit, as regards both repayment of the loan and the payment of interest, from the unconditional and irrevocable guarantee of a State or of one of a State's federated States, national legislation or the competent authorities may authorize the abridgement of the information provided for in Chapters 3 and 5 of Schedule B.

2. The possibility of abridgement provided for in paragraph 1 may also be applied to companies set up or governed by a special law or pursuant to such law which have the power to levy charges on their consumers.

SECTION III. ARRANGEMENTS FOR THE SCRUTINY AND
PUBLICATION OF LISTING PARTICULARS

Article 18.   1. Member States shall appoint one or more competent authorities and shall notify the Commission of the appointments of such authorities, giving details of any division of powers among them. Member States shall also ensure that this Directive is applied.

2. No listing particulars may be published until they have been approved by the competent authorities.

3. The competent authorities shall approve the publication of listing particulars only if they are of the opinion that they satisfy all the requirements set out in this Directive.

Member States shall ensure that the competent authorities have the powers necessary for them to carry out their task.

4. This Directive shall not affect the competent authorities' liability, which shall continue to be governed solely by the national law.

Article 19. The competent authorities shall decide whether to accept the audit report of the official auditor provided for in heading 1.3 of Schedules A and B or, if necessary, to require an additional report.

The requirement for the additional report must be the outcome of an examination of each case on its merits. At the request of the official auditor and/or of the issuer, the competent authorities must disclose to them the reasons justifying this requirement.

Article 20. 1. Listing particulars must be published either:

— by insertion in one or more newspapers circulated throughout the Member State in which the admission to official listing of securities is sought, or widely circulated therein, or

— in the form of a brochure to be made available, free of charge, to the public at the offices of the stock exchange or stock exchanges on which the securities are being admitted to official listing, at the registered office of the issuer and at the offices of the financial organizations retained to act as the latter's paying agents in the Member State in which the admission of securities to official listing is sought.

2. In addition, either the complete listing particulars or a notice stating where the listing particulars have been published and where they may be obtained by the public must be inserted in a publication designated by the Member State in which the admission of securities to official listing is sought.

Article 21. 1. Listing particulars must be published within a reasonable period, to be laid down in national legislation or by the competent authorities before the date on which official listing becomes effective.

Moreover, where the admission of securities to official listing is preceded by trading of the pre-emptive subscription rights giving rise to dealings recorded in the official list, the listing particulars must be published within a reasonable period, to be laid down by the competent authorities before such trading starts.

2. In exceptional, properly justified cases, the competent authorities may allow the postponement of the publication of the listing particulars until after:

— the date on which official listing becomes effective, in the case of securities of a class already listed on the same stock exchange issued in consideration of transfers of assets other than cash,

— the date of the opening of trading in pre-emptive subscription rights.

3. If the admission of debt securities to official listing coincides with their public issue and if some of the terms of the issue are not finalized until the last moment, the competent authorities may merely require the publication, within a reasonable period, of listing particulars omitting information as to these terms but indicating how it will be given. Such information must be published before the date on which official listing starts, except where debt securities are issued on a continuous basis at varying prices.

Article 22.   Where listing particulars are, or will be, published in accordance with Articles 1 and 3 for the admission of securities to official listing, the notices, bills, posters and documents announcing this operation and indicating the essential characteristics of these securities, and all other documents relating to their admission and intended for publication by the issuer or on his behalf, must first be communicated to the competent authorities. The latter shall decide whether they should be submitted to scrutiny before publication.

The abovementioned documents must state that listing particulars exist and indicate where they are being, or will be, published in accordance with Article 20.

Article 23.   Every significant new factor capable of affecting assessment of the securities which arises between the time when the listing particulars are adopted and the time when stock exchange dealings begin shall be covered by a supplement to the listing particulars, scrutinized in the same way as the latter and published in accordance with procedures to be laid down by the competent authorities.

SECTION IV. COOPERATION BETWEEN THE MEMBER STATES

Article 24.   1. Where applications for admission of the same securities to official listing on stock exchanges situated or operating within several Member States are made simultaneously, or within short intervals of one another, the competent authorities shall exchange information and use their best endeavours to achieve maximum coordination of their requirements concerning listing particulars, to avoid a multiplicity of formalities and to agree to a single text requiring at the most translation, where appropriate, and the issue of supplements as necessary to meet the individual requirements of each Member State concerned.

2. Where an application for admission to official listing is made for securities which have been listed in another Member State less than six months previously, the competent authorities to whom application is made shall contact the competent authorities which have already admitted the securities to official listing and shall, as far as possible, exempt the issuer of those securities from the preparation of new listing particulars, subject to any need for updating, translation or the issue of supplements in accordance with the individual requirements of the Member State concerned.

Article 25. 1. Member States shall provide that all persons employed or formerly employed by the competent authorities shall be bound by professional secrecy. This means that any confidential information received in the course of their duties may not be divulged to any person or authority except by virtue of provisions laid down by law.

2. Paragraph 1 shall not, however, preclude the competent authorities of the various Member States from exchanging information as provided for in this Directive. Information thus exchanged shall be covered by the obligation of professional secrecy to which the persons employed or formerly employed by the competent authorities receiving the information are subject.

SECTION V. CONTACT COMMITTEE

Article 26. 1. The Contact Committee set up by Article 20 of Council Directive 79/279/EEC of 5 March 1979 coordinating the conditions for the admission of securities to official stock exchange listing[1] shall also have as its function:

(a) without prejudice to Articles 169 and 170 of the EEC Treaty to facilitate the harmonized implementation of this Directive through regular consultations on any practical problems arising from its application on which exchanges of views are deemed useful;
(b) to facilitate consultation between the Member States on the supplements and improvements to the listing particulars which the competent authorities are entitled to require or recommend at national level;
(c) to advise the Commission, if necessary, on any additions or amendments to be made to this Directive.

2. It shall not be the function of the Contact Committee to appraise the merits of decisions taken by the competent authorities in individual cases.

---

[1] OJ No L 66, 16. 3. 1979, p. 21.

SECTION VI. FINAL PROVISIONS

Article 27. 1. Member States shall take the measures necessary to comply with this Directive within 30 months of its notification. They shall forthwith inform the Commission thereof.

2. As from the notification of this Directive, the Member States shall communicate to the Commission the texts of the main laws, regulations and administrative provisions which they adopt in the field covered by this Directive.

Article 28. This Directive is addressed to the Member States.

Done at Brussels, 17 March 1980.

For the Council, The President, J. Santer

ANNEX

SCHEDULE A

Layout for Listing Particulars for the Admission of Shares to Official Stock Exchange Listing

Chapter 1. Information concerning those responsible for listing particulars and the auditing of accounts

1.1. Name and function of natural persons and name and registered office of legal persons responsible for the listing particulars or, as the case may be, for certain parts of them, with, in the latter case, an indication of those parts.

1.2. Declaration by those responsible referred to in heading 1.1 that, to the best of their knowledge, the information given in that part of the listing particulars for which they are responsible is in accordance with the facts and contains no omissions likely to affect the import of the listing particulars.

1.3. Names, addresses and qualifications of the official auditors who have audited the company's annual accounts for the preceding three financial years in accordance with national law.

Statement that the annual accounts have been audited. If audit reports on the annual accounts have been refused by the official auditors or if they contain qualifications, such refusal or such qualifications shall be reproduced in full and the reasons given.

Indication of other information in the listing particulars which has been audited by the auditors.

Chapter 2. Information concerning admission to official listing and the shares for the admission of which application is being made

2.1. Indication that the admission applied for is admission to official listing of shares already marketed or admission to listing with a view to stock exchange marketing.

2.2. Information concerning the shares in respect of which application for official listing is being made:

2.2.0. Indication of the resolutions, authorizations and approvals by virtue of which the shares have been or will be created and/or issued.

Nature of the issue and amount thereof.

Number of shares which have been or will be created and/or issued, if predetermined.

2.2.1. In the case of shares issued in connection with a merger, the division of a company, the transfer of all or part of an undertaking's assets and liabilities, a takeover offer, or as consideration for the transfer of assets other than cash, indication of where the documents describing the terms and conditions of such operations are available for inspection by the public.

2.2.2. A concise description of the rights attaching to the shares, and in particular the extent of the voting rights, entitlement to share in the profits and to share in any surplus in the event of liquidation and any privileges.

Time limit after which dividend entitlement lapses and indication of the party in whose favour this entitlement operates.

2.2.3. Tax on the income from the shares withheld at source in the country of origin and/or the country of listing.

Indication as to whether the issuer assumes responsibility for the withholding of tax at source.

2.2.4. Arrangements for transfer of the shares and any restrictions on their free negotiability (e.g. clause establishing approval requirement).

2.2.5. Date on which entitlement to dividends arises.

2.2.6. The stock exchanges where admission to official listing is or will be sought.

2.2.7. The financial organizations which, at the time of admission of shares to official listing, are the paying agents of the issuer in the Member States where admission has taken place.

2.3 In so far as it is relevant, information concerning issue and placing, public or private, of the shares in respect of which the application for admission to official listing is made where such issue or placing has been effected within the 12 months preceding admission:

2.3.0. Indication of the exercise of the right of pre-emption of shareholders or of the restriction or withdrawal of such right.

Indication, where applicable, of the reasons for restriction or withdrawal of such right; in such cases, justification of the issue price, where an issue is for cash; indication of the beneficiaries if the restriction or withdrawal of the right of pre-emption is intended to benefit specific persons.

2.3.1. The total amount of the public or private issue or placing and the number of shares offered, where applicable by category.

2.3.2. If the public or private issue or placing were or are being made simultaneously on the markets of two or more States and if a tranche has been or is being reserved for certain of these, indication of any such tranche.

2.3.3. The issue price or the offer or placing price, stating the nominal value or, in its absence, the accounting par value or the amount to be capitalized; the issue premium and the amount of any expenses specifically charged to the subscriber or purchaser.

The methods of payment of the price, particularly as regards the paying-up of shares which are not fully paid.

2.3.4. The procedure for the exercise of any right of pre-emption; the negotiability of subscription rights; the treatment of subscription rights not exercised.

2.3.5. Period of the opening of the issue or offer of shares, and names of the financial organizations responsible for receiving the public's subscriptions.

2.3.6. Methods of and time limits for delivery of the shares, possible creation or provisional certificates.

2.3.7. Names, addresses and descriptions of the natural or legal persons underwriting or guaranteeing the issue for the issuer. Where not all of the issue is underwritten or guaranteed, a statement of the portion not covered.

2.3.8. Indication or estimate of the overall amount and/or of the amount per share of the charges relating to the issue operation, stating the total remuneration of the financial intermediaries, including the underwriting commission or margin, guarantee commission, placing commission or selling agent's commission.

2.3.9. Net proceeds accruing to the issuer from the issue and intended application of such proceeds, e.g., to finance the investment programme or to strengthen the issuer's financial position.

2.4 Information concerning admission of shares to official listing:

2.4.0. Description of the shares for which admission to official listing is applied, and in particular the number of shares and nominal value per share, or, in the absence of nominal value, the accounting par value or the total nominal value, the exact designation or class, and coupons attached.

2.4.1. If the shares are to be marketed on the stock exchange and no such shares have previously been sold to the public, a statement of the number of shares made available to the market and of their nominal value, or, in the absence of nominal value, of their accounting par value, or a statement of the total nominal value and, where applicable, a statement of the minimum offer price.

2.4.2. If known, the dates on which the new shares will be listed and dealt in.

2.4.3. If shares of the same class are already listed on one or more stock exchanges, indication of these stock exchanges.

2.4.4. If shares of the same class have not yet been admitted to official listing but are dealt in on one or more other markets which are subject to regulation, are in regular operation and are recognized and open, indication of such markets.

2.4.5. Indication of any of the following which have occurred during the last financial year and the current financial year:

— public takeover offers by third parties in respect of the issuer's shares,
— public takeover offers by the issuer in respect of other companies' shares.

The price or exchange terms attaching to such offers and the outcome thereof are to be stated.

2.5. If, simultaneously or almost simultaneously with the creation of shares for which admission to official listing is being sought, shares of the same class are subscribed for or placed privately or if shares of other classes are created for public or private placing, details are to be given of the nature of such operations and of the number and characteristics of the shares to which they relate.

Chapter 3. General information about the issuer and its capital

3.1. General information about the issuer:

3.1.0. Name, registered office and principal administrative establishment if different from the registered office.

3.1.1. Date of incorporation and the length of life of the issuer, except where indefinite.

3.1.2. Legislation under which the issuer operates and legal form which it has adopted under that legislation.

3.1.3. Indication of the issuer's objects and reference to the clause of the memorandum of association in which they are described.

3.1.4. Indication of the register and of the entry number therein.

3.1.5. Indication of where the documents concerning the issuer which are referred to in the listing particulars may be inspected.

3.2. General information about the capital:

3.2.0. The amount of the issued capital, the number and classes of the shares of which it is composed with details of their principal characteristics; the part of the issued capital still to be paid up, with an indication of the number, or total nominal value, and the type of the shares not yet fully paid up, broken down where applicable according to the extent to which they have been paid up.

3.2.1. Where there is authorized but unissued capital or an undertaking to increase the capital, *inter alia* in connection with convertible loans issued or subscription options granted, indication of:

— the amount of such authorized capital or capital increase and, where appropriate, the duration of the authorization,

— the categories of persons having preferential subscription rights for such additional portions of capital,

— the terms and arrangements for the share issue corresponding to such portions.

3.2.2. If there are shares not representing capital, the number and main characteristics of such shares are to be stated.

3.2.3. The amount of any convertible debt securities, exchangeable debt securities or debt securities with warrants, with an indication of the conditions governing and the procedures for conversion, exchange or subscription.

3.2.4. Conditions imposed by the memorandum and articles of association governing changes in the capital and in the respective rights of the various classes of shares, where such conditions are more stringent than is required by law.

3.2.5. Summary description of the operations during the three preceding years which have changed the amount of the issued capital and/or the number and classes of shares of which it is composed.

3.2.6. As far as they are known to the issuer, indication of the natural or legal persons who, directly or indirectly, severally or jointly, exercise or could exercise control over the issuer, and particulars of the proportion of the capital held giving a right to vote.

Joint control shall mean control exercised by more than one company or by more than one person having concluded an agreement which may lead to their adopting a common policy in respect of the issuer.

3.2.7. In so far as they are known to the issuer, indication of the shareholders who, directly or indirectly, hold a proportion of the issuer's capital which the Member States may not fix at more than 20%.

3.2.8. If the issuer belongs to a group of undertakings, a brief description of the group and of the issuer's position within it.

3.2.9. Number, book value and nominal value or, in the absence of a nominal value, the accounting par value of any of its own shares which the issuer or another company in which it has a direct or indirect holding of more than 50% has acquired and is holding, if such securities do not appear as a separate item on the balance sheet.

Chapter 4. Information concerning the issuer's activities

4.1. The issuer's principal activities:

4.1.0. Description of the issuer's principal activities, stating the main categories of products sold and/or services performed.

Indication of any significant new products and/or activities.

4.1.1. Breakdown of net turnover during the past three financial years by categories of activity and into geographical markets in so far as, taking account of the manner in which the sale of products and the provision of services falling within the issuer's ordinary activities are organized, these categories and markets differ substantially from one another.

4.1.2. Location and size of the issuer's principal establishments and summary information about real estate owned. Any establishment which accounts for more than 10% of turnover or production shall be considered a principal establishment.

4.1.3. For mining, extraction of hydrocarbons, quarrying and similar activities in so far as significant, description of deposits, estimate of economically exploitable reserves and expected period of working.

Indication of the periods and main terms of concessions and the economic conditions for working them.

Indication of the progress of actual working.

4.1.4. Where the information given pursuant to headings 4.1.0 to 4.1.3 has been influenced by exceptional factors, that fact should be mentioned.

4.2. Summary information regarding the extent to which the issuer is dependent, if at all, on patents or licences, industrial, commercial or financial contracts or new manufacturing processes, where such factors are of fundamental importance to the issuer's business or profitability.

4.3. Information concerning policy on the research and development of new products and processes over the past three financial years, where significant.

4.4. Information on any legal or arbitration proceedings which may have or have had a significant effect on the issuer's financial position in the recent past.

4.5. Information on any interruptions in the issuer's business which may have or have had a significant effect on the issuer's financial position in the recent past.

4.6. Average numbers employed and changes therein over the past three financial years, if such changes are material, with, if possible, a breakdown of persons employed by main categories of activity.

4.7. Investment policy:

4.7.0. Description, with figures, of the main investments made, including interests such as shares, debt securities, etc., in other undertakings over the past three financial years and the months already elapsed of the current financial year.

4.7.1. Information concerning the principal investments being made with the exception of interests being acquired in other undertakings.

Distribution of these investments geographically (home and abroad).

Method of financing (internal or external).

4.7.2. Information concerning the issuer's principal future investments, with the exception of interests to be acquired in other undertakings on which its management bodies have already made firm commitments.

Chapter 5. Information concerning the issuer's assets and liabilities, financial position and profits and losses

5.1. Accounts of the issuer:

5.1.0. The last three balance sheets and profit and loss accounts drawn up by the company set out as a comparative table. The notes on the annual accounts for the last financial year.

The draft listing particulars must be filed with the competent authorities not more than 18 months after the end of the financial year to which the last annual accounts published relate. The competent authorities may extend that period in exceptional cases.

5.1.1. If the issuer prepares consolidated annual accounts only, it shall include those accounts in the listing particulars in accordance with heading 5.1.0.

If the issuer prepares both own and consolidated annual accounts, it shall include both sets of accounts in the listing particulars in accordance with heading 5.1.0. However, the competent authorities may allow the issuer to include either the own or the consolidated annual accounts, on condition that the accounts which are not included do not provide any significant additional information.

5.1.2. The profit or loss per share of the issuing company, for the financial year, arising out of the company's ordinary activities, after tax, for the last three financial years, where the company includes its own annual accounts in the listing particulars.

Where the issuer includes only consolidated annual accounts in the listing particulars, it shall indicate the consolidated profit or loss per share, for the financial year, for the last three financial years. This information shall appear in addition to that provided in accordance with the preceding subparagraph where the issuer also includes its own annual accounts in the listing particulars.

If in the course of the abovementioned period of three financial years the number of shares in the issuing company has changed as a result, for example, of an increase or decrease in capital or the rearrangement of splitting of shares, the profit or loss per share referred to in the first and second paragraph above shall be adjusted to make them comparable; in that event the adjustment formulae used shall be disclosed.

5.1.3. The amount of the dividend per share of the last three financial years, adjusted, if necessary, to make it comparable in accordance with the third subparagraph of heading 5.1.2.

5.1.4. Where more than nine months have elapsed since the end of the financial year to which the last published own annual and/or consolidated annual accounts relate, an interim financial statement covering at least the first six months shall be included in the listing particulars or appended to them. If such an interim financial statement is unaudited, that fact must be stated.

Where the issuer prepares consolidated annual accounts, the competent authorities shall decide whether the interim financial statement to be submitted must be consolidated or not.

Any significant change which has occurred since the end of the last financial year or the preparation of the interim financial statement must be described in a note inserted in the listing particulars or appended thereto.

5.1.5. If the own or consolidated annual accounts do not comply with the Council Directives on undertakings' annual discounts and do not give a true and fair view of the issuer's assets and liabilities, financial position and profits and losses, more detailed and/or additional information must be given.

5.1.6. A table showing the sources and application of funds over the past three financial years.

5.2. Individual details listed below relating to the undertakings in which the issuer holds a proportion of the capital likely to have a significant effect on the assessment of its own assets and liabilities, financial position or profits and losses.

The items of information listed below must be given in any event for every undertaking in which the issuer has a direct or indirect participating interest, if the book value of that participating interest represents at least 10% of the capital and reserves or accounts for at least 10% of the net profit or loss of the issuer or, in the case of a group, if the book value of that participating interest represents at least 10% of the consolidated net assets or accounts for at least 10% of the consolidated net profit or loss of the group.

The items of information listed below need not be given provided that the issuer proves that its holding is of a purely provisional nature.

Similarly, the information required under points (e) and (f) may be omitted where the undertaking in which a participating interest is held does not publish its annual accounts.

Pending subsequent coordination of provisions relating to consolidated annual accounts, the Member States may authorize the competent authorities to permit the omission of the information prescribed in points (d) to (j) if the annual accounts of the undertakings in which the participating interests are held are consolidated into the group annual accounts or if the value attributable to the interest under the equity method is disclosed in the annual accounts, provided that, in the opinion of the competent authorities, the omission of that information is not likely to mislead the public with regard to the facts and circumstances, knowledge of which is essential for the assessment of the security in question.

The information provided for under points (g) and (j) may be omitted if, in the opinion of the competent authorities, such omission does not mislead investors.

(a) Name and registered office of the undertaking.
(b) Field of activity.
(c) Proportion of capital held.
(d) Issued capital.
(e) Reserves.
(f) Profit or loss arising out of ordinary activities, after tax, for the last financial year.
(g) Value at which the issuer obliged to publish listing particulars shows shares held in its accounts.
(h) Amount still to be paid up on shares held.
(i) Amount of dividends received in the course of the last financial year in respect of shares held.
(j) Amount of the debts owed to and by the issuer with regard to the undertaking.

5.3. Individual details relating to the undertakings not referred to in heading 5.2 in which the issuer holds at least 10% of the capital. These details may be omitted when they are of negligible importance for the purpose of the objective set in Article 4 of this Directive:

(a) name and registered office of the undertaking;
(b) proportion of capital held.

5.4. When the listing particulars comprise consolidated annual accounts, disclosure:

(a) of the consolidation principles applied. These shall be described explicitly where the Member State has no laws governing the consolidation of annual accounts or where such principles are not in conformity with such laws or with a generally accepted method in use in the Member State in which the stock exchange on which admission to official listing is requested is situated or operates;

(b) of the names and registered offices of the undertakings included in the consolidation, where that information is important for the purpose of assessing the assets and liabilities, the financial position and the profits and losses of the issuer. It is sufficient to distinguish them by a sign in the list of undertakings of which details are required in heading 5.2;

(c) for each of the undertakings referred to in (b):

— the total proportion of third-party interests, if annual accounts are consolidated globally;

— the proportion of the consolidation calculated on the basis of interests, if consolidation has been effected on a *pro rata* basis.

5.5. Where the issuer is a dominant undertaking forming a group with one or more dependent undertakings, the details provided for in Chapters 4 and 7 shall be given for that issuer and group.

The competent authorities may permit the provision of that information for the issuer alone or for the group alone, provided that the details which are not provided are not material.

5.6 If certain information provided for under Schedule A is given in the annual accounts provided in accordance with this Chapter, it need not be repeated.

Chapter 6. Information concerning administration, management and supervision

6.1. Names, addresses and functions in the issuing company of the following persons and an indication of the principal activities performed by them outside that company where these are significant with respect to that company:

(a) members of the administrative, management or supervisory bodies;

(b) partners with unlimited liability, in the case of a limited partnership with a share capital;

(c) founders, if the company has been established for fewer than five years.

6.2. Interests of the members of the administrative, management and supervisory bodies in the issuing company:

6.2.0. Remuneration paid and benefits in kind granted, during the last completed financial year under any heading whatsoever, and charged to overheads or the profit appropriation account, to members of the administrative, management and supervisory bodies, these being total amounts for each category of body.

The total remuneration paid and benefits in kind granted to all members of the administrative, management and supervisory bodies of the issuer by all the dependent undertakings with which it forms a group must be indicated.

6.2.1. Total number of shares in the issuing company held by the members of its administrative, management and supervisory bodies and options granted to them on the company's shares.

6.2.2. Information about the nature and extent of the interests of members of the administrative, management and supervisory bodies in transactions effected by the issuer which are unusual in their nature or conditions (such as purchases outside normal activity, acquisition or disposal of fixed asset items) during the preceding financial year and the current financial year. Where such unusual transactions were concluded in the course of previous financial years and have not been definitively concluded, information on those transactions must also be given.

6.2.3. Total of all the outstanding loans granted by the issuer to the persons referred to in heading 6.1 (a) and also of any guarantees provided by the issuer for their benefit.

6.3. Schemes for involving the staff in the capital of the issuer.

Chapter 7. Information concerning the recent development and prospects of the issuer

7.1. Except in the event of a derogation granted by the competent authorities, general information on the trend of the issuer's business since the end of the financial year to which the last published annual accounts relate, in particular:

— the most significant recent trends in production, sales and stocks and the state of the order book, and

— recent trends in costs and selling prices.

7.2. Except in the event of a derogation granted by the competent authorities, information on the issuer's prospects for at least the current financial year.

SCHEDULE B

Layout for Listing Particulars for the Admission of Debt Securities to Official Stock Exchange Listing

Chapter 1. Information concerning those responsible for listing particulars and the auditing of accounts

1.1. Names and addresses of the natural or legal persons responsible for the listing particulars or, as the case may be, for certain parts of them with, in the latter case, an indication of those parts.

1.2. Declaration by those responsible, as referred to in heading 1.1, that, to the best of their knowledge, the information given in that part of the listing particulars for which they are responsible is in accordance with the facts and contains no omissions likely to affect the import of the listing particulars.

1.3 Names, addresses and qualifications of the official auditors who have audited the annual accounts for the preceding three financial years in accordance with national law.

Statement that the annual accounts have been audited. If audit reports on the annual accounts have been refused by the official auditors or if they contain qualifications, such refusal or such qualifications must be reproduced in full and the reasons given.

Indication of other information in the listing particulars which has been audited by the auditors.

Chapter 2. Information concerning loans and the admission of debt securities to official listing

2.1 Conditions of the loan:

2.1.0. The nominal amount of the loan; if this amount is not fixed, a statement to this effect be made.

The nature, number and numbering of the debt securities and the denominations.

2.1.1. Except in the case of continuous issues, the issue and redemption prices and the nominal interest rate; if several interest rates are provided for, an indication of the conditions for changes in the rate.

2.1.2. Procedures for the allocation of any other advantages; the method of calculating such advantages.

2.1.3. Tax on the income from the debt securities withheld at source in the country of origin and/or the country of listing.

Indication as to whether the issuer assumes responsibility for the withholding of tax at source.

2.1.4. Arrangements for the amortization of the loan, including the repayment procedures.

2.1.5. The financial organizations which, at the time of admission to official listing are the paying agents of the issuer in the Member State of admission.

2.1.6. Currency of the loan; if the loan is denominated in units of account, the contractual status of these; currency option.

2.1.7. Time limits:
(a) period of the loan and any interim due dates;
(b) the date from which interest becomes payable and the due dates for interest;
(c) the time limit on the validity of claims to interest and repayment of principal;
(d) procedures and time limits for delivery of the debt securities, possible creation of provisional certificates.

2.1.8. Except in the case of continuous issues, an indication of yield. The method whereby that yield is calculated shall be described in summary form.

2.2. Legal information:

2.2.0. Indication of the resolutions, authorizations and approvals by virtue of which the debt securities have been or will be created and/or issued.

Type of operation and amount thereof.

Number of debt securities which have been or will be created and/or issued, if predetermined.

2.2.1. Nature and scope of the guarantees, sureties and commitments intended to ensure that the loan will be duly serviced as regards both the repayment of the debt securities and the payment of interest.

Indication of the places where the public may have access to the texts of the contracts relating to these guarantees, sureties and commitments.

2.2.2. Organization of trustees or of any other representation for the body of debt security holders.

Name and function and description and head office of the representative of the debt security holders, the main conditions of such representation and in particular the conditions under which the representative may be replaced.

Indication of where the public may have access to the contracts relating to these forms of representation.

2.2.3. Mention of clauses subordinating the loan to other debts of the issuer already contracted or to be contracted.

2.2.4. Indication of the legislation under which the debt securities have been created and of the courts competent in the event of litigation.

2.2.5. Indication as to whether the debt securities are registered or bearer.

2.2.6. Any restrictions on the free transferability of the debt securities.

2.3. Information concerning the admission of the debt securities to official listing.

2.3.0. The stock exchanges where admission to official listing is, or will be, sought.

2.3.1. Names, addresses and description of the natural or legal persons underwriting or guaranteeing the issue for the issuer. Where not all of the issue is underwritten or guaranteed, a statement of the portion not covered.

2.3.2. If the public or private issue or placing were or are being made simultaneously on the markets of two or more States and if a tranche has been or is being reserved for certain of these, indication of any such tranche.

2.3.3. If debt securities of the same class are already listed on one or more stock exchanges, indication of these stock exchanges.

2.3.4. If debt securities of the same class have not yet been admitted to official listing but are dealt in one or more other markets which are subject to regulation, are in regular operation and are recognized and open, indication of such markets.

2.4. Information concerning the issue of it is concomitant with official admission or if it took place within the three months preceding such admission.

2.4.0. The procedure for the exercise of any right of pre-emption; the negotiability of subscription rights; the treatment of subscription rights not exercised.

2.4.1. Method of payment of the issue or offer price.

2.4.2. Except in the case of continuous debt security issues, period of the opening of the issue or offer and any possibilities of early closure.

2.4.3. Indication of the financial organizations responsible for receiving the public's subscriptions.

2.4.4. Reference, where necessary, to the fact that the subscriptions may be reduced.

2.4.5. Except in the case of continuous debt security issues, indication of the net proceeds of the loan.

2.4.6. Purpose of the issue and intended application of its proceeds.

Chapter 3. General information about the issuer and its capital

3.1. General information about the issuer.

3.1.0. Name, registered office and principal administrative establishment if different from the registered office.

3.1.1. Date of incorporation and the length of life of the issuer, expect where indefinite.

3.1.2. Legislation under which the issuer operates and legal form which it has adopted under that legislation.

3.1.3. Indication of the issuer's objects and reference to the clause in the memorandum of association in which they are described.

3.1.4. Indication of the register and of the entry number therein.

3.1.5. Indication of where the documents concerning the issuer which are referred to in the listing particulars may be inspected.

3.2. General information about capital:

3.2.0. The amount of the issued capital and the number and classes of the securities of which it is composed with details of their principal characteristics.

The part of the issued capital still to be paid up, with an indication of the number, or total nominal value, and the type of securities not yet fully paid up, broken down where applicable according to the extent to which they have been paid up.

3.2.1. The amount of any convertible debt securities, exchangeable debt securities or debt securities with warrants, with an indication of the conditions governing and the procedures for conversion, exchange or subscription.

3.2.2. If the issuer belongs to a group of undertakings, a brief description of the group and of the issuer's position within it.

3.2.3. Number, book value and nominal value or, in the absence of a nominal value, the accounting par value of any of its own shares which the issuer or another company in which the issuer has a direct or indirect holding of more than 50% has acquired and is holding, if such securities do not appear as a separate item on the balance sheet, in so far as they represent a significant part of the issued capital.

Chapter 4. Information concerning the issuer's activities

4.1. The issuer's principal activities.

4.1.0. Description of the issuer's principal activities, stating the main categories of products sold and/or services performed.

Indication of any significant new products and/or activities.

4.1.1. Net turnover during the past two financial years.

4.1.2. Location and size of the issuer's principal establishments and summary information about real estate owned. Any establishment which accounts for more than 10% of turnover or production shall be considered a principal establishment.

4.1.3. For mining, extraction of hydrocarbons, quarrying and similar activities in so far as significant, description of deposits, estimate of economically exploitable reserves and expected period of working.

Indication of the periods and main terms of concessions and the economic conditions for working them.

Indication of the progress of actual working.

4.1.4. Where the information given pursuant to headings 4.1.0 to 4.1.3 has been influenced by exceptional factors, that fact should be mentioned.

4.2. Summary information regarding the extent to which the issuer is dependent, if at all, on patents or licences, industrial, commercial or financial contracts or new manufacturing processes, where such factors are of fundamental importance to the issuer's business or profitability.

4.3. Information on any legal or arbitration proceedings which may have or have had a significant effect on the issuer's financial position in the recent past.

4.4. Investment policy:

4.4.0. Description, with figures, of the main investments made, including interests such as shares, debt securities, etc., in other undertakings, over the past three financial years and the months already elapsed of the current financial year.

4.4.1. Information concerning the principal investments being made with the exception of interests being acquired in other undertakings.

Distribution of these investments geographically (home and abroad).

Method of financing (internal or external).

4.4.2. Information concerning the issuer's principal future investments, with the exception of interests to be acquired in other undertakings, on which its management bodies have already made firm commitments.

Chapter 5. Information concerning the issuer's assets and liabilities, financial position and profits and losses

5.1. Accounts of the issuer:

5.1.0. The last two balance sheets and profit and loss accounts drawn up by the issuer set out as a comparative table. The notes on the annual accounts for the last financial year.

The draft listing particulars must be filed with the competent authorities not more than 18 months after the end of the financial year to which the last annual accounts published relate. The competent authorities may extend that period in exceptional cases.

5.1.1. If the issuer prepares consolidated annual accounts only, it shall include those accounts in the listing particulars in accordance with heading 5.1.0.

If the issuer prepares both own and consolidated annual accounts, it shall include both sets of accounts in the listing particulars in accordance with heading 5.1.0. However, the competent authorities may allow the issuer to include either the own or the consolidated annual accounts, on condition that the accounts which are not included do not provide any significant additional information.

5.1.2. Where more than nine months have elapsed since the end of the financial year to which the last published own annual and/or consolidated annual accounts relate, an interim financial statement covering at least the first six months shall be included in the listing particulars or appended to them. If the interim financial statement is unaudited, that fact must be stated.

Where the issuer prepares consolidated annual accounts, the competent authorities shall decide whether the interim financial statement to be submitted must be consolidated or not.

Any significant change which has occurred since the end of the last financial year or the preparation of the aforementioned interim financial statement must be described in a note inserted in or appended to the listing particulars.

5.1.3. If the own annual or consolidated annual accounts do not comply with the Council Directives on undertakings' annual accounts and do not give a true and fair view of the issuer's assets and liabilities, financial position and profits and losses, more detailed and/or additional information must be given.

5.1.4. Indication as at the most recent date possible (which must be stated) of the following, if material:

— the total amount of any loan capital outstanding, distinguishing between loans guaranteed (by the provision of security or otherwise, by the issuer or by third parties) and loans not guaranteed,

— the total amount of all other borrowings and indebtedness in the nature of borrowing, distinguishing between guaranteed and unguaranteed borrowings and debts,

— the total amount of any contingent liabilities.

An appropriate negative statement shall be given, where relevant, in the absence of any such loan capital, borrowings and indebtedness and contingent liabilities.

If the issuer prepares consolidated annual accounts, the principles laid down in heading 5.1.1 shall apply.

As a general rule, no account should be taken of liabilities between undertakings within the same group, a statement to that effect being made if necessary.

5.1.5. A table showing the sources and application of funds over the past three financial years.

5.2. Individual details listed below relating to the undertakings in which the issuer holds a proportion of the capital likely to have a significant effect on the assessment of its own assets and liabilities, financial position or profits and losses.

The items of information listed below must be given in any event for every undertaking in which the issuer has a direct or indirect participating interest, if the book value of that participating interest represents at least 10% of the capital and reserves or accounts for at least 10% of the net profit or loss of the issuer, or in the case of a group, if the book value of that participating interest represents at least 10% of the consolidated net assets or accounts for at least 10% of the consolidated net profit or loss of the group.

The items of information listed below need not be given provided that the issuer proves that its holding is of a purely provisional nature.

Similarly, the information required under points (e) and (f) may be omitted where the undertaking in which a participating interest is held does not publish its annual accounts.

Pending coordination of provisions relating to consolidated annual accounts, the Member States may authorize the competent authorities to permit the omission of the information prescribed in points (d) to (h) if the annual acounts of the undertakings in which the participating interests are held are consolidated into the group annual acounts or if the value attributable to the interest under the equity method is disclosed in the annual accounts, provided that in the opinion of the competent author-ities, the omission of that information is not likely to mislead the public with regard to the facts and circumstances knowledge of which is essential for the assessment of the security in question.

(a) Name and registered office of the undertaking.
(b) Field of activity.
(c) Proportion of capital held.
(d) Issued capital.
(e) Reserves.

(f) Profit or loss arising out of ordinary activities, after tax, for the last financial year.

(g) Amount still to be paid up on shares held.

(h) Amount of dividends received in the course of the last financial year in respect of shares held.

5.3. When the listing particulars comprise consolidated annual accounts, disclosure:

(a) of the consolidation principles applied. These shall be described explicitly where the Member State has no laws governing the consolidation of annual accounts or where such principles are not in conformity with such laws or with a generally accepted method in use in the Member State in which the stock exchange on which admission to official listing is requested is situated or operates;

(b) of the names and registered offices of the undertakings included in the consolidation, where that information is important for the purpose of assessing the assets and liabilities, the financial position and the profits and losses of the issuer. It is sufficient to distinguish them by a sign in the list of companies for which details are required in heading 5.2;

(c) for each of the undertakings referred to in (b):

— the total proportion of third-party interests, if annual accounts are consolidated globally,

— the proportion of the consolidation calculated on the basis of interests, if consolidation has been effected on a *pro rata* basis.

5.4. Where the issuer is a dominant undertaking forming a group with one or more dependent undertakings, the details provided for in Chapters 4 and 7 shall be given for that issuer and group.

The competent authorities may permit the provision of that information for the issuer alone or for the group alone, provided that the details which are not provided are not material.

5.5. If certain information provided for under Schedule B is given in the annual accounts provided in accordance with this Chapter, it need not be repeated.

Chapter 6. Information concerning administration, management and supervision

6.1. Names, addresses and functions in the issuing undertaking of the following persons, and an indication of the principal activities performed by them outside that undertaking where these are significant with respect to that undertaking:

(a) members of the administrative, management or supervisory bodies;

(b) partners with unlimited liability, in the case of a limited partnership with a share capital.

Chapter 7. Information concerning the recent development and prospects of the issuer

7.1. Except in the event of a derogation granted by the competent authorities, general information on the trend of the issuer's business since the end of the financial year to which the last published annual accounts relate, in particular:

— the most significant recent trends in production, sales and stocks and the state of the order book, and
— recent trends in costs and selling prices.

7.2. Except in the event of a derogation granted by the competent authorities, information on the issuer's prospects for at least the current financial year.

SCHEDULE C

Layout for Listing Particulars for the Admission of Certificates Representing Shares to Official Stock Exchange Listing

Chapter 1. General information about the issuer

1.1. Name, registered office and principal administrative establishment if different from the registered office.

1.2. Date of incorporation and length of life of the issuer, except where indefinite.

1.3. Legislation under which the issuer operates and legal form which it has adopted under that legislation.

1.4. The amount of the issued capital and the number and classes of the securities of which it is composed with details of their principal characteristics.

The part of the issued capital still to be paid up, with an indication of the number, or total nominal value, and the type of the securities not yet fully paid up, broken down where applicable according to the extent to which they have been paid up.

1.5. Indication of the principal holders of the capital.

1.6. Names, addresses and functions in the issuing body of the following persons, and an indication of the principal activities performed by them outside that body where these are significant with respect to that body, and also the functions held:

(a) members of the administrative, management or supervisory bodies;

(b) partners with unlimited liability, in the case of a limited partnership with a share capital.

1.7. The company's objects. If the issue of certificates representing shares is not the sole object of the company, the nature of its other activities must be described, those of a purely trustee nature being dealt with separately.

1.8. A summary of the annual accounts relating to the last completed financial year.

Where more than nine months have elapsed since the end of the last financial year to which the last published own annual and/or consolidated annual accounts relate, an interim financial statement covering at least the first six months shall be included in the listing particulars or appended to them. If the interim financial statement is unaudited, that fact must be stated.

Where the issuer prepares consolidated annual accounts, the competent authorities shall decide whether the interim financial statement to be submitted must be consolidated or not.

Any significant change which has occurred since the end of the last financial year or the preparation of the interim financial statement must be described in a note inserted in the listing particulars or appended thereto.

Chapter 2. Information on the certificates themselves

2.1. Legal status: Indication of the rules governing the issue of the certificates and mention of the date and place of their publication.

2.1.0. Exercise of and benefit from the rights attaching to the original securities, in particular voting rights—conditions on which the issuer of the certificates may exercise such rights, and measures envisaged to obtain the instructions of the certificate holders—and the right to share in profits and any liquidation surplus.

2.1.1. Bank or other guarantees attached to the certificates and intended to underwrite the issuer's obligations.

2.1.2. Possibility of obtaining the conversion of the certificates into original securities and procedure for such conversion.

2.2. The amount of the commissions and costs to be borne by the holder in connection with:

— the issue of the certificate,
— the payment of the coupons,
— the creation of additional certificates,
— the exchange of the certificates for original securities.

2.3. Transferability of the certificates:

(a) The stock exchanges where admission to official listing is, or will be, sought;

(b) Any restrictions on the free transferability of the certificates.

2.4. Supplementary information for admission to official listing:

(a) If the certificates are to be placed on a stock exchange the number of certificates made available to the market and/or the total nominal value; the minimum sale price, if such a price is fixed;

(b) Date on which the new certificates will be listed, if known.

2.5. Indication of the tax arrangements with regard to any taxes and charges to be borne by the holders and levied in the countries where the certificates are issued.

2.6. Indication of the legislation under which the certificates have been created and of the courts competent in the event of litigation.

Council Directive

of 3 March 1982 amending Directive 79/279/EEC coordinating the conditions for the admission of securities to official stock exchange listing and Directive 80/390/EEC coordinating the requirements for the drawing up, scrutiny and distribution of the listing particulars to be published for the admission of securities to official stock exchange listing

(82/148/EEC)

The Council of the European Communities,

Having regard to the Treaty establishing the European Economic Community, and in particular Articles 54 (3) (g) and 100 thereof,

Having regard to the proposal from the Commission,

Having regard to the opinion of the European Parliament,[1]

Having regard to the opinion of the Economic and Social Committee,[2]

Whereas Member States must comply with Directive 79/279/EEC[3] within two years of its notification; whereas such notification took place on 8 March 1979; whereas the period therefore expired on 8 March 1981; whereas, however, the period was extended by one year in the case of Member States

---

[1] Opinion delivered on 19 February 1982 (not yet published in the Official Journal).
[2] Opinion delivered on 25 February 1982 (not yet published in the Official Journal).
[3] OJ No L 66, 16. 3. 1979, p. 21.

simultaneously introducing Directives 79/279/EEC and 80/390/EEC;[4] whereas such period expires, in these circumstances, on 8 March 1982;

Whereas Member States must comply with Directive 80/390/EEC within 30 months of its notification; whereas such notification took place on 19 March 1980; whereas the period therefore expires on 19 September 1982; whereas, however, the period will expire on the earlier date of 8 March 1982 in the case of Member States simultaneously introducing Directives 79/279/EEC and 80/390/EEC;

Whereas Member States must comply by 30 June 1983 at the latest with Council Directive 82/121/EEC of 15 February 1982 on information to be published on a regular basis by companies the shares of which have been admitted to official stock-exchange listing;[5]

Whereas there is a close link between these three Directives, not only because the purpose of all three is to coordinate a number of rules relating to securities which have been admitted to official stock exchange listing or whose admission to such official listing is requested, but above all because the three Directives aim to establish at Community level a coordinated information policy on the securities in question;

Whereas Member States should therefore be given the possibility of implementing the three Directives simultaneously so that they do not have to initiate several legislative or rule-making procedures in one and the same area at very short intervals, which might constitute an unacceptable extra burden for national parliaments or national stock exchange authorities;

Whereas Directives 79/279/EEC and 80/390/EEC should therefore be amended to allow Member States to implement them on the same date as Directive 82/121/EEC, namely by 30 June 1983 at the latest,

Has adopted this directive:

Article 1.   The following subparagraph shall be added to Article 22 (1) of Directive 79/279/EEC:

However, this period shall be extended to 30 June 1983 in the case of Member States simultaneously introducing this Directive and Directives 80/390/EEC and 82/121/EEC.

Article 2.   The following subparagraph shall be added to Article 27 (1) of Directive 80/390/EEC:

This period shall be extended to 30 June 1983 in the case of Member States simultaneously introducing this Directive and Directives 79/279/EEC and 82/121/EEC.

[4] OJ No L 100, 17. 4. 1980, p. 1.
[5] OJ No L 48, 20. 2. 1982, p. 26.

Article 3.   This Directive is addressed to the Member States.
Done at Brussels, 3 March 1982.

For the Council, The President, L. Tindemans

Council Directive

of 22 June 1987 amending Directive 80/390/EEC coordinating the requirements for the drawing-up, scrutiny and distribution of the listing particulars to be published for the admission of securities to official stock exchange listing

(87/345/EEC)

The Council of the European Communities,

Having regard to the Treaty establishing the European Economic Community, and in particular Article 54 (2) thereof,

Having regard to the proposal from the Commission,

Having regard to the opinion of the European Parliament,[1]

Having regard to the opinion of the Economic and Social Committee,[2]

Whereas, on 17 November 1986, the Council adopted Directive 86/566/EEC amending the First Directive of 11 May 1960 for the implementation of Article 67 of the Treaty;[3] whereas, as a consequence, the number of cross-border applications for admission to listing is likely to increase;

Whereas Article 24 of Directive 80/390/EEC,[4] as amended by Directive 82/148/EEC,[5] provides that, where securities are to be admitted to official listing on stock exchanges in two or more Member States, the competent authorities of such Member States are to cooperate and endeavour to agree a single text for the listing particulars for use in all the Member States concerned;

Whereas that provision does not result in the full mutual recognition of listing particulars and it is therefore appropriate to amend Directive 80/390/EEC so as to achieve that recognition;

Whereas mutual recognition represents an important step forward in the creation of the Community's internal market;

---

[1] OJ No C 125, 11. 5. 1987, p. 173.   [2] OJ No C 150, 9. 6. 1987, p. 18.
[3] OJ No L 332, 26. 11. 1986, p. 22.   [4] OJ No L 100, 17. 4. 1980, p. 1.
[5] OJ No L 62, 5. 3. 1982, p. 22.

Whereas, in this connection, it is necessary to specify which authorities are competent to check and approve listing particulars in the event of simultaneous applications for admission to official listing in two or more Member States;

Whereas mutual recognition can be effective only in so far as Directive 80/390/EEC and the Directives to which it refers have been incorporated in the national legislation of the Member State the competent authorities of which approve the listing particulars;

Whereas the mutual recognition of listing particulars does not in itself confer a right to admission;

Whereas it is advisable to provide for the extension, by means of agreements to be concluded by the Community with non-member countries, of the recognition of listing particulars from those countries on a reciprocal basis;

Whereas provision should be made for a transitional period for the Kingdom of Spain and the Portuguese Republic to take account of the periods accorded to those Member States under Article 2 (2) of Directive 86/566/EEC,

Has adopted this directive:

Article 1. Section IV of Directive 80/390/EEC is replaced by the following Sections and Sections V and VI shall become Sections VIII and IX, respectively:

SECTION IV. DETERMINATION OF THE COMPETENT AUTHORITY

Article 24. Where, for the same securities, applications for admission to official listing on stock exchanges situated or operating in two or more Member States, including the Member State in which the issuer's registered office is situated, are made simultaneously or within a short interval, listing particulars shall be drawn up in accordance with the rules laid down in this Directive in the Member State in which the issuer has its registered office and approved by the competent authorities of that State; if the issuer's registered office is not situated in one of those Member States, the issuer must choose one of those States under the legislation of which the listing particulars will be drawn up and approved.

SECTION V. MUTUAL RECOGNITION

Article 24a. 1. Once approved in accordance with Article 24, listing particulars must, subject to any translation, be recognized by the other Member States in which admission to official listing has been applied for, without its being necessary to obtain the approval of the competent authorities of those States and without their being able to require that additional information be included in the listing particulars. The competent authorities may, however, require that listing particulars include information specific to the market of the country of admission concerning in particular the income tax system, the financial organizations retained to act as paying agents for the issuer in that country, and the way in which notices to investors are published.

2. Listing particulars approved by the competent authorities within the meaning of Article 24 must be recognized in another Member State in which application for admission to official listing is made, even if partial exemption or partial derogation has been granted pursuant to this Directive, provided that:

(a) the partial exemption or partial derogation in question is of a type that is recognized in the rules of the other Member State concerned, and

(b) the conditions that justify the partial exemption or partial derogation also exist in the other Member State concerned and that there are no other conditions concerning such exemption or derogation which might lead the competent authority in that Member State to refuse them.

Even if the conditions laid down in (a) and (b) are not fulfilled, the Member State concerned may allow its competent authorities to recognize the listing particulars approved by the competent authorities within the meaning of Article 24.

3. When approving listing particulars, the competent authorities within the meaning of Article 24 shall provide the competent authorities of the other Member States in which application for official listing is made with a certificate of approval. If partial exemption or partial derogation has been granted pursuant to this Directive, the certificate shall state that fact and the reasons for it.

4. When application for admission to official listing is made, the issuer shall communicate to the competent authorities in each of the other Member States in which it is applying for admission the draft listing particulars which it intends to use in that State.

5. Member States may restrict the application of this Article to listing particulars of issuers having their registered office in a Member State.

Article 24b. 1. Where the securities for which applications for admission to official listing on stock exchanges situated in two or more Member States have been made simultaneously or within a short interval have been the subject of a prospectus drawn up and approved in accordance with this Directive, at the time of the public offer, by the competent authorities within the meaning of Article 24 in the three months preceding the application for admission in that State, that prospectus must, subject to any translation, be recognized as listing particulars in the other Member States in which application for admission to official listing is made, without its being necessary to obtain the approval of the competent authorities of those Member States and without their being able to require that additional information be included in the listing particulars. The competent authorities may, however, require that listing particulars include information specific to the market of the country of admission concerning, in particular, the income tax system, the financial organizations retained to act as paying agents for the issuer in the country of admission and the ways in which notices to investors are published.

2. Article 24a (2), (3), (4) and (5) shall apply in the eventuality referred to in paragraph 1 of this Article.

3. Article 23 shall apply to all changes occurring between the time when the content of the prospectus referred to in paragraph 1 of this Article is adopted and the time when stock exchange dealings begin.

SECTION VI. COOPERATION

Article 24c.   1. The competent authorities shall cooperate wherever necessary for the purpose of carrying out their duties and shall exchange any information required for that purpose.

2. Where an application for admission to official listing concerning securities giving a right to participate in company capital, either immediately or at the end of the maturity period, is made in one or more Member States other than that in which the registered office of the issuer of the shares to which those securities give entitlement is situated, while that issuer's shares have already been admitted to official listing in that Member State, the competent authorities of the Member State of admission may act only after having consulted the competent authorities of the Member State in which the registered office of the issuer of the shares in question is situated.

3. Where an application for admission to official listing is made for securities which have been listed in another Member State less than six months previously, the competent authorities to whom application is made shall contact the competent authorities which have already admitted the securities to official listing and shall, as far as possible, exempt the issuer of those securities from the preparation of new listing particulars, subject to any need for updating, translation or the issue of supplements in accordance with the individual requirements of the Member State concerned.

Article 25.   1. Member States shall provide that all persons employed or formerly employed by the competent authorities shall be bound by professional secrecy. This means that any confidential information received in the course of their duties may not be divulged to any person or authority except by virtue of provisions laid down by law.

2. Paragraph 1 shall not, however, preclude the competent authorities of the various Member States from exchanging information as provided for in this Directive. Information thus exchanged shall be covered by the obligation of professional secrecy to which the persons employed or formerly employed by the competent authorities receiving the information are subject.

3. Without prejudice to cases covered by criminal law, the competent authorities receiving information pursuant to Article 24c (1) may use it only for the performance of their duties or in the context of administrative appeals or legal proceedings relating to such performance.

SECTION VII. NEGOTIATIONS WITH NON-MEMBER COUNTRIES

Article 25a.   The Community may, by means of agreements concluded with one or more non-member countries pursuant to the Treaty, recognize listing particulars drawn up and checked, in accordance with the rules of the non-member country or countries, as meeting the requirements of this Directive, subject to reciprocity, provided that the rules concerned give investors protection equivalent to that afforded by this Directive, even if those rules differ from the provisions of this Directive.

Article 2. 1. Member States shall take the measures necessary for them to comply with this Directive by 1 January 1990. They shall forthwith inform the Commission thereof. However, for the Kingdom of Spain the date 1 January 1990 shall be replaced by 1 January 1991 and for the Portuguese Republic by 1 January 1992.

2. Member States shall communicate to the Commission the texts of the main laws, regulations and administrative provisions which they adopt in the field covered by this Directive.

Article 3. This Directive is addressed to the Member States.
Done at Luxembourg, 22 June 1987.

For the Council, The President, L. Tindemans

Council Directive

of 23 April 1990 amending Directive 80/390/EEC in respect of the mutual recognition of public-offer prospectuses as stock-exchange listing particulars

(90/211/EEC)

The Council of the European Communities,
Having regard to the Treaty establishing the European Economic Community, and in particular Article 54 thereof.
Having regard to the proposal from the Commission,[1]
In cooperation with the European Parliament,[2]
Having regard to the opinion of the Economic and Social Committee,[3]
Whereas Article 21 of Directive 89/298/EEC[4] provides that where public offers are made simultaneously or within short intervals of one another in two or more Member States, a public-offer prospectus drawn up and

---

[1] OJ No C 101, 22. 4. 1989, p. 13.
[2] OJ No C 304, 8. 12. 1989, p. 34, OJ No C 38, 19. 2. 1990, p. 40
[3] OJ No C 201, 7. 8. 1989, p. 5.   [4] OJ No L 124, 5. 5. 1989, p. 8.

approved in accordance with Article 7, 8 or 12 of that Directive must be recognized as a public-offer prospectus in the other Member States concerned on the basis of mutual recognition;

Whereas it is also desirable to provide the recognition of a public-offer prospectus as listing particulars where admission to official stock-exchange listing is requested within a short period of the public offer;

Whereas, therefore, it is appropriate to amend Article 24b of Directive 80/390/EEC,[5] as last amended by Directive 87/345/EEC;[6]

Whereas the mutual recognition of public-offer prospectuses does not in itself confer the right to admission to official stock-exchange listing,

Has adopted this directive,

Article 1.   The following is hereby added to the beginning of Article 6 of Directive 80/390/EEC:

Without prejudice to Article 24b (1).

Article 2.   Paragraph 1 of Article 24b of Directive 80/390/EEC is hereby replaced by the following:

1. Where application for admission to official listing in one or more Member States is made and the securities have been the subject of a public-offer prospectus drawn up and approved in any Member State in accordance with Article 7, 8 or 12 of Directive 89/298/EEC* in the three months preceding the application for admission, the public-offer prospectus shall be recognized, subject to any translation, as listing particulars in the Member State or States in which application for admission to official listing is made, without its being necessary to obtain the approval of the competent authorities of that Member State or those Member States and without their being able to require that additional information be included in the prospectus. The competent authorities may, however, require that the prospectus include information specific to the market of the country of admission concerning, in particular, the income tax system, the financial organizations retained to act as paying agents for the issuer in the country of admission and the ways in which notices to investors are published.

Article 3.   1. The Member States shall take the measures necessary for them to comply with this Directive by 17 April 1991. They shall forthwith inform the Commission thereof.

2. The Member State shall communicate to the Commission the texts of

---

[5] OJ No L 100, 17. 4. 1980, p. 1.   [6] OJ No L 185, 4. 7. 1987, p. 81.
* OJ No L 124, 5. 5. 1989, p. 8.

the main laws, regulations or administrative provisions which they adopt in the field covered by this Directive.

Article 4.   This Directive is addressed to the Member States.
  Done at Luxembourg, 23 April 1990.

For the Council, The President, A. Reynolds

Council Directive

of 15 February 1982 on information to be published on a
regular basis by companies the shares of which have
been admitted to official stock-exchange listing

(82/121/EEC)

The Council of the European Communities,

Having regard to the Treaty establishing the European Economic Community, and in particular Articles 54 (3) (g) and 100 thereof,

Having regard to the proposal from the Commission,[1]

Having regard to the opinion of the European Parliament,[2]

Having regard to the opinion of the Economic and Social Committee,[3]

Whereas Council Directive 80/390/EEC of 17 March 1980 coordinating the requirements for the drawing up, scrutiny and distribution of the listing particulars to be published for the admission of securities to official stock-exchange listing[4] seeks to ensure improved protection of investors and a greater degree of equivalence in the protection provided, by coordinating requirements as to the information to be published at the time of admission;

Whereas, in the case of securities admitted to official stock-exchange listing, the protection of investors requires that the latter be supplied with appropriate regular information throughout the entire period during which the securities are listed; whereas coordination of requirements for this regular information has similar objectives to those envisaged for the listing particulars, namely to improve such protection and to make it more equivalent, to facilitate the listing of the Community, and in so doing to contribute towards the establishment of a genuine Community capital market by permitting a fuller interpretation of securities markets;

Whereas, under Council Directive 79/279/EEC of 5 March 1979 coordinating the conditions for the admission of securities to official stock-exchange listing,[5] listed companies must as soon as possible make available to investors their annual accounts and report giving information on the company for the whole of the financial year; whereas the fourth Directive 78/660/EEC[6] has coordinated the laws, regulations and administrative provisions of the Member States concerning the annual accounts of certain types of companies;

---

[1] OJ No C 29, 1. 2. 1979, p. 5 and OJ No C 210, 16. 8. 1980, p. 5.
[2] OJ No C 85, 8. 4. 1980, p. 69.   [3] OJ No C 53, 3. 3. 1980, p. 54.
[4] OJ No L 100, 17. 4. 1980, p. 1.   [5] OJ No L 66, 16. 3. 1979, p. 21.
[6] OJ No L 222, 14. 8. 1978, p. 11.

Whereas companies should also, at least once during each financial year, make available to investors reports on their activities; whereas this Directive can, consequently, be confined to coordinating the content and distribution of a single report covering the first six months of the financial year;

Whereas, however, in the case of ordinary debentures, because of the rights they confer on their holders, the protection of investors by means of the publication of a half-yearly report is not essential; whereas, by virtue of Directive 79/279/EEC, convertible or exchangeable debentures and debentures with warrants may be admitted to official listing only if the related shares are already listed on the same stock exchange or on another regulated, regularly operating, recognized open market or are so admitted simultaneously; whereas the Member States may derogate from this principle only if their competent authorities are satisfied that holders have at their disposal all the information necessary to form an opinion concerning the value of the shares to which these debentures relate; whereas, consequently, regular information needs to be coordinated only for companies whose shares are admitted to official stock-exchange listing;

Whereas the half-yearly report must enable investors to make an informed appraisal of the general development of the company's activities during the period covered by the report; whereas, however, this report need contain only the essential details on the financial position and general progress of the business of the company in question;

Whereas, in order to take account of difficulties resulting from the current state of laws in certain Member States, companies may be allowed a longer period to implement the provisions of this Directive than that laid down for the adaptation of national laws;

Whereas, so as to ensure the effective protection of investors and the proper operation of stock exchanges, the rules relating to regular information to be published by companies, the shares of which are admitted to official stock-exchange listing within the Community, should apply not only to companies from Member States, but also to companies from non-member countries.

Has adopted this directive:

SECTION I. GENERAL PROVISIONS AND SCOPE

Article 1. 1. This Directive shall apply to companies the shares of which are admitted to official listing on a stock exchange situated or operating in a Member State, whether the admission is of the shares themselves or of certificates representing them and whether such admission precedes or follows the date on which this Directive enters into force.

2. This Directive shall not, however, apply to investment companies other than those of the closed-end type.

For the purposes of this Directive 'investment companies other than those of the closed-end type' shall mean investment companies:

— the object of which is the collective investment of capital provided by the public, and which operate on the principle of risk spreading, and
— the shares of which are, at the holders' request, repurchased or redeemed, directly or indirectly, out of those companies' assets. Action taken by such companies to ensure that the stock-exchange value of their shares does not significantly vary from their net asset value shall be regarded as equivalent to such repurchase or redemption.

3. The Member States may exclude central banks from the scope of this Directive.

Article 2.   The Member States shall ensure that the companies publish half-yearly reports on their activities and profits and losses during the first six months of each financial year.

Article 3.   The Member States may subject companies to obligations more stringent than those provided for by this Directive or to additional obligations, provided that they apply generally to all companies or to all companies of a given class.

SECTION II. PUBLICATION AND CONTENTS OF THE HALF-YEARLY REPORT

Article 4.   1. The half-yearly report shall be published within four months of the end of the relevant six-month period.

2. In exceptional, duly substantiated cases, the competent authorities shall be permitted to extend the time limit for publication.

Article 5.   1. The half-yearly report shall consist of figures and an explanatory statement relating to the company's activities and profits and losses during the relevant six-month period.

2. The figures, presented in table form, shall indicate at least:

— the net turnover, and
— the profit or loss before or after deduction of tax.

These terms shall have the same meanings as in the Council Directives on company accounts.

3. The Member States may allow the competent authorities to authorize companies, exceptionally and on a case-by-case basis, to supply estimated figures for profits and losses, provided that the shares of each such company are listed officially in only one Member State. The use of this procedure must be indicated by the company in its report and must not mislead investors.

4. Where the company has paid or proposes to pay an interim dividend, the figures must indicate the profit or loss after tax for the six-month period and the interim dividend paid or proposed.

5. Against each figure there must be shown the figure for the corresponding period in the preceding financial year.

6. The explanatory statement must include any significant information enabling investors to make an informed assessment of the trend of the company's activities and profits or losses together with an indication of any special factor which has influenced those activities and those profits or losses during the period in question, and enable a comparison to be made with the corresponding period of the preceding financial year.

It must also, as far as possible, refer to the company's likely future development in the current financial year.

7. Where the figures provided for in paragraph 2 are unsuited to the company's activities, the competent authorities shall ensure that appropriate adjustments are made.

Article 6. Where a company publishes consolidated accounts it may publish its half-yearly report in either consolidated or unconsolidated form. However, the Member States may allow the competent authorities, where the latter consider that the form not adopted would have contained additional material information, to require the company to publish such information.

Article 7. 1. The half-yearly report must be published in the Member State or Member States where the shares are admitted to official listing by insertion in one or more newspapers distributed throughout the State or widely distributed therein or in the national gazette, or shall be made available to the public either in writing in places indicated by announcement to be published in one or more newspapers distributed throughout the State or widely distributed therein, or by other equivalent means approved by the competent authorities.

2. A half-yearly report must be drawn up in the official language or languages or in one of the official languages or in another language, provided that, in the Member State concerned, such official language or languages or such other language are customary in the sphere of finance and are accepted by the competent authorities.

3. The company shall send a copy of its half-yearly report simultaneously to the competent authorities of each Member State in which its shares are admitted to official listing. It shall do so not later than the time when the half-yearly report is published for the first time in a Member State.

Article 8. Where the accounting information has been audited by the official auditor of the company's accounts, that auditor's report and any qualifications he may have shall be reproduced in full.

SECTION III. POWERS OF THE COMPETENT AUTHORITIES

Article 9.   1. Member States shall appoint one or more competent authorities and shall notify the Commission of the appointment of such authorities, giving details of any division of powers among them. Member States shall also ensure that this Directive is applied.

2. The Member States shall ensure that the competent authorities have the necessary powers to carry out their task.

3. Where particular requirements of this Directive are unsuited to a company's activities or circumstances, the competent authorities shall ensure that suitable adaptations are made to such requirements.

4. The competent authorities may authorize the omission from the half-yearly report of certain information provided for in this Directive if they consider that disclosure of such information would be contrary to the public interest or seriously detrimental to the company, provided that, in the latter case, such omission would not be likely to mislead the public with regard to facts and circumstances knowledge of which is essential for the assessment of the shares in question.

The company or its representatives shall be responsible for the correctness and relevance of the facts on which any application for such exemption is based.

5. Paragraphs 3 and 4 shall also apply to the more stringent or additional obligations imposed pursuant to Article 3.

6. If a company governed by the law of a non-member country publishes a half-yearly report in a non-member country, the competent authorities may authorize it to publish that report instead of the half-yearly report provided for in this Directive, provided that the information given is equivalent to that which would result from the application of this Directive.

7. This Directive shall not affect the competent authorities' liability, which shall continue to be governed solely by national law.

SECTION IV. COOPERATION BETWEEN MEMBER STATES

Article 10.   1. The competent authorities shall cooperate whenever necessary for the purpose of carrying out their duties and shall exchange any information required for that purpose.

2. Where a half-yearly report has to be published in more than one Member State, the competent authorities of these Member States shall, by way of derogation from Article 3, use their best endeavours to accept as a single text the text which meets the requirements of the Member State in

which the company's shares were admitted to official listing for the first time or the text which most closely approximates to that text. In cases of simultaneous admission to official listing on two or more stock exchanges situated or operating in different Member States, the competent authorities of the Member States concerned shall use their best endeavours to accept as a single text the text of the report which meets the requirements of the Member State in which the company's head office is situated; if the company's head office is situated in a non-member country, the competent authorities of the Member States concerned shall use their best endeavours to accept a single version of the report.

SECTION V. CONTACT COMMITTEE

Article 11. 1. The Contact Committee set up by Article 20 of Directive 79/279/EEC shall also have as its function:

(a) without prejudice to Articles 169 and 170 of the Treaty to facilitate the harmonized implementation of this Directive through regular consultations on any practical problems arising from its application on which exchanges of views are deemed useful;

(b) to facilitate consultation between the Member States on the more stringent or additional obligations which they may impose pursuant to Article 3 with a view to the ultimate convergence of obligations imposed in all Member States, in accordance with Article 54 (3) (g) of the Treaty;

(c) to advise the Commission, if necessary, on any additions or amendments to be made to this Directive; in particular, the Committee shall consider the possible modification of Articles 3 and 5 in the light of progress towards the convergence of obligations referred to in (b) above.

2. Within five years of notification of this Directive, the Commission shall, after consulting the Contact Committee, submit to the Council a report on the application of Articles 3 and 5 and on such modifications as it would be possible to make thereto.

SECTION VI. FINAL PROVISIONS

Article 12. 1. Member States shall bring into force the measures necessary to comply with this Directive not later than 30 June 1983. They shall forthwith inform the Commission thereof.

2. Member States may postpone application of the measures referred to in paragraph 1 until 36 months from the date on which they bring such measures into force.

3. As from the notification of this Directive, Member States shall

communicate to the Commission the main provisions of the laws, regulations and administrative provisions which they adopt in the field governed by this Directive.

Article 13.   This Directive is addressed to the Member States.
  Done at Brussels, 15 February 1982.

For the Council, The President, P. de Keersmaeker

Council Directive

of 12 December 1988 on the information to be published
when a major holding in a listed company is acquired or
disposed of

(88/627/EEC)

The Council of the European Communities,

Having regard to the Treaty establishing the European Economic
Community, and in particular Article 54 thereof,

Having regard to the proposal from the Commission,[1]

In cooperation with the European Parliament,[2]

Having regard to the opinion of the Economic and Social Committee,[3]

Whereas a policy of adequate information of investors in the field of
transferable securities is likely to improve investor protection, to increase
investors' confidence in securities markets and thus to ensure that securities
markets function correctly;

Whereas, by making such protection more equivalent, coordination of
that policy at Community level is likely to make for greater inter-penetration
of the Member States' transferable securities markets and therefore help to
establish a true European capital market;

Whereas to that end investors should be informed of major holdings and
of changes in those holdings in Community companies the shares of which
are officially listed on stock exchanges situated or operating within the
Community;

Whereas coordinated rules should be laid down concerning the detailed
content and the procedure for applying that requirement;

Whereas companies, the shares of which are officially listed on a Community stock exchange, can inform the public of changes in major holdings
only if they have been informed of such changes by the holders of those
holdings;

Whereas most Member States do not subject holders to such a requirement and where such a requirement exists there are appreciable differences
in the procedures for applying it; whereas coordinated rules should
therefore be adopted at Community level in this field,

Has adopted this directive:

---

[1] OJ No C 351, 31. 12. 1985, p. 35, and OJ No C 255, 25. 9. 1987, p. 6.
[2] OJ No C 125, 11. 5. 1987, p. 144, and OJ No C 309, 5. 12. 1988.
[3] OJ No C 263, 20. 10. 1986, p. 1.

Article 1. 1. Member States shall make subject to this Directive natural persons and legal entities in public or private law who acquire or dispose of, directly or through intermediaries, holdings meeting the criteria laid down in Article 4 (1) which involve changes in the holdings of voting rights in companies incorporated under their law the shares of which are officially listed on a stock exchange or exchanges situated or operating within one or more Member States.

2. Where the acquisition or disposal of a major holding such as referred to in paragraph 1 is effected by means of certificates representing shares, this Directive shall apply to the bearers of those certificates, and not to the issuer.

3. This Directive shall not apply to the acquisition or disposal of major holdings in collective investment undertakings.

4. Paragraph 5 (c) of Schedule C of the Annex to Council Directive 79/279/EEC of 5 March 1979 coordinating the conditions for the admission of securities to official stock exchange listing,[4] as last amended by Directive 82/148/EEC,[5] is hereby replaced by the following:

(c) The company must inform the public of any changes in the structure (shareholders and breakdowns of holdings) of the major holdings in its capital as compared with information previously published on that subject as soon as such changes come to its notice.

In particular, a company which is not subject to Council Directive 88/627/EEC of 12 December 1988 on the information to be published when a major holding in a listed company is acquired or disposed of* must inform the public within nine calendar days whenever it comes to its notice that a person or entity has acquired or disposed of a number of shares such that his or its holding exceeds or falls below one of the thresholds laid down in Article 4 of that Directive.

Article 2. For the purposes of Directive, 'acquiring a holding' shall mean not only purchasing a holding, but also acquisition by any other means whatsoever, including acquisition in one of the situations referred to in Article 7.

Article 3. Member States may subject the natural persons, legal entities and companies referred to in Article 1 (1) to requirements stricter than those provided for in this Directive or to additional requirements, provided that such requirements apply generally to all those acquiring or disposing of holdings and all companies or to all those falling within a particular category acquiring or disposing of holdings or of companies.

---

[4] OJ No L 66, 16. 3. 1979, p. 21.   [5] OJ No L 62, 5. 3. 1982, p. 22.
* OJ No L 348, 17. 12. 1988, p. 62.

Article 4. 1. Where a natural person or legal entity referred to in Article 1 (1) acquires or disposes of a holding in a company referred to in Article 1 (1) and where, following that acquisition or disposal, the proportion of voting rights held by that person or legal entity reaches, exceeds or falls below one of the thresholds of 10%, 20%, 1/3, 50% and 2/3, he shall notify the company and at the same time the competent authority or authorities referred to in Article 13 within seven calendar days of the proportion of voting rights he holds following that acquisition or disposal. Member States need not apply:

— the thresholds of 20% and 1/3 where they apply a single threshold of 25%,
— the threshold of 2/3 where they apply the threshold of 75%.

The period of seven calendar days shall start from the time when the owner of the major holding learns of the acquisition or disposal, or from the time when, in view of the circumstances, he should have learnt of it.

Member States may further provide that a company must also be informed in respect of the proportion of capital held by a natural person or legal entity.

2. Member States shall, if necessary, establish in their national law, and determine in accordance with it, the manner in which the voting rights to be taken into account for the purposes of applying paragraph 1 are to be brought to the notice of the natural persons and legal entities referred to in Article 1 (1).

Article 5. Member States shall provide that at the first annual general meeting of a company referred to in Article 1 (1) to take place more than three months after this Directive has been transposed into national law, any natural person or legal entity as referred to in Article 1 (1) must notify the company concerned and at the same time the competent authority or authorities where he holds 10% or more of its voting rights, specifying the proportion of voting rights actually held unless that person or entity has already made a declaration in accordance with Article 4.

Within one month of that general meeting, the public shall be informed of all holdings of 10% or more in accordance with Article 10.

Article 6. If the person or entity acquiring or disposing of a major holding as defined in Article 4 is a member of a group of undertakings required under Directive 83/349/EEC[1] to draw up a consolidated accounts, that person or entity shall be exempt from the obligation to make the declaration provided for in Article 4 (1) and in Article 5 if it is made by the parent undertaking or, where the parent undertaking is itself a subsidiary undertaking, by its own parent undertaking.

---

[1] OJ No L 193, 18. 7. 1983, p. 1.

Article 7. For the purposes of determining whether a natural person or legal entity as referred to in Article 1 (1) is required to make a declaration as provided for in Article 4 (1) and in Article 5, the following shall be regarded as voting rights held by that person or entity:

— voting rights held by other persons or entities in their own names but on behalf of that person or entity,
— voting rights held by an undertaking controlled by that person or entity;
— voting rights held by a third party with whom that person or entity has concluded a written agreement which obliges them to adopt, by concerted exercise of the voting rights they hold, a lasting common policy towards the management of the company in question.
— voting rights held by a third party under a written agreement concluded with that person or entity or with an undertaking controlled by that person or entity providing for the temporary transfer for consideration of the voting rights in question,
— voting rights attaching to shares owned by that person or entity which are lodged as security, except where the person or entity holding the security controls the voting rights and declares his intention of exercising them, in which case they shall be regarded as the latter's voting rights,
— voting rights attaching to shares of which that person or entity has the life interest,
— voting rights which that person or entity or one of the other persons or entities mentioned in the above indents is entitled to acquire, on his own initiative alone, under a formal agreement; in such cases, the notification prescribed in Article 4 (1) shall be effected on the date of the agreement,
— voting rights attaching to shares deposited with that person or entity which that person or entity can exercise at its discretion in the absence of specific instructions from the holders.

By way of derogation from Article 4 (1), where a person or entity may exercise voting rights referred to in the last indent of the preceding subparagraph in a company and where the totality of these voting rights together with the other voting rights held by that person or entity in that company reaches or exceeds one of the thresholds provided for in Article 4 (1), Member States may lay down that the said person or entity is only obliged to inform the company concerned 21 calendar days before the general meeting of that company.

Article 8. 1. For the purposes of this Directive, 'controlled undertaking' shall mean any undertaking in which a natural person or legal entity:

(a) has a majority of the shareholders' or members' voting rights; or
(b) has the right to appoint or remove a majority of the members of the administrative, management or supervisory body and is at the same

time a shareholder in, or member of, the undertaking in question; or

(c) is a shareholder or member and alone controls a majority of the shareholders' or members' voting rights pursuant to an agreement entered into with other shareholders or members of the undertaking.

2. For the purposes of paragraph 1, a parent undertaking's rights as regards voting, appointment and removal shall include the rights of any other controlled undertaking and those of any person or entity acting in his own name but on behalf of the parent undertaking or of any other controlled undertaking.

Article 9.   1. The competent authorities may exempt from the declaration provided for in Article 4 (1) the acquisition or disposal of a major holding, as defined in Article 4, by a professional dealer in securities, in so far as that acquisition or disposal is effected in his capacity as a professional dealer in securities and in so far as the acquisition is not used by the dealer to intervene in the management of the company concerned.

2. The competent authorities shall require the professional dealers in securities referred to in paragraph 1 to be members of a stock exchange situated or operating within a Member State or to be approved or supervised by a competent authority such as referred to in Article 12.

Article 10.   1. A company which has received a declaration referred to in the first subparagraph of Article 4 (1) must in turn disclose it to the public in each of the Member States in which its shares are officially listed on a stock exchange as soon as possible but not more than nine calendar days after the receipt of that declaration.

A Member State may provide for the disclosure to the public, referred to in the first subparagraph, to be made not by the company concerned but by the competent authority, possibly in cooperation with that company.

2. The disclosure referred to in paragraph 1 must be made by publication in one or more newspapers distributed throughout or widely in the Member State or States concerned or be made available to the public either in writing in places indicated by announcements to be published in one or more newspapers distributed throughout or widely in the Member State or States concerned or by other equivalent means approved by the competent authorities.

The said disclosure must be made by publication in the official language or languages, or in one of the official langauges or in another language, provided that in the Member State in question the official language or languages or such other language is or are customary in the sphere of finance and accepted by the competent authorities.

Article 11.   The competent authorities may, exceptionally, exempt the companies referred to in Article 1 (1) from the obligation to notify the public set out in Article 10 where those authorities consider that the disclosure of such information would be contrary to the public interest or seriously detrimental to the companies concerned, provides that, in the latter case, such omission would not be likely to mislead the public with regard to the facts and circumstances knowledge of which is essential for the assessment of the transferable securities in question.

Article 12.   1. Member States shall designate the competent authority or authorities for the purposes of this Directive and shall inform the Commission accordingly, specifying, where appropriate, and division of duties between those authorities.

2. Member States shall ensure that the competent authorities have such powers as may be necessary for the performance of their duties.

3. The competent authorities in the Member States shall cooperate wherever necessary for the purpose of performing their duties and shall exchange any information useful for that purpose.

Article 13.   For the purpose of this Directive, the competent authorities shall be those of the Member State the law of which governs the companies referred to in Article 1 (1).

Article 14.   1. Member States shall provide that every person who carries on or has carried on an activity in the employment of a competent authority shall be bound by professional secrecy. This means that no confidential information received in the course of their duties may be divulged to any person or authority except by virtue of provisions laid down by law.

2. Paragraph 1 shall not, however, preclude the competent authorities of the various Member States from exchanging information as provided for in this Directive. Information thus exchanged shall be covered by the obligation of professional secrecy to which persons employed or previously employed by the competent authorities receiving the information are subject.

3. A competent authority which receives confidential information pursuant to paragraph 2 may use it solely for the performance of its duties.

Article 15.   Member States shall provide for appropriate sanctions in cases where the natural persons or legal entities and the companies referred to in Article 1 (1) do not comply with the provisions of this Directive.

Article 16.   1. The Contact Committee set up by Article 20 of Directive 79/279/EEC shall also have as its function:

(a) to permit regular consultations on any practical problems which arise from the application of this Directive and on which exchanges of view are deemed useful;

(b) to facilitate consultations between the Member States on the stricter or additional requirements which they may lay down in accordance with Article 3, so that the requirements imposed in all the Member States may be brought into line, in accordance with Article 54 (3) (g) of the Treaty;

(c) to advise the Commission, if necessary, on any additions or amendments to be made to this Directive.

Article 17. 1. Member States shall take the measures necessary for them to comply with this Directive before 1 January 1991. They shall forthwith inform the Commission thereof.

2. Member States shall communicate to the Commission the provisions of national law which they adopt in the field governed by this Directive.

Article 18. This Directive is addressed to the Member States.

Done at Brussels, 12 December 1988.

For the Council, The President, P. Roumeliotis

Council Directive

of 17 April 1989 coordinating the requirements for the
drawing-up, scrutiny and distribution of the prospectus
to be published when transferable securities are offered
to the public

(89/298/EEC)

The Council of the European Communities,

Having regard to the Treaty establishing the European Economic
Community, and in particular Article 54 thereof,

Having regard to the proposal from the Commission,[1]

In cooperation with the European Parliament,[2]

Having regard to the opinion of the Economic and Social Committee,[3]

Whereas investment in transferable securities, like any other form of
investment, involves risks; whereas the protection of investors requires that
they be put in a position to make a correct assessment of such risks so as to be
able to take investment decisions in full knowledge of the facts;

Whereas the provision of full, appropriate information concerning transferable securities and the issuers of such securities promotes the protection
of investors;

Whereas, moreover, such information is an effective means of increasing
confidence in transferable securities and thus contributes to the proper
functioning and development of transferable securities markets;

Whereas a genuine Community information policy relating to transferable securities should therefore be introduced; whereas, by virtue of the
safeguards that it offers investors and its impact on the proper functioning of
transferable securities markets, such an information policy is capable of
promoting the interpenetration of national transferable securities markets
and thus encouraging the creation of a genuine European capital market;

Whereas Council Directive 80/390/EEC of 17 March 1980 coordinating
the requirements for the drawing-up, scrutiny and distribution of the listing
particulars to be published for the admission of securities to official stock
exchange listing,[4] as last amended by Directive 87/345/EEC,[5] represents an
important step in the implementation of such a Community information
policy; whereas that Directive coordinates the information to be published
when securities are admitted to stock exchange listing concerning the nature

[1] OJ No C 226, 31. 8. 1982, p. 4.
[2] OJ No C 125. 17. 5. 1982, p. 176 and OJ No C 69, 20. 3. 1989.
[3] OJ No C 310, 30. 11. 1981, p. 50.   [4] OJ No L 100, 17. 4. 1980, p. 1.
[5] OJ No L 185, 4. 7. 1987, p. 81.

of the securities offered and the issuers of such securities, so as to enable investors to make an informed assessment of the assets and liabilities, financial position, profits and losses and prospects of issuers and of the rights attaching to such securities;

Whereas such an information policy also requires that when transferable securities are offered to the public for the first time in a Member State, whether by, or on behalf of the issuer or a third party, whether or not they are subsequently listed, a prospectus containing information of this nature must be made available to investors; whereas it is also necessary to co-ordinate the contents of that prospectus in order to achieve equivalence of the minimum safeguards afforded to investors in the various Member States;

Whereas, so far, it has proved impossible to furnish a common definition of the term 'public offer' and all its constituent parts;

Whereas, in cases where a public offer is of transferable securities which are to be admitted to official listing on a stock exchange, information similar to that required by Directive 80/390/EEC, whilst being adapted to the circumstances of the public offer, must be supplied; whereas, for public offers of transferable securities that are not to be admitted to official stock exchange listing, less detailed information can be required so as not to burden small and medium-sized issuers unduly; whereas, for public offers of transferable securities that are to be admitted to official stock exchange listing, the degree of coordination achieved is such that a prospectus approved by the competent authorities of a Member State can be used for public offers of the same securities in another Member State on the basis of mutual recognition; whereas mutual recognition should also apply where public offer prospectuses comply with the basic standards laid down in Directive 80/390/EEC and are approved by the competent authorities even in the absence of a request for admission to official stock exchange listing;

Whereas in order to ensure that the purposes of this Directive will be fully realized it is necessary to include within the scope of this Directive transferable securities issued by companies of firms governed by the laws of third countries;

Whereas it is advisable to provide for the extension, by means of agreements to be concluded by the Community with third countries, of the recognition of prospectuses from those countries on a reciprocal basis;

Has adopted this directive.

SECTION I. GENERAL PROVISIONS

Article 1. 1. This Directive shall apply to transferable securities which are offered to the public for the first time in a Member State provided that these securities are not already listed on a stock exchange situated or operating in that Member State.

2. Where an offer to the public is for part only of the transferable securities from a single issue, the Member States need not require that another prospectus be published if the other part is subsequently offered to the public.

Article 2.   This Directive shall not apply:
 1. to the following types of offer:
(a) where transferable securities are offered to persons in the context of their trades, professions or occupations, and/or
(b) where transferable securities are offered to a restricted circle of persons, and/or
(c) where the selling price of all the transferable securities offered does not exceed ECU 40000, and/or
(d) where the transferable securities ofered can be acquired only for a consideration of at least ECU 40000 per investor;
 2. to transferable securities of the following types:
(a) to transferable securities offered in individual denominations of at least ECU 40000;
(b) to units issued by collective investment undertakings other than of the closed-end type;
(c) to transferable securities issued by a State or by one of a State's regional or local authorities or by public international bodies of which one or more Member States are members;
(d) to transferable securities offered in connection with a take-over bid;
(e) to transferable securities offered in connection with a merger;
(f) to shares allotted free of charge to the holders of shares;
(g) to shares or transferable securities equivalent to shares offered in exchange for shares in the same company if the offer of such new securities does not involve any overall increase in the company's issued shares capital;
(h) to transferable securities offered by their employer or by an affiliated undertaking to or for the benefit of serving or former employees;
(i) to transferable securities resulting from the conversion of convertible debt securities or from the exercise of the rights conferred by warrants or to shares offered in exchange for exchangeable debt securities, provided that a public offer prospectus or listing particulars relating to those convertible or exchangeable debt securities or those warrants were published in the same Member State;
(j) to transferable securities issued, with a view to their obtaining the means necessary to achieve their disinterested objectives, by associations with legal status or non-profit-making bodies, recognized by the State;

(k) to shares or transferable securities equivalent to shares, ownership of which entitles the holder to avail himself of the services rendered by bodies such as 'building societies', 'Crédits populaires', 'Genossen-schaftsbanken', or 'Industrial and Provident Societies', or to become a member of such a body:

(l) to Euro-securities which are not the subject of a generalized campaign of advertising or canvassing.

Article 3. For the purposes of this Directive:

(a) 'collective investment undertakings other than of the closed-end type' shall mean unit trusts and investment companies:

— the object of which is the collective investment of capital provided by the public, and which operate on the principle of risk spreading, and

— the units of which are, at the holders' request, repurchased or redeemed, directly or indirectly, out of the assets of those under-takings. Action taken by such undertakings to ensure that the stock exchange value of their units does not significantly vary from their net asset value shall be regarded as equivalent to such repurchase or redemption;

(b) 'units of a collective investment undertaking' shall mean transferable securities issued by a collective investment undertaking representing the rights of the participants in such an undertaking over its assets;

(c) 'issuers' shall mean companies and other legal persons and any under-takings the transferable securities of which are offered to the public;

(d) 'credit institution' shall mean an undertaking the business of which is to receive deposits or other repayable funds from the public and to grant credits for its own account, including credit institutions such as referred to in Article 2 of Directive 77/780/EEC,[1] as last amended by Directive 86/524/EEC;[2]

(e) 'transferable securities' shall mean shares in companies and other transferable securities equivalent to shares in companies, debt securities having a maturity of at least one year and other transferable securities equivalent to debt securities, and any other transferable security giving the right to acquire any such transferable securities by subscription or exchange;

(f) 'Euro-securities' shall mean transferable securities which:

— are to be underwritten and distributed by a syndicate at least two of the members of which have their registered offices in different States, and

— are offered on a significant scale in one or more States other than that of the issuer's registered office, and

---

[1] OJ No L 322, 17. 12. 1977, p. 30.   [2] OJ No L 309, 4. 11. 1986, p. 15.

— may be subscribed for or initially acquired only through a credit institution or other financial institution.

Article 4.   Member States shall ensure that any offer of transferable securities to the public within their territories is subject to the publication of a prospectus by the person making the offer.

Article 5.   Member States may provide for partial or complete exemption from the obligation to publish a prospectus where the transferable securities being offered to the public are:

(a) debt securities or other transferable securities equivalent to debt securities issued in a continuous or repeated manner by credit institutions or other financial institutions equivalent to credit institutions which regularly publish their annual accounts and which, within the Community, are set up or governed by a special law or pursuant to such a law, or are subject to public supervision intended to protect savings;

(b) debt securities or other transferable securities equivalent to debt securities issued by companies and other legal persons which are nationals of a Member State and which:

— in carrying on their business, benefit from State monopolies, and
— are set up or governed by a special law or pursuant to such a law or whose borrowings are unconditionally and irrevocably guaranteed by a Member State or one of a Member State's regional or local authorities;

(c) debt securities issued by legal persons, other than companies, which are nationals of a Member State, and

— were set up by special law, and
— whose activities are governed by that law and consist solely in

(i) raising funds under state control through the issues of debt securities; and
(ii) financing production by means of the resources which they have raised and resources provided by a Member State and/or acquiring a holding in such production, and

— the debt securities of which are, for the purposes of admission to official listing, considered by national law as debt securities issued or guaranteed by the State.

Article 6.   If a full prospectus has been published in a Member State within the previous 12 months, the following prospectus drawn up by the same issuer in the same State, but relating to different transferable securities, may indicate only those changes likely to influence the value of the securities which have occurred since publication of the full prospectus.

However, that prospectus may be made available only accompanied by the full prospectus to which it relates or by a reference thereto.

SECTION II. CONTENTS AND ARRANGEMENTS FOR THE SCRUTINY AND DISTRIBUTION OF THE PROSPECTUS FOR TRANSFERABLE SECURITIES FOR WHICH ADMISSION TO OFFICIAL STOCK EXCHANGE LISTING IS SOUGHT

Article 7. Where a public offer relates to transferable securities which at the time of the offer are the subject of an application for admission to official listing on a stock exchange situated or operating within the same Member State, the contents of the prospectus and the procedures for scrutinizing and distributing it shall, subject to adaptations appropriate to the circumstances of a public offer, be determined in accordance with Directive 80/390/EEC.

Article 8. 1. Where a public offer is made in one Member State and admission is sought to official listing on a stock exchange situated in another Member State, the person making the public offer shall have the possibility in the Member State in which the public offer is to be made of drawing up a prospectus the contents and procedures for scrutiny and distribution of which shall, subject to adaptations appropriate to the circumstances of a public offer, be determined in accordance with Directive 80/390/EEC.

2. Paragraph 1 shall apply only in those Member States which in general provide for the prior scrutiny of public offer prospectuses.

Article 9. A prospectus must be published or made available to the public not later than the time when an offer is made to the public.

Article 10. 1. Where a prospectus in accordance with Article 7 or 8 is or is to be published, the advertisements, notices, posters and documents announcing the public offer must be communicated in advance to the competent authorities. The aforementioned documents must mention that there is a prospectus and state where the prospectus is published.

2. If the Member States authorize the distribution of the documents referred to in paragraph 1 before the prospectus is available, those documents must state that a prospectus will be published and indicate where members of the public will be able to obtain it.

3. The prospectus must be published either:

— by insertion in one or more newspapers circulated throughout the Member State in which the public offer is made, or

— in the form of a brochure to be made available, free of charge, to the public in the Member State in which the public offer is made and at the registered office of the person making the public offer and at the offices of the financial organizations retained to act as paying agents of the latter in the Member State where the offer is made.

4. In addition, either the complete prospectus or a notice stating where the prospectus has been published and where it may be obtained by the public must be inserted in a publication designated by the Member State in which the public offer is made.

SECTION III. CONTENTS AND ARRANGEMENTS FOR THE DISTRIBUTION OF THE PROSPECTUS FOR TRANSFERABLE SECURITIES FOR WHICH ADMISSION TO OFFICIAL STOCK-EXCHANGE LISTING IS NOT SOUGHT

Article 11. 1. Where a public offer relates to transferable securities other than those referred to in Articles 7 and 8, the prospectus must contain the information which, according to the particular nature of the issuer and of the transferable securities offered to the public, is necessary to enable investors to make an informed assessment of the assets and liabilities, financial position, profits and losses and prospects of the issues and of the rights attaching to the transferable securities.

2. In order to fulfil the obligation referred to in paragraph 1, the prospectus shall, subject to the possibilities for exemption provided for in Articles 5 and 13, contain in as easily analysable and comprehensible a form as possible, at least the information listed below:

(a) those responsible for the prospectus (names, functions and declarations by them that to the best of their knowledge the information contained in the prospectus is in accordance with the facts and that the prospectus makes no omission likely to affect its import);

(b) the offer to the public and the transferable securities being offered (nature of the securities being offered, the amount and purpose of the issue, the number of securities issued and the rights attaching to them; the income tax withheld at source; the period during which the offer is open; the date on which entitlement to dividends or interest arises; the persons underwriting or guaranteeing the offer; any restrictions on the free transferability of the securities being offered and the markets on which they may be traded; the establishments serving as paying agents; if known, the price at which the securities are offered, or else, if national rules so provide, the procedure and timetable for fixing the price if it is not known when the prospectus is being drawn up; methods of payment; the procedure for the exercise of any right of pre-emption and the methods of and time-limits for delivery of the securities);

(c) the issuer (name, registered office; its date of incorporation, the legislation applicable to the issuer and the issuer's legal form, its objects, indication of the register and of the entry number therein) and its capital (amount of the subscribed capital, the number and main particulars of the securities of which the capital consists and any part of the capital still to be paid up; the amount of any convertible debt securities, exchange-able debt securities or debt securities with warrants and the procedures for conversion, exchange or subscription; where appropriate, the group of undertakings to which the issuer belongs; in the case of shares, the following additional information must be supplied: any shares not representing capital, the amount of the authorized capital and the duration of the authorization; in so far as they are known, indication of the shareholders who directly or indirectly exercise or could exercise a determining role in the management of the issuer);

(d) the issuer's principal activities (description of its principal activities, and, where appropriate, any exceptional factors which have influenced its activities; any dependence on patents, licences or contracts if these are of fundamental importance; information regarding investments in progress where they are significant; any legal proceedings having an important effect on the issuer's financial position);

(e) the issuer's assets and liabilities, financial position and profits and losses (own accounts and, where appropriate, consolidated accounts; if the issuer prepares consolidated annual accounts only, it shall include those accounts in the prospectus; if the issuer prepares both own and consol-idated accounts, it shall include both types of account in the prospectus; however, the issuer may include only one of the two, provided that the accounts which are not included do not provide any significant addi-tional information); interim accounts if any have been published since the end of the previous financial year; the name of the person respons-ible for auditing the accounts; if that person has qualified them or refused an audit report, the fact must be stated and the reasons given;

(f) the issuer's admininstration, management and supervision (names, addresses, functions; in the case of an offer to the public of shares in a limited-liability company, remuneration of the members of the issuer's administrative, management and supervisory bodies);

(g) to the extent that such information would have a significant impact on any assessment that might be made of the issuer, recent developments in its business and prospects (the most significant recent trends concerning the development of the issuer's business since the end of the preceding financial year, information on the issuer's prospects for at least the current financial year).

3. Where a public offer relates to debt securities guaranteed by one or more legal persons, the information specified in paragraph 2 (c) to (g) must also be given with respect to the guarantor or guarantors.

4. Where a public offer relates to convertible debt securities, exchangeable debt securities or debt securities with warrants or to the warrants themselves, information must also be given with regard to the nature of the shares or debt securities to which they confer entitlement and the conditions of and procedures for conversion, exchange or subscription. Where the issuer of the shares or debt securities is not the issuer of the debt securities or warrants the information specified in paragraph 2 (c) to (g) must also be given with respect to the issuer of the shares or debt securities.

5. If the period of existence of the issuer is less than any period mentioned in paragraph 2, the information need be provided only for the period of the issuer's existence.

6. Where certain information specified in paragraph 2 is found to be inappropriate to the issuer's sphere of activity or its legal form or to the transferable securities being offered, a prospectus giving equivalent information must be drawn up.

7. Where shares are offered on a pre-emptive basis to shareholders of the issue on the occasion of their admission to dealing on a stock exchange market, the Member States or bodies designated by them may allow some of the information specified in paragraph 2 (d), (e) and (f) to be omitted, provided that investors already possess up-to-date information about the issuer equivalent to that required by Section III as a result of stock exchange disclosure requirements.

8. Where a class of shares has been admitted to dealing on a stock exchange market, the Member States or bodies designated by them may allow a partial or complete exemption from the obligation to publish a prospectus if the number or estimated market value or the nominal value or, in the absence of a nominal value, the accounting par value of the shares offered amounts to less than 10% of the number or of the corresponding value of shares of the same class already admitted to dealing, provided that investors already possess up-to-date information about the issuer equivalent to that required by Section III as a result of stock exchange disclosure requirements.

Article 12.   1. However, the Member States may provide that the person making a public offer shall have the possibility of drawing up a prospectus the contents of which shall, subject to adaptations appropriate to the circumstances of a public offer, be determined in accordance with Directive 80/390/EEC.

2. The prior scrutiny of the prospectus referred to in paragraph 1 must be carried out by the bodies designated by the Member States even in the absence of a request for admission to official stock-exchange listing.

Article 13.   1. The Member States or the bodies designated by them may authorize the omission from the prospectus referred to in Article 11 of certain information prescribed by this Directive:

(a) if that information is of minor importance only and is not likely of influence assessment of the issuer's assets and liabilities, financial position, profits and losses and prospects; or

(b) if disclosure of that information would be contrary to the public interest or seriously detrimental to the issuer, provided that, in the latter case, omission would not be likely to mislead the public with regard to facts and circumstances essential for assessment of the transferable securities.

2. Where the initiator of an offer is neither the issuer nor a third party acting on the issuer's behalf, the Member States or the bodies designated by them may authorize omission from the prospectus of certain information which would not normally be in the initiator's possession.

3. The Member States or the bodies designated by them may provide for partial or complete exemption from the obligation to publish a prospectus where the information which those making the offer are required to supply by law, regulation or rules made by bodies enabled to do so by national laws is available to investors not later than the time when the prospectus must be or should have been published or made available to the public, in accordance with this Directive, in the form of documents giving information at least equivalent to that required by Section III.

Article 14. A prospectus must be communicated, before its publication, to the bodies designated for that purpose in each Member State in which the transferable securities are offered to the public for the first time.

Article 15. A prospectus must be published or made available to the public in the Member State in which an offer to the public is made in accordance with the procedures laid down by that Member State.

Article 16. A prospectus must be published or made available to the public not later than the time when an offer is made to the public.

Article 17. 1. When a prospectus complying with Article 11 or 12 is or must be published, the advertisements, notices, posters and documents announcing the public offer distributed or made available to members of the public by the person making the public offer, must be communicated in advance to the bodies designated in accordance with Article 14, if such bodies carry out prior scrutiny of public offer prospectuses. In such a case, the latter shall determine whether the documents concerned should be checked before publication. Such documents must state that a prospectus exists and indicate where it is published.

2. If Member States authorize the dissemination of the documents referred to in paragraph 1 before the prospectus is available, those documents must state that a prospectus will be published and indicate where members of the public will be able to obtain it.

Article 18.   Any significant new factor or significant inaccuracy in a prospectus capable of affecting assessment of the transferable securities which arises or is noted between the publication of the prospectus and the definitive closure of a public offer must be mentioned or rectified in a supplement to the prospectus, to be published or made available to the public in accordance with at least the same arrangements as were applied when the original prospectus was disseminated or in accordance with procedures laid down by the Member States or by the bodies designated by them.

SECTION IV. COOPERATION BETWEEN MEMBER STATES

Article 19.   The Member States shall designate the bodies, which may be the same as those referred to in Article 14, which shall cooperate with each other for the purposes of the proper application of this Directive and shall use their best endeavours, within the framework of their responsibilities, to exchange all the information necessary to that end. Member States shall inform the Commission of the bodies thus designated. The Commission shall communicate that information to the other Member States.

Member States shall ensure that the bodies designated have the powers required for the accomplishment of their task.

Article 20.   1. Where, for the same transferable securities, public offers are made simultaneously or within a short interval of one another in two or more Member States and where a public offer prospectus is drawn up in accordance with Article 7, 8 or 12, the authority competent for the approval of the prospectus shall be that of the Member State in which the issuer has its registered office if the public offer or any application for admission to official listing on a stock exchange is made in that Member State.

2. However, if the Member State referred to in paragraph 1 does not provide in general for the prior scrutiny of public offer prospectuses and if only the public offer or an application for admission to listing is made in that Member State, as well as in all other cases, the person making the public offer must choose the supervisory authority from those in the Member States in which the public offer is made and which provide in general for the prior scrutiny of public offer prospectuses.

SECTION V. MUTUAL RECOGNITION

Article 21. 1. If approved in accordance with Article 20, a prospectus must, subject to translation if required, be recognized as complying or be deemed to comply with the laws of the other Member States in which the same transferable securities are offered to the public simultaneously or within a short interval of one another, without being subject to any form of approval there and without those States being able to require that additional information be included in the prospectus. Those Member States may, however, require that the prospectus include information specific to the market of the country in which the public offer is made concerning in particular the income tax system, the financial organizations retained to act as paying agents for the issuer in that country, and the way in which notices to investors are published.

2. A prospectus approved by the competent authorities within the meaning of Article 24a of Directive 80/390/EEC must be recognized as complying or be deemed to comply with the laws of another Member State in which the public offer is made, even if partial exemption or partial derogation has been granted pursuant to this Directive, provided, however, that:

(a) the partial exemption or partial derogation in question is of a type that is recognized in the rules of the other Member State concerned; and

(b) the circumstances that justify the partial exemption or partial derogation also exist in the other Member State concerned.

Even if the conditions laid down in (a) and (b) of the first subparagraph are not fulfilled, the Member State concerned may deem a prospectus approved by the competent authorities within the meaning of Article 20 to comply with its laws.

3. The person making the public offer shall communicate to the bodies designated by the other Member States in which the public offer is to be made the prospectus that it intends to use in that State. That prospectus must be the same as the prospectus approved by the authority referred to in Article 20.

4. The Member States may restrict the application of this Article to prospectuses concerning transferable securities of issuers who have their registered office in a Member State.

SECTION VI. COOPERATION

Article 22. 1. The competent authorities shall cooperate wherever necessary for the purpose of carrying out their duties and shall exchange any information required for that purpose.

2. Where a public offer concerning transferable securities giving a right to participate in company capital, either immediately or at the end of a

maturity period, is made in one or more Member States other than that in which the registered office of the issuer of the shares to which those securities give entitlement is situated, while that issuer's shares have already been admitted to official listing in that Member State, the competent authorities of the Member State of the offer may act only after having consulted the competent authorities of the Member State in which the registered office of the issuer of the shares in question is situated in cases where the public offer prospectus is scrutinized.

Article 23. 1. Member States shall provide that all persons then or previously employed by the authorities referred to in Article 20 shall be bound by the obligation of professional secrecy. This shall mean that they may not divulge any confidential information received in the course of their duties to any person or authority whatsoever, except by virtue of provisions laid down by law.

2. Paragraph 1 shall not prevent the various Member State authorities referred to in Article 20 from forwarding information as provided for in this Directive. The information thus exchanged shall be covered by the obligation of professional secrecy applying the persons employed then or previously by the authority receiving such information.

3. Without prejudice to cases covered by criminal law, the authorities referred to in Article 20 receiving information pursuant to Article 21 may use it only to carry out their functions or in the context of an administrative appeal or in court proceedings relating to the carrying out of those functions.

SECTION VII. NEGOTIATIONS WITH NON-MEMBER COUNTRIES

Article 24. The Community may, by means of agreements with one or more non-member countries concluded pursuant to the Treaty, recognize public offer prospectuses drawn up and scrutinized in accordance with the rules of the non-member country or countries concerned as meeting the requirements of this Directive, subject to reciprocity, provided that the rules concerned give investors protections equivalent to that afforded by this Directive, even if those rules differ from the provisions of this Directive.

SECTION VIII. CONTACT COMMITTEE

Article 25. 1. The Contact Committee set up by Article 20 of Council Directive 79/279/EEC of 5 March 1979 coordinating the conditions for the admission of transferable securities to official stock-exchange listing,[1] as last amended by Directive 82/148/EEC,[2] shall also have as its function:

[1] OJ No L 66, 16. 3. 1979, p. 1.   [2] OJ No L 62, 5. 3. 1982, p. 22.

(a) to facilitate, without prejudice to Articles 169 and 170 of the Treaty, the harmonized implementation of this Directive through regular consultations on any practical problems arising from its application on which exchanges of views are deemed useful;
(b) to facilitate consultation between the Member States on the supplements and improvements to prospectuses which they are entitled to require or recommend at national level;
(c) to advise the Commission, if necessary, on any additions or amendments to be made to this Directive.

2. It shall not be the function of the Contact Committee to appraise the merits of decisions taken in individual cases.

SECTION IX. FINAL PROVISIONS

Article 26. 1. Member States shall take the measures necessary for them to comply with this Directive by 17 April 1991. They shall forthwith inform the Commission thereof.

2. Member States shall communicate to the Commission the texts of the main provisions of national law which they adopt in the field governed by this Directive.

Article 27. This Directive is addressed to the Member States.
Done at Luxembourg, 17 April 1989.

For the Council, The President, C. Solchaga Catalan

Council Directive

of 13 November 1989 coordinating regulations
on insider dealing

(89/592/EEC)

The Council of the European Communities,

Having regard to the Treaty establishing the European Economic Community, and in particular Article 100a thereof,

Having regard to the proposal from the Commission,[1]

In cooperation with the European Parliament,[2]

Having regard to the opinion of the Economic and Social Committee,[3]

Whereas Article 100a (1) of the Treaty states that the Council shall adopt the measures for the approximation of the provisions laid down by law, regulation or administrative action in Member States which have as their object the establishment and functioning of the internal market;

Whereas the secondary market in transferable securities plays an important role in the financing of economic agents;

Whereas, for that market to be able to play its role effectively, every measure should be taken to ensure that market operates smoothly;

Whereas the smooth operation of that market depends to a large extent on the confidence it inspires in investors;

Whereas the factors on which such confidence depends include the assurance afforded to investors that they are placed on an equal footing and that they will be protected against the improper use of inside information;

Whereas, by benefiting certain investors as compared with others, insider dealing is likely to undermine that confidence and may therefore prejudice the smooth operation of the market;

Whereas the necessary measures should therefore be taken to combat insider dealing;

Whereas in some Member States there are no rules or regulations prohibiting insider dealing and whereas the rules or regulations that do exist differ considerably from one Member State to another;

Whereas it is therefore advisable to adopt coordinated rules at a Community level in this field;

Whereas such coordinated rules also have the advantage of making it possible, through cooperation by the competent authorities, to combat transfrontier insider dealing more effectively;

[1] OJ No C 153, 11. 6. 1987, p. 8 and OJ No C 277, 27. 10. 1988, p. 13.

[2] OJ No C 187, 18. 7. 1987, p. 93 and Decision of 11 October 1989 (not yet published in the Official Journal).   [3] OJ No C 35, 8. 2. 1989, p. 22.

Whereas, since the acquisition or disposal of transferable securities necessarily involves a prior decision to acquire or to dispose taken by the person who undertakes one or other of these operations, the carrying-out of this acquisition or disposal does not constitute in itself the use of inside information;

Whereas insider dealing involves taking advantage of inside information; whereas the mere fact that market-makers, bodies authorized to act as *contrepartie*, or stockbrokers with inside information confine themselves, in the first two cases, to pursuing their normal business of buying or selling securities or, in the last, to carrying out an order should not in itself be deemed to constitute use of such inside information; whereas likewise the fact of carrying out transactions with the aim of stabilizing the price of new issues or secondary offers of transferable securities should not in itself be deemed to constitute use of inside information;

Whereas estimates developed from publicly available data cannot be regarded as inside information and whereas, therefore, any transaction carried out on the basis of such estimates does not constitute insider dealing within the meaning of this Directive;

Whereas communication of inside information to an authority, in order to enable it to ensure that the provisions of this Directive or other provisions in force are respected, obviously cannot be covered by the prohibitions laid down by this Directive,

Has adopted this directive:

Article 1. For the purposes of this Directive:

1. 'inside information' shall mean information which has not been made public of a precise nature relating to one or several issuers of transferable securities or to one or several transferable securities, which, if it were made public, would be likely to have a significant effect on the price of the transferable security or securities in question;

2. 'transferable securities' shall mean:

(a) shares and debt securities, as well as securities equivalent to shares and debt securities;

(b) contracts or rights to subscribe for, acquire or dispose of securities referred to in (a);

(c) futures contracts, options and financial futures in respect of securities referred to in (a);

(d) index contracts in respect of securities referred to in (a),

when admitted to trading on a market which is regulated and supervised by authorities recognized by public bodies, operates regularly and is accessible directly or indirectly to the public.

Article 2.   1. Each Member State shall prohibit any person who:

— by virtue of his membership of the administrative, management or supervisory bodies of the issuer,
— by virtue of his holding in the capital of the issuer, or
— because he has access to such information by virtue of the exercise of his employment, profession or duties,

possesses inside information from taking advantage of that information with full knowledge of the facts by acquiring or disposing of for his own account or for the account of a third party, either directly or indirectly, transferable securities of the issuer or issuers to which that information relates.

2. Where the person referred to in paragraph 1 is a company or other type of legal person, the prohibition laid down in that paragraph shall apply to the natural persons who take part in the decision to carry out the transaction for the account of the legal person concerned.

3. The prohibition laid down in paragraph 1 shall apply to any acquisition or disposal of transferable securities effected through a professional intermediary.

Each Member State may provide that this prohibition shall not apply to acquisitions or disposals of transferable securities effected without the involvement of a professional intermediary outside a market as defined in Article 1 (2) *in fine.*

4. This Directive shall not apply to transactions carried out in pursuit of monetary, exchange-rate or public debt-management policies by a sovereign State, by its central bank or any other body designated to that effect by the State, or by any person acting on their behalf. Member States may extend this exemption to their federated States or similar local authorities in respect of the management of their public debt.

Article 3.   Each Member State shall prohibit any person subject to the prohibition laid down in Article 2 who possesses inside information from:

(a) disclosing that inside information to any third party unless such disclosure is made in the normal course of the exercise of his employment, profession or duties;
(b) recommending or procuring a third party, on the basis of that inside information, to acquire or dispose of transferable securities admitted to trading on its securities markets as referred to in Article 1 (2) *in fine.*

Article 4.   Each Member State shall also impose the prohibition provided for in Article 2 on any person other than those referred to in that Article who with full knowledge of the facts possesses inside information, the direct or indirect source of which could not be other than a person referred to in Article 2.

Article 5. Each Member State shall apply the prohibitions provided for in Articles 2, 3 and 4, at least to actions undertaken within its territory to the extent that the transferable securities concerned are admitted to trading on a market of a Member State. In any event, each Member State shall regard a transaction as carried out within its territory if it is carried out on a market, as defined in Article 1 (2) *in fine*, situated or operating within that territory.

Article 6. Each Member State may adopt provisions more stringent than those laid down by this Directive or additional provisions, provided that such provisions are applied generally. In particular it may extend the scope of the prohibition laid down in Article 2 and impose on persons referred to in Article 4 the prohibitions laid down in Article 3.

Article 7. The provisions of Schedule C5 (a) of the Annex to Directive 79/279/EEC[1] shall also apply to companies and undertakings the transferable securities of which, whatever their nature, are admitted to trading on a market as referred to in Article 1 (2) *in fine* of this Directive.

Article 8. 1. Each Member State shall designate the administrative authority or authorities competent, if necessary in collaboration with other authorities to ensure that the provisions adopted pursuant to this Directive are applied. It shall so inform the Commission which shall transmit that information to all Member States.

2. The competent authorities must be given all supervisory and investigatory powers that are necessary for the exercise of their functions, where appropriate in collaboration with other authorities.

Article 9. Each Member State shall provide that all persons employed or formerly employed by the competent authorities referred to in Article 8 shall be bound by professional secrecy. Information covered by professional secrecy may not be divulged to any person or authority except by virtue of provisions laid down by law.

Article 10. 1. The competent authorities in the Member States shall cooperate with each other whenever necessary for the purpose of carrying out their duties, making use of the powers mentioned in Article 8 (2). To this end, and notwithstanding Article 9, they shall exchange any information required for that purpose, including information relating to actions prohibited, under the options given to Member States by Article 5 and by the second sentence of Article 6, only by the Member State requesting cooperation. Information thus exchanged shall be covered by the obligation of professional secrecy to which the persons employed or formerly employed by the competent authorities receiving the information are subject.

[1] OJ No L 66, 16. 3. 1979, p. 21.

2. The competent authorities may refuse to act on a request for information:

(a) where communication of the information might adversely affect the sovereignty, security or public policy of the State addressed;

(b) where judicial proceedings have already been initiated in respect of the same actions and against the same persons before the authorities of the State addressed or where final judgment has already been passed on such persons for the same actions by the competent authorities of the State addressed.

3. Without prejudice to the obligations to which they are subject in judicial proceedings under criminal law, the authorities which receive information pursuant to paragraph 1 may use it only for the exercise of their functions within the meaning of Article 8 (1) and in the context of administrative or judicial proceedings specifically relating to the exercise of those functions. However, where the competent authority communicating information consents thereto, the authority receiving the information may use it for other purposes or forward it to other States' competent authorities.

Article 11.   The Community may, in conformity with the Treaty, conclude agreements with non-member countries on the matters governed by this Directive.

Article 12.   The Contact Committee set up by Article 20 of Directive 79/279/EEC shall also have as its function:

(a) to permit regular consultation on any practical problems which arise from the application of this Directive and on which exchanges of view are deemed useful;

(b) to advise the Commission, if necessary, on any additions or amendments to be made to this Directive.

Article 13.   Each Member State shall determine the penalties to be applied for infringement of the measures taken pursuant to this Directive. The penalties shall be sufficient to promote compliance with those measures.

Article 14.   1. Member States shall take the measures necessary to comply with this Directive before 1 June 1992. They shall forthwith inform the Commission thereof.

2. Member States shall communicate to the Commission the provisions of national law which they adopt in the field governed by this Directive.

Article 15.   This Directive is addressed to the Member States.
Done at Brussels, 13 November 1989.

For the Council, The President, P. Bérégovoy

The Convention on Insider Trading

PREAMBLE

The member States of the Council of Europe, signatories hereto,

Considering that the aim of the Council is to achieve a greater unity between its members;

Considering that certain financial transactions in securities traded on stock exchanges are carried out by persons seeking to avoid losses or to make profits by using the privileged information available to them, thus undermining equality of opportunity as between investors and the credibility of the market;

Considering that such behaviour is also proving dangerous for the economies of the member States concerned and in particular for the proper functioning of the stock markets;

Considering that, because of the internationalization of markets and the ease of present-day communications, operations of this nature are carried out sometimes on the market of a State by persons not resident in that State or acting through persons not resident there;

Considering that efforts to counter such practices which are already being made on the domestic level in many member States make it essential to set up specific machinery to deal with these situations and co-ordinate endeavours at international level;

Have agreed as follows:

CHAPTER I. DEFINITIONS

Article 1. 1. For the purposes of this Convention an irregular operation of insider trading means an irregular operation carried out by a person:

(a) who is the president or chairman, or a member of a board of directors or other administrative or supervisory organ, or is the authorized agent or in the employment of an issuer of securities, and has effected or caused to be effected an operation on an organized stock market knowingly using information not yet disclosed to the public, the possession of which he obtained by reason of his occupation and the disclosure of which was likely to have a significant influence on the market, with a view to securing an advantage for himself or a third party.

(b) who has entered into the transactions described above knowingly using not yet disclosed information which he obtained in the performance of his duties or in the course of his occupation;

(c) who has entered into the transactions described above knowingly using not yet disclosed information communicated to him by one of the persons mentioned in (a) or (b) above.

2. For the purposes of applying this Convention:

(a) the expression 'organized stock market' signifies stock markets subject to regulations established by authorities recognized by the Government for the purpose;

(b) the term 'stock' signifies transferable securities issued according to the national legislation of each Party by business firms or companies or other issuers, where such securities may be bought and sold on a market organized in accordance with the provisions of paragraph (a) above, as well as other transferable securities admitted on that market in conformity with the national rules applicable to it;

(c) the expression 'operation' signifies any act on an organized stock market which gives or may give entitlement to stock as provided for in paragraph (b) above.

CHAPTER II. EXCHANGE OF INFORMATION

Article 2.   The Parties undertake, in accordance with the provisions of this Chapter, to provide each other with the greatest possible measure of mutual assistance in the exchange of information relating to matters establishing or giving rise to the belief that irregular operations of insider trading have been carried out.

Article 3.   Each Party may, by a declaration to the Secretary General of the Council of Europe, undertake to provide other Parties, subject to reciprocity, with the greatest possible measure of mutual assistance in the exchange of information necessary for the surveillance of operations carried out in the organized stock markets which could adversely affect equal access to information for all users of the stock market or the quality of the information supplied to investors in order to ensure honest dealing.

Article 4.   1. Each Party shall designate one or more authorities actually responsible for submitting any request for assistance, and for receiving and taking action on requests for assistance from the corresponding authorities designated by each Party.

2. Each Party shall, in a declaration addressed to the Secretary General of the Council of Europe, indicate the name and address of the authority or authorities designated in accordance with the provisions of this Article and any modification thereto.

3. The Secretary General shall notify these declarations to the other Parties.

Article 5. 1. Reasons shall be given for making a request for assistance.

2. The request shall contain a description of the facts establishing or giving rise to the belief that irregular operations of insider trading have been carried out or, if assistance is requested according to the rules laid down by Parties under Article 3, reference to the principles mentioned in that Article which have been violated.

3. The request shall contain reference to the provisions by virtue of which the operations are irregular in the State of the requesting authority.

4. The request shall be in or translated into one of the official languages of the State of the requested authority, or in one of the official languages of the Council of Europe.

5. The request shall specify:

(a) the requesting authority and the requested authority;

(b) the information sought by the requesting authority, the persons or bodies which may be in possession of it, or the place where it may be available;

(c) the reasons for and the purpose of the requesting authority's application, and the use it will make of the information under its national law; and

(d) how soon a response is required and, in cases of urgency, the reasons therefor.

Article 6. 1. The execution of requests for assistance by the requested authority is carried out in accordance with the rules and procedures laid down by the law of the Party in which that authority operates.

2. When the search for information so requires, and in the absence of specific provisions, the rules laid down by national law for obtaining evidence shall be capable of being applied by the requested authority or on its behalf. Sanctions laid down for breaches of professional secrecy shall not apply in regard to the information provided compulsorily in the course of enquiries.

3. These provisions shall not prejudice the rights accorded to the defendant by national law.

4. Save to the extent strictly necessary to carry out the request, the requested authority and the persons seeking the information requested are bound to maintain secrecy about the request, the component parts of the request and the information so gathered.

5. However, at the time of the designation of the authority, provided for by Article 4, each Party shall declare the derogations to the principle set forth in paragraph 4 of this Article possibly imposed or permitted by national law:

— either to guarantee free access of citizens to the files of the administration;
— or when the designated authority is obliged to denounce to other
administrative or judicial authorities information communicated or
gathered within the framework of the request;
— or, provided the requesting authority has been informed, to investigate
violations of the law of the requested Party or to secure compliance with
such law.

Article 7. 1. The requesting authority may not use the information
supplied for purposes other than those set out in its request.

2. The requested authority may refuse to supply the requested information or subsequently oppose its use for purposes set out in the request or fix
certain conditions unless:

(a) the facts are within the scope of Article 1 and
(b) the purposes set out are in conformity with the aims defined in Article 2
and
(c) the facts constitute in each State an irregularity as regards the rules of
both States.

3. When the requesting authority wishes to use the information supplied
for purposes other than those set out in the initial request it must inform in
advance the requested authority who may refuse to consent to such use
unless the conditions in paragraph 2 above are fulfilled.

4. The information supplied may be used before a criminal court only in
cases where it could have been obtained by application of Chapter III.

5. No authority of the requesting Party may use or transmit this information for tax, customs or currency purposes unless otherwise provided in a
declaration by the requested Party.

Article 8. The requested authority may refuse to give effect to the request
for assistance or to supply the information obtained, if:

(a) the request is not in conformity with this Convention;
(b) the communication of the information obtained might constitute an
infringment of the sovereignty, security, essential interests or public
policy (ordre public) of the requested Party;
(c) the irregularities to which the requested information relates or the
sanctions provided for such irregularities are time-barred under the law
of the requesting or of the requested Party;
(d) the requested information relates to matters which arose before the
Convention entered into force for the requesting or the requested Party;
(e) proceedings have already been commenced before the authorities in the
requested Party in respect of the same matters and against the same

persons, or if they have been finally adjudicated upon in respect of the same matters by the competent authorities of the requested Party;

(f) the authorities of the requested Party have decided not to commence proceedings or to stop proceedings in respect of the same matters.

Article 9.   The requested authority shall, in so far as it is able to do so, supply the information requested by the requesting authority in the form desired by that authority or in the form currently in use between them.

Article 10.   1. Any Party which has ascertained that there has been a substantial breach by the requesting authority of the confidentiality of the information provided may suspend the application of Chapter II of this Convention with respect to the Party which has failed to discharge its obligation and shall notify the Secretary General of the Council of Europe of its decision. The Party may lift the suspension at any time and shall notify the Secretary General accordingly.

2.   Any Party which intends to make use of the procedure provided for in paragraph 1 must first give an opportunity to the Party concerned to make observations on the alleged breach of confidentiality.

3. The Secretary General of the Council of Europe shall inform the Member States and the Parties to this Convention of any use made of the procedure provided for in paragraph 1.

Article 11.   Parties may agree that, notwithstanding the provisions of Article 5.4, requests for assistance and replies thereto may be drawn up in the language of their choice and made according to simplified procedures or by employing means of communication other than the exchange of written correspondence.

CHAPTER III. MUTUAL ASSISTANCE IN CRIMINAL MATTERS

Article 12.   1. The Parties undertake to afford each other the widest measure of mutual assistance in criminal matters relating to offences involving insider trading.

2. Nothing in this Convention shall be construed as restricting or prejudicing the application of the European Convention on Mutual Assistance in Criminal Matters and the Additional Protocol thereto among States party to these instruments or of specific agreements or arrangements on mutual assistance in criminal matters in force between Parties.

CHAPTER IV. FINAL PROVISIONS

Article 13.   This Convention shall be open for signature by the Member

States of the Council of Europe. It shall be subject to ratification, acceptance or approval. Instruments of ratification, acceptance or approval shall be deposited with the Secretary General of the Council of Europe.

Article 14.   1. This Convention shall enter into force on the first day of the month following the expiration of a period of three months after the date on which three member States of the Council of Europe have expressed their consent to be bound by the Convention in accordance with the provisions of Article 13.

2. In respect of any member State which subsequently expresses its consent to be bound by it, the Convention shall enter into force on the first day of the month following the expiration of a period of three months after the date of the deposit of the instrument of ratification, acceptance or approval.

Article 15.   1. After the entry into force of this Convention, the Committee of Ministers of the Council of Europe may invite any State not a member of the Council of Europe or any international intergovernmental organization to accede to this Convention, by a decision taken by the majority provided for in Article 20d of the Statute of the Council of Europe and by the unanimous vote of the representatives of the Contracting States entitled to sit on the Committee.

2. In respect of any acceding State or international intergovernmental organisation, the Convention shall enter into force on the first day of the month following the expiration of a period of three months after the date of deposit of the instrument of accession with the Secretary General of the Council of Europe.

Article 16.   1. Any State may at the time of signature or when depositing its instrument of ratification, acceptance, approval or accession, specify the territory or territories to which this Convention shall apply.

2. Any Contracting State may at any later date, by a declaration addressed to the Secretary General of the Council of Europe, extend the application of this Convention to any other territory specified in the declaration. In respect of such territory the Convention shall enter into force on the first day of the month following the expiration of a period of three months after the date of receipt of such declaration by the Secretary General.

3. Any declaration made under the two preceding paragraphs may, in respect of any territory specified in such declaration, be withdrawn by a notification addressed to the Secretary General. The withdrawal shall become effective on the first day of the month following the expiration of a period of three months after the date of receipt of such notification by the Secretary General.

Article 17.   With prejudice to the application of Article 6 no reservation may be made to the Convention.

Article 18.   1. After the entry into force of the present Convention, a group of experts representing the Parties to the Convention and the member States of the Council of Europe not being Parties to the Convention shall be convened at the request of at least two Parties or on the initiative of the Secretary General of the Council of Europe.

2. This group shall have the task of preparing an evaluation of the application of the Convention and making appropriate suggestions.

Article 19.   Difficulties with regard to the interpretation and application of this Convention shall be settled by direct consultation between the competent administrative authorities and, if the need arises, through diplomatic channels.

Article 20.   1. Any Party may at any time denounce this Convention by means of a notification addressed to the Secretary General of the Council of Europe.

2. Such denunciation shall become effective on the first day of the month following the expiration of a period of three months after the date of receipt of the notification by the Secretary General; denunciation shall not prejudice requests already in progress at the time of denunciation.

Article 21.   The Secretary General of the Council of Europe shall notify the member States of the Council and any Party to this Convention, of:

(a) any signature;
(b) the deposit of any instrument of ratification, acceptance, approval or accession;
(c) any date of entry into force of this Convention in accordance with Articles 14, 15 and 16;
(d) any other act, notification or communication relating to this Convention.

In witness whereof the undersigned, being duly authorized thereto, have signed this Convention.

Done at Strasbourg, the 20th April 1989, in English and French, both texts being equally authentic, in a single copy which shall be desposited in the archives of the Council of Europe. The Secretary General of the Council of Europe shall transmit certified copies to each Member State of the Council of Europe and to any State and any international intergovernmental organisation invited to accede to this Convention.

Commission Recommendation

of 25 July 1977 concerning a European code of conduct
relating to transactions in transferable securities

(77/534/EEC)

EXPLANATORY MEMORANDUM

1. The objectives set out in Article 2 of the Treaty of Rome, particularly the harmonious development of economic activities in the Community, can only be achieved if sufficient capital is available, and the sources of capital are sufficiently diversified to enable investments in the common market to be financed as rationally as possible.

The role of the securities markets is to permit a very free interplay at all times between supply and demand for capital. Consequently, the proper working and the interpenetration of these markets must be regarded as an essential aspect of the establishment of a 'common market' in capital.

2. Although the existing differences between the various financial markets in the nine Member States have not so far constituted an insuperable barrier to a number of international transactions, the lack of full information on the securities themselves and ignorance or misunderstanding of the rules governing the various markets have certainly helped to confine the investments of the great majority of savers to the markets of the countries in which they live or to a few well-known major international securities.

A reduction in these disparities would therefore tend to encourage the interpenetration of the member countries' markets, particularly if this is accompanied by improving the safeguards available to savers.

I. THE EUROPEAN CODE OF CONDUCT IN THE CONTEXT OF APPROXIMATING THE LAWS OF THE MEMBER STATES

3. On the basis of a Decision adopted in 1968 on the provision of information to the public on securities and conditions governing transactions in them, the Commission has already carried out a certain amount of harmonization work in this sector, covering various specific aspects such as 'the content, checking and distribution of the prospectus to be published when securities issued by companies . . . are admitted to official stock exchange quotation'[1] and coordination of 'the conditions for the admission of securities to official stock exchange quotation'.[2]

---

[1] OJ No C 131, 13. 12. 1972.   [2] OJ No C 56, 10. 3. 1976.

4. In parallel with the work of harmonization by Directives, and without prejudice to this method which is the only one capable of attaining the objective of true European integration, the Commission is of the opinion that it could recommend to the Member States—in a document covering a range of problems connected with dealing in securities—that they should ensure the observation of certain basic principles. These principles are already widely recognized in all the countries of Europe, but restating and applying them will help to create a common set of professional ethics in an ever-changing field; this, in its turn, will considerably facilitate the process of harmonization through Directives by making clear in advance the approach the Commission will be adopting.

5. This code of conduct, to be issued in the form of a Commission recommendation, must be seen separately from the Commission's other harmonization work in this sector:

— because the ethical approach has been given priority over the legislative approach;
— because the Commission is anxious to take full account of the dynamics of the financial market and of business life, and consciously to adopt a positive attitude which seeks to improve the machinery of the market and the effectiveness of those operating on it;
— because some of the topics dealt with in a very general way in the code may be, and in some cases already are, the subject of proposals for Directives where a strict legal framework will be appropriate.

II. JURIDICIAL SCOPE OF THE COMMISSION'S RECOMMENDATION

6. The purpose of the present recommendation to the Member States is that they should ensure that those who are in a position to influence the workings of securities markets comply with the principles of the code of conduct; the Commission has consulted those involved and has ascertained that there is already broad support for the principles of the code.

7. Although most States are now conscious of the need to supervise financial markets, it is only too obvious that methods of supervision still differ widely.

The recommendation allows for these differences; it does not require the Member States to create special supervisory authorities, but merely to coordinate at national level the action of the various associations and bodies concerned.

8. It must, however, be stressed that the introduction of a code of conduct for securities transactions by means of a recommendation can in no way be an obstacle to the subsequent adoption of Directives or Regulations in one or other of the fields covered by it. A number of such instruments are in fact already under preparation.

9. In the same light, it is not impossible that certain States may feel legislation on some or all of the subjects covered by the code is necessary in order to comply with the recommendation.

III. THE CONTENT OF THE CODE

10. The code sets out a fundamental objective, certain general principles and a number of supplementary principles.

11. *The general principles* are the key provisions of the code and are of overriding importance.

They take priority over and go well beyond the detailed principles which follow them, and which are merely illustrations of them.

It is the general principles which will enable the fundamental objective of the code to be complied with; the content of the code must be understood and interpreted in the light of the general principles and not only by reference to the letter of the various supplementary principles.

A. *The first general principle* emphasizes the importance of this aspect of the interpretation of the code. It recalls that any transaction on the securities market must be carried out in compliance with the rules and practices in each State designed to ensure the proper working of the markets, the principles of the present code supplementing or strengthening such rules and practices.

B. *The second general principle* is that information provided to savers must be complete and accurate, since lack of knowledge is a source of imperfection in any market.

If the information is not provided, or if it is incomprehensible or wrongly interpreted by those for whom it is intended, or if it is deliberately slanted or distorted, the prices quoted may well become completely artificial and the market may cease to fulfil its role. Consequently, a large number of principles, in the second part, have been worked out to cover this problem (supplementary principles 7 to 15).

The need for properly distributed information covers a wide range of situations, as different as the issue or the negotiation of securities. Proposals for Directives have also been made in this connection (including a proposal concerning rules for admission to quotation).

C. *The third general principle* relates to equality of treatment for shareholders. Despite some criticism, the Commission has taken the view that the principle of equality of treatment should be retained, illustrating its application by two supplementary principles, with the accent mainly on a specific obligation to disclose information.

Supplementary principle 17 mentions equality of treatment for other shareholders where a controlling holding is transferred, but accepts that the protection of such shareholders could be achieved by other means; this takes account of the existence in Germany of a law limiting the powers of the dominant shareholder. It is important to realize that the fundamental principle of the equality of shareholders goes well beyond the scope of the code. It is not confined, even in the code, to the transfer of blocks of shares or to the few supplementary principles in the second part which may refer to this principle, such as the use of undisclosed information to the detriment of those not having access to it or the compartmentation of markets making it possible to give advantages to certain purchasers or sellers of securities over others.

Obviously, only a few of the situations in which such a principle might be relevant can be mentioned; any attempt to give a more detailed list of the cases in which the principle would involve the risk of leaving loopholes which would probably soon be exploited. This principle lays down an approach and a spirit in which certain transactions must be carried out.

D. *The fourth, fifth and sixth general principles* are more particularly concerned with certain categories of persons the importance of whose role in the realization of the code's objectives is beyond doubt, namely the members of companies' supervisory boards, company directors and company managers (principle 4), financial intermediaries and persons concerned professionally in transactions in securities (principles 5 and 6).

The fourth general principle recalls first that the code applies in particular to the members of companies' supervisory boards, company directors and company managers and then mentions more particularly their duty to refrain from any action liable to hamper the proper working of the market in their security or to harm the other shareholders.

Objectionable action on the market in the securities of a company by directors or managers is a term to be interpreted in the broad sense, since there may well be instances of failure to act which are just as reprehensible, or more reprehensible, than positive action.

The fifth general principle recommends that persons professionally engaged in stock exchange transactions, or at least all 'persons dealing regularly on the securities markets', avoid jeopardizing, by seeking immediate and unfair profit, the credibility and the effectiveness of the market which it is in their own interest to foster.

Conflicts of interest liable to arise, e.g. in the various departments of a bank, because of the diversity of the roles which a banker has to play for his various customers, led to the enunciation of the *sixth general principle*.

While conceding that it is very difficult to lay down precise limits as far as discretion is concerned, it should be emphasized that ways and means must be sought of avoiding conflicts of this nature. An example will illustrate how difficult it is to define the scope of this rule: should confidential information be kept so secret in a financial establishment that it would be wrong to advise against an investment (through without saying why the investment would be a bad one) when the aim would be not to achieve a ggain but to avoid a loss? In such a case, the banker should be free to give such informed advice to the customer, and this does indeed seem to be a reasonable solution; however, only practice will show whether this interpretation of supplementary principle 8 can become the source of impropriety, and whether the Commission's recommendation will have to be strengthened on this specific point.

12. *The supplementary principles*: as their name suggests, their purpose is to supplement the general principles by making them clearer and illustrating them. They are not exhaustive; they can be supplemented through the meetings of the liaison committee responsible for applying the code, in the light of actual situations encountered on the various European markets. The supplementary principles can be divided into two parts.

A. *The first supplementary principles* indicate a number of aspects of what the expression 'fair behaviour' by financial intermediaries is to be taken to mean.

In addition to compliance with laws, regulations and current practice, supplementary principles 1 to 6 describe a number of rules of conduct specific to intermediaries.

The main rule concerns, of course, the recommendation to carry out orders on an organized market and the limits set to acting as counter-party and to offsetting orders. The Commission's recommendation does not advise formally against these operations, but it is felt that they should be brought under the supervision of the supervisory authorities where these authorities can in fact assume responsibility for them.

B. *The following supplementary principles* from rule 7 onwards until the end refer to the need for information.

It is clear that many improprieties would be avoided if accurate information were disclosed very quickly and the time during which important information was kept secret were thus cut to a minimum.

The principles relating to information can themselves be divided into several parts depending on whether they refer:

(a) to the creation of an artificial market (principle 7);
(b) to the improper use of price-sensitive information (principles 8 to 10);

(c) to information to be provided to the public by the market authorities and companies (principles 11 to 14);

(d) to equality of information to which all investors must be entitled (principles 15 and 16); and lastly,

(e) to information to be provided where there is acquisition or, where appropriate, sale of a holding conferring *de jure* or *de facto* control of a company (principles 17 and 18).

IV. IMPLEMENTATION OF THE EUROPEAN CODE OF CONDUCT

13. In recommending the European code of conduct to the Member States, the Commission is of course well aware that a recommendation does not bind the States as to the results to be achieved; the successful implementation of the code will therefore depend to a great extent on the active cooperation of those affected by it, in particular on the authority of the body or bodies which are to supervise implementation.

14. An essential feature is that, on the basis of existing structures, there should be in each Member State at least one body (supervisory authority, professional association, etc.) responsible for supervising the implementation of the code at national level.

However, the choice of the appropriate body is a matter for the Member State concerned.

The code does not require that these supervisory bodies should have the power normally vested in public authorities, since the code will not carry penal sanctions.

15. However, since the code should be complied with throughout the Community, it will be desirable that representatives of each of the supervisory bodies should come together in a liaison committee.

The committee could advise the Commission on the development of the code, in the light of the problems and practices encountered in its application.

For these reasons, under the provisions of the Treaty establishing the European Economic Community, and in particular Article 155 thereof, the Commission recommends the Member States, without prejudice to the Regulations or administrative provisions already in existence:

1. to ensure that those who operate on securities markets, or who are in a position to influence the working of these markets, respect the fundamental objective, the general principles and the supplementary provisions of the European code of conduct annexed hereto;

2. to this end, to coordinate the action of the professional associations and the national authorities charged, in each State, with the supervision of the proper functioning of the market and the conduct of those who operate on it;

3. to appoint one or more representatives from these associations or authorities who shall be responsible for informing the Commission each year, beginning one year after the transmission of this recommendation, of any measures adopted to implement it and of the experience in applying them, of any difficulties encountered and of any suggestions for additions or amendments to the European code of conduct;
4. to take any other measures they may consider necessary to promote the principles of the code and to supervise their application.

Done at Brussels, 25 July 1977.

For the Commission, Christopher Tugendhat, *Member of the Commission*

ANNEX

European Code of Conduct Relating to Transactions in Transferable Securities

Fundamental objective

This code of conduct is to be seen in the general context of the development and integration of securities markets within the European Community, and seeks to establish certain general principles, supported by supplementary guidelines.

The code's objective is to establish standards of ethical behaviour on a Community-wide basis, so as to promote the effective functioning of securities markets (i.e. by creating the best possible conditions for matching supply and demand for capital), and to safeguard the public interest.

Definitions

In the code, the following expressions shall have the meanings ascribed to them below:

— 'transferable securities' shall mean all securities which are or may be the subject of dealings on an organized market;
— 'financial intermediaries' shall mean all persons professionally concerned in transactions in transferable securities;
— 'principles' shall mean all persons who give orders to buy or sell transferable securities and in particular those occupying a strategic position with regard to a security and the market in it (e.g. company directors or managers, holders or acquirers of major shareholdings);*

---

* Corrected version of this indent supplied from OJ 1977, L 294/28.

— 'securities markets' shall mean the official stock exchange and all the markets organized by or under the supervision of the competent authorities and also all transactions in transferable securities as defined above including privately negotiated dealings between individuals in transferable securities—the word 'market' (in the singular) being used only for the official stock exchange and the organized markets;

— 'competent authorities' are those who have the tasks of ensuring the proper working of the market and the proper flow of information for the market at national level—principally the stock exchange authorities and supervisory agencies.

General principles

1. The objective of this code and the general principles should be observed even in cases not expressly covered by supplementary principles. Every transaction carried out on the securities markets should be in conformity with not only the letter but also the spirit of the laws and regulations in force in each Member State, and also the principles of good conduct already applying to these markets, or recommended by this code.

2. Information should be available to the public which is fair, accurate, clear, adequate and which is given in good time.

The information should be provided in such a way that its significance and intent can be easily understood. Any person, who by virtue of his profession or duties has the duty or the means of informing the public, is under a special obligation to ensure that it is kept properly informed, and that no particular class of persons attains a privileged position.

3. Equality of treatment should be guaranteed to all holders of securities of the same type issued by the same company; in particular, any act resulting directly or indirectly in the transfer of a holding conferring *de jure* or *de facto* control of a company whose securities are dealt in on the market, should have regard to the right of all shareholders to be treated in the same fashion.

4. When the securities of a company are dealt in on the market, the members of its supervisory board, its directors, managers, and persons exercising *de jure* or *de facto* control, should act in such manner as to ensure that the fundamental objective of this code of conduct is realized. They have a particular duty to avoid any action which would operate to the detriment of fair dealings in the securities concerned, or prejudice the rights of other shareholders.

5. Persons dealing regularly on the securities markets should act fairly in accordance with the code's objective, even if this could in certain cases result in their having to forgo short-term gains.

6. Financial intermediaries should endeavour to avoid all conflicts of interest, whether as between themselves and their clients or other persons

with whom they have a fiduciary relationship, or as between these two last-mentioned categories of persons. If, however, such a conflict arises, they should not seek to gain a direct or indirect personal advantage from the situation, and should avoid any prejudice to their clients or other persons with whom they have fiduciary relationship.

Supplementary principles

1. All persons dealing regularly on the securities markets have a duty to promote investors' confidence in the fairness of the market by observance of the best standards of commercial probity and professional conduct.

2. Financial intermediaries have a special responsibility to observe the fundamental objective and the general principles of this code of conduct. In particular, they should not connive at any breach by other persons of the provisions and principles referred to in the second paragraph of general principle 1, and they should not engage in manipulation which could distort the normal operation of the market.

3. No person should incite another person, whether or not an intermediary, to contravene the provisions and principles referred to in the second paragraph of general principle 1, nor exert pressure to obtain:

(1) information which is not public and which cannot be divulged without contravening rules relating to such information, or
(2) the carrying out of an irregular or dishonest transaction.

4. Financial intermediaries should seek out and recommend the best conditions for their clients for the execution of orders which are given to them, while observing the fundamental objective and general principles of the code.

They should execute the orders which they are given on an organized market, unless the principal has given express instructions to the contrary. However, if the circumstances of the transaction or the nature of the securities makes it difficult even impossible to execute orders on an organized market, financial intermediaries may act as counterparties to their clients or offset orders outside the market, provided that they ensure that this does not prejudice their clients' interests, and provided that they are in a position to reply to any request on the part of the competent authorities as regards the justification for, the number of, and the conditions applying to, transactions carried out in this manner.

5. Financial intermediaries should refrain from encouraging sales or purchases with the sole object of generating commission.

6. Financial intermediaries should not disclose the identity of their principals except in cases when this is required by national regulations or the

control authorities (and also in the investigation of crimes or other serious misdeeds).

7. Any attempt or manipulation by persons acting separately or in concert with others, which aims at or results in the rise or fall in the price of securities by fraudulent means, is contrary to the fundamental objective of this code.

Fraudulent means are considered in particular to be the publication or diffusion of information which is false, exaggerated or tendentious, and also the use of other devices aimed at disrupting the markets' normal operation.

Financial intermediaries and members of the supervisory board, the directors and managers of companies whose securities are dealt in on the securities markets, who become aware of any such attempt or manipulation should endeavour to take the necessary steps to thwart it. They should inform the competent authorities and the companies concerned without delay.

8. Financial intermediaries should endeavour to keep secret, even as between different departments or services of the same organization, information which they acquire in the course of carrying out their duties which is not yet public and which is price-sensitive.

In particular, financial intermediaries should not use such information in transactions which they carry out for their own account on the securities markets, nor in transactions upon which they advise their clients or carry out for their account.

9. Any person who comes into possession of information, in exercising his profession or carrying out his duties, which is not public and which relates to a company or to the market in its securities or to any event of general interest to the market, which is price-sensitive, should refrain from carrying out, directly or indirectly, any transaction in which such information is used, and should refrain from giving the information to another person so that he may profit from it before the information becomes public.

10. Securities markets should be sufficiently open to prevent their being fragmented, whereby the same security can be dealt in at the same time on different markets in different prices.

11. When a security is dealt in on the market the public should be informed not only of the different prices at which transactions take place, but also of the volume of dealings, unless the organization of the market makes it possible for the public to assess the liquidity of its investment by some other means.

12. Every company whose securities are dealt in on the market should publish periodically, and at least every six months, information which is clear, precise, complete and up-to-date concerning its business operations, results, and financial position. Any fact or important decision capable of

having an appreciable effect on the price of securities should also be made public without delay.

13. When a fact or important decision, referred to in the preceding provision, cannot be made public without delay, for example because certain formalities have not yet been completed or because the company would be seriously prejudiced as a result, but the company nevertheless considers that there is a risk of leaks, the company should inform the competent authorities of the position. The latter should take the necessary steps to safeguard the market's proper operation until the relevant fact or decision can be made public. In particular they may, if this step appears unavoidable, suspend transactions for the necessary period.

14. It is desirable that a public issue of securities should be preceded by the publication of a prospectus. The existence of the prospectus and the place or places where it may be obtained should be indicated in any publicity concerning such issue.

15. No investor or group of investors should be given more favourable treatment as regards information than other investors or the public. All investors should have free access to information.

16. On the occasion of each issue of securities of the same type which are or may be dealt in on several markets at the same time, the issuer should endeavour not to give more favourable treatment to one market than to another.

17. Any transaction resulting in the transfer of a holding conferring control in the sense referred to in general principle 3 should not be carried out in a surreptitious fashion without informing the other shareholders and the market control authorities.

It is desirable that all the shareholders of the company whose control has changed hands should be offered the opportunity of disposing of their securities on identical conditions, unless they have the benefit of alternative safeguards which can be regarded as equivalent.

18. Any acquisition, or attempted acquisition on the market, separately or by concerted action, of a holding conferring control in the sense referred to in general principle 3, without informing the public, is against the objective of this code.

E

European Economic Interest Grouping[1]

---

[1] See *The European Economic Interest Grouping Regulations 1989* (SI 1989, No. 638).

Council Regulation

of 25 July 1985 on the European Economic Interest
Grouping (EEIG)

(85/2137/EEC)

The Council of the European Communities,

Having regard to the Treaty establishing the European Economic
Community, and in particular Article 235 thereof,

Having regard to the proposal from the Commission,[1]

Having regard to the opinion of the European Parliament,[2]

Having regard to the opinion of the Economic and Social Committee,[3]

Whereas a harmonious development of economic activities and a continuous and balanced expansion throughout the Community depend on the
establishment and smooth functioning of a common market offering conditions analogous to those of a national market; whereas to bring about this
single market and to increase its unity a legal framework which facilitates the
adaptation of their activities to the economic conditions of the Community
should be created for natural persons, companies, firms and other legal
bodies in particular; whereas to that end it is necessary that those natural
persons, companies, firms and other legal bodies should be able to
cooperate effectively across frontiers;

Whereas cooperation of this nature can encounter legal, fiscal or psycho-
logical difficulties; whereas the creation of an appropriate Community legal
instrument in the form of a European Economic Interest Grouping would
contribute to the achievement of the abovementioned objectives and
therefore proves necessary;

Whereas the Treaty does not provide the necessary powers for the
creation of such a legal instrument;

Whereas a grouping's ability to adapt to economic conditions must be
guaranteed by the considerable freedom for its members in their contractual
relations and the internal organization of the grouping;

Whereas a grouping differs from a firm or company principally in its
purpose, which is only to facilitate or develop the economic activities of its
members to enable them to improve their own results, whereas, by reason of
that ancillary nature, a grouping's activities must be related to the economic

---

[1] OJ C 14, 15. 2. 1974, p. 30, and OJ C 103, 28. 4. 1978, p. 4.

[2] OJ C 163, 11. 7. 1977, p. 17.

[3] OJ C 108, 15. 5. 1975, p. 46.

activities of its members but not replace them so that, to that extent, for example, a grouping may not itself, with regard to third parties, practise a profession, the concept of economic activities being interpreted in the widest sense;

Whereas access to grouping form must be made as widely available as possible to natural persons, companies, firms and other legal bodies, in keeping with the aims of this Regulation; whereas this Regulation shall not, however, prejudice the application at national level of legal rules and/or ethical codes concerning the conditions for the pursuit of business and professonal activities;

Whereas this Regulation does not itself confer on any person the right to participate in a grouping, even where the conditions it lays down are fulfilled;

Whereas the power provided by this Regulation to prohibit or restrict participation in a grouping on grounds of public interest is without prejudice to the laws of Member States which govern the pursuit of activities and which may provide further prohibitions or restrictions or otherwise control or supervise participation in a grouping by any natural person, company, firm or other legal body or any class of them;

Whereas, to enable a grouping to achieve its purpose, it should be endowed with legal capacity and provision should be made for it to be represented *vis-à-vis* third parties by an organ legally separate from its membership;

Whereas the protection of third parties requires widespread publicity; whereas the members of a grouping have unlimited joint and several liability for the grouping's debts and other liabilities, including those relating to tax or social security, without, however, that principle's affecting the freedom to exclude or restrict the liability of one or more of its members in respect of a particular debt or other liability by means of a specific contract between the grouping and a third party;

Whereas matters relating to the status or capacity of natural persons and to the capacity of legal persons are governed by national law;

Whereas the grounds for winding up which are peculiar to the grouping should be specific while referring to national law for its liquidation and the conclusion thereof;

Whereas groupings are subject to national laws relating to insolvency and cessation of payments; whereas such laws may provide other grounds for the winding up of groupings;

Whereas this Regulation provides that the profits or losses resulting from the activities of a grouping shall be taxable only in the hands of its members; whereas it is understood that otherwise national tax laws apply, particularly as regards the apportionment of profits, tax procedures and any obligations imposed by national tax law;

Whereas in matters not covered by this Regulation the laws of the Member States and Community law are applicable, for example with regard to:

(a) social and labour laws,
(b) competition law,
(c) intellectual property law;

Whereas the activities of groupings are subject to the provisions of Member States' laws on the pursuit and supervision of activities; whereas in the event of abuse or circumvention of the laws of a Member State by a grouping or its members that Member State may impose appropriate sanctions;

Whereas the Member States are free to apply or to adopt any laws, regulations or administrative measures which do not conflict with the scope or objectives of this Regulation;

Whereas this Regulation must enter into force immediately in its entirety; whereas the implementation of some provisions must nevertheless be deferred in order to allow the Member States first to set up the necessary machinery for the registration of groupings in their territories and the disclosure of certain matters relating to groupings; whereas, with effect from the date of implementation of this Regulation, groupings set up may operate without territorial restrictions,

Has adopted this regulation:

Article 1. 1. European Economic Interest Groupings shall be formed upon the terms, in the manner and with the effects laid down in this Regulation.

Accordingly, parties intending to form a grouping must conclude a contract and have the registration provided for in Article 6 carried out.

2. A grouping so formed shall, from the date of its registration as provided for in Article 6, have the capacity, in its own name, to have rights and obligations of all kinds, to make contracts or accomplish other legal acts, and to sue and be sued.

3. The Member States shall determine whether or not groupings registered at their registries, pursuant to Article 6, have legal personality.

Article 2. 1. Subject to the provisions of this Regulation, the law applicable, on the one hand, to the contract for the formation of a grouping, except as regards matters relating to the status or capacity of natural persons and to the capacity of legal persons and, on the other hand, to the internal organization of a grouping shall be the internal law of the State in which the official address is situated, as laid down in the contract for the formation of the grouping.

2. Where a State comprises several territorial units, each of which has its own rules of law applicable to the matters referred to in paragraph 1, each territorial unit shall be considered as a State for the purposes of identifying the law applicable under this Article.

Article 3.   1. The purpose of a grouping shall be to facilitate or develop the economic activities of its members and to improve or increase the results of those activities; its purpose is not to make profits for itself.

Its activity shall be related to the economic activities of its members and must not be more than ancillary to those activities.

2. Consequently, a grouping may not:

(a) exercise, directly or indirectly, a power of management or supervision over its members' own activities or over the activities of another undertaking, in particular in the fields of personnel, finance and investment;

(b) directly or indirectly, on any basis whatsoever, hold shares of any kind in a member undertaking; the holding of shares in another undertaking shall be possible only in so far as it is necessary for the achievement of the grouping's objects and if it is done on its members' behalf;

(c) employ more than 500 persons;

(d) be used by a company to make a loan to a director of a company, or any person connected with him, when the making of such loans is restricted or controlled under the Member States' laws governing companies. Nor must a grouping be used for the transfer of any property between a company and a director, or any person connected with him, except to the extent allowed by the Member States' laws governing companies. For the purposes of this provision the making of a loan includes entering into any transaction or arrangement of similar effect, and property includes moveable and immoveable property;

(e) be a member of another European Economic Interest Grouping.

Article 4.   1. Only the following may be members of a grouping:

(a) companies or firms within the meaning of the second paragraph of Article 58 of the Treaty and other legal bodies governed by public or private law, which have been formed in accordance with the law of a Member State and which have their registered or statutory office and central administration in the Community; where, under the law of a Member State, a company, firm or other legal body is not obliged to have a registered or statutory office, it shall be sufficient for such a company, firm or other legal body to have its central administration in the Community;

(b) natural persons who carry on any industrial, commercial, craft or agricultural activity or who provide professional or other services in the Community.

2. A grouping must comprise at least:

(a) two companies, firms or other legal bodies, within the meaning of paragraph 1, which have their central administrations in different Member States, or

(b) two natural persons, within the meaning of paragraph 1, who carry on their principal activities in different Member States, or

(c) a company, firm or other legal body within the meaning of paragraph 1 and a natural person, of which the first has its central administration in one Member State and the second carries on his principal activity in another Member State.

3. A Member State may provide that groupings registered at its registries in accordance with Article 6 may have no more than 20 members. For this purpose, that Member State may provide that, in accordance with its laws, each member of a legal body formed under its laws, other than a registered company, shall be treated as a separate member of a grouping.

4. Any Member State may, on grounds of that State's public interest, prohibit or restrict participation in groupings by certain classes of natural persons, companies, firms, or other legal bodies.

Article 5. A contract for the formation of a grouping shall include at least:

(a) the name of the grouping preceded or followed either by the words 'European Economic Interest Grouping', or by the initials 'EEIG', unless those words or initials already form part of the name;

(b) the official address of the grouping;

(c) the objects for which the grouping is formed;

(d) the name, business name, legal form, permanent address or registered office, and the number and place of registration, if any, of each member of the grouping;

(e) the duration of the grouping, except where this is indefinite.

Article 6. A grouping shall be registered in the State in which it has its official address, at the registry designated pursuant to Article 39 (1).

Article 7. A contract for the formation of a grouping shall be filed at the registry referred to in Article 6.

The following documents and particulars must also be filed at that registry:

(a) any amendment to the contract for the formation of a grouping, including any change in the composition of a grouping;

(b) notice of the setting up or closure of any establishment of the grouping;

(c) any judicial decision establishing or declaring the nullity of a grouping, in accordance with Article 15;

(d) notice of the appointment of the manager or managers of a grouping, their names and any other identification particulars required by the law of the Member State in which the register is kept, notification that they may act alone or must act jointly, and the termination of any manager's appointment;

(e) notice of a member's assignment of his participation in a grouping or a proportion thereof, in accordance with Article 22 (1);

(f) any decision by members ordering or establishing the winding up of a grouping, in accordance with Article 31, or any judicial decision ordering such winding up, in accordance with Articles 31 or 32;

(g) notice of the appointment of the liquidator or liquidators of a grouping, as referred to in Article 35, their names and any other identification particulars required by the law of the Member State in which the register is kept, and the termination of any liquidator's appointment;

(h) notice of the conclusion of a grouping's liquidation, as referred to in Article 35 (2);

(i) any proposal to transfer the official address, as referred to in Article 14 (1);

(j) any clause exempting a new member from the payment of debts and other liabilities which originated prior to his admission, in accordance with Article 26 (2).

Article 8.   The following must be published, as laid down in Article 39, in the gazette referred to in paragraph 1 of that Article:

(a) the particulars which must be included in the contract for the formation of a grouping pursuant to Article 5, and any amendments thereto;

(b) the number, date and place of registration as well as notice of the termination of that registration;

(c) the documents and particulars referred to in Article 7 (b) to (j).

The particulars referred to in (a) and (b) must be published in full. The documents and particulars referred to in (c) may be published either in full or in extract form or by means of a reference to their filing at the registry, in accordance with the national legislation applicable.

Article 9.   1. The documents and particulars which must be published pursuant to this Regulation may be relied on by a grouping as against third parties under the conditions laid down by the national law applicable pursuant to Article 3 (5) and (7) of Council Directive 68/151/EEC of 9 March 1968 on coordination of safeguards which, for the protection of the interests of members and others, are required by Member States of companies within the meaning of the second paragraph of Article 58 of the Treaty, with a view to making such safeguards equivalent throughout the Community.[1]

2. If activities have been carried on on behalf of a grouping before its registration in accordance with Article 6 and if the grouping does not, after its registration, assume the obligations arising out of such activities, the natural persons, companies, firms or other legal bodies which carried on those activities shall bear unlimited joint and several liability for them.

Article 10. Any grouping establishment situated in a Member State other than that in which the official address is situated shall be registered in that State. For the purpose of such registration, a grouping shall file, at the appropriate registry in that Member State, copies of the documents which must be filed at the registry of the Member State in which the official address is situated, together, if necessary, with a translation which conforms with the practice of the registry where the establishment is registered.

Article 11. Notice that a grouping has been formed or that the liquidation of a grouping has been concluded stating the number, date and place of registration and the date, place and title of publication, shall be given in the *Official Journal of the European Communities* after it has been published in the gazette referred to in Article 39 (1).

Article 12. The official address referred to in the contract for the formation of a grouping must be situated in the Community.

The official address must be fixed either:

(a) where the grouping has its central administration, or
(b) where one of the members of the grouping has its central administration or, in the case of a natural person, his principal activity, provided that the grouping carries on an activity there.

Article 13. The official address of a grouping may be transferred within the Community.

When such a transfer does not result in a change in the law applicable pursuant to Article 2, the decision to transfer shall be taken in accordance with the conditions laid down in the contract for the formation of the grouping.

Article 14. 1. When the transfer of the official address results in a change in the law applicable pursuant to Article 2, a transfer proposal must be drawn up, filed and published in accordance with the conditions laid down in Articles 7 and 8.

[1] OJ L 65, 14. 3. 1968, p. 8.

No decision to transfer may be taken for two months after publication of the proposal. Any such decision must be taken by the members of the grouping unanimously. The transfer shall take effect on the date on which the grouping is registered, in accordance with Article 6, at the registry for the new official address. That registration may not be effected until evidence has been produced that the proposal to transfer the official address has been published.

2. The termination of a grouping's registration at the registry for its old official address may not be effected until evidence has been produced that the grouping has been registered at the registry for its new official address.

3. Upon publication of a grouping's new registration the new official address may be relied on as against third parties in accordance with the conditions referred to in Article 9 (1); however, as long as the termination of the grouping's registration at the registry for the old official address has not been published, third parties may continue to rely on the old official address unless the grouping proves that such third parties were aware of the new official address.

4. The laws of a Member State may provide that, as regards groupings registered under Article 6 in that Member State, the transfer of an official address which would result in a change of the law applicable shall not take effect if, within the two-month period referred to in paragraph 1, a competent authority in that Member State opposes it. Such opposition may be based only on grounds of public interest. Review by a judicial authority must be possible.

Article 15.   1. Where the law applicable to a grouping by virtue of Article 2 provides for the nullity of that grouping, such nullity must be established or declared by judicial decision. However, the court to which the matter is referred must, where it is possible for the affairs of the grouping to be put in order, allow time to permit that to be done.

2. The nullity of a grouping shall entail its liquidation in accordance with the conditions laid down in Article 35.

3. A decision establishing or declaring the nullity of a grouping may be relied on as against third parties in accordance with the conditions laid down in Article 9 (1).

Such a decision shall not of itself affect the validity of liabilities, owed by or to a grouping, which originated before it could be relied on as against third parties in accordance with the conditions laid down in the previous subparagraph.

Article 16.   1. The organs of a grouping shall be the members acting collectively and the manager or managers.

A contract for the formation of a grouping may provide for other organs; if it does it shall determine their powers.

2. The members of a grouping, acting as a body, may take any decision for the purpose of achieving the objects of the grouping.

Article 17. 1. Each member shall have one vote. The contract for the formation of a grouping may, however, give more than one vote to certain members, provided that no one member holds a majority of the votes.

2. A unanimous decision by the members shall be required to:

(a) alter the objects of a grouping;
(b) alter the number of votes allotted to each member;
(c) alter the conditions for the taking of decisions;
(d) extend the duration of a grouping beyond any period fixed in the contract for the formation of the grouping;
(e) alter the contribution by every member or by some members to the grouping's financing;
(f) alter any other obligation of a member, unless otherwise provided by the contract for the formation of the grouping;
(g) make any alteration to the contract for the formation of the grouping not covered by this paragraph, unless otherwise provided by that contract.

3. Except where this Regulation provides that decisions must be taken unanimously, the contract for the formation of a grouping may prescribe the conditions for a quorum and for a majority, in accordance with which the decisions, or some of them, shall be taken. Unless otherwise provided for by the contract, decisions shall be taken unanimously.

4. On the initiative of a manager or at the request of a member, the manager or managers must arrange for the members to be consulted so that the latter can take a decision.

Article 18. Each member shall be entitled to obtain information from the manager or managers concerning the grouping's business and to inspect the grouping's books and business records.

Article 19. 1. A grouping shall be managed by one or more natural persons appointed in the contract for the formation of the grouping or by decision of the members.

No person may be a manager of a grouping if:

(a) by virtue of the law applicable to him, or
(b) by virtue of the internal law of the State in which the grouping has its official address, or

(c) following a judicial or administrative decision made or recognized in a Member State

he may not belong to the administrative or management body of a company, may not manage an undertaking or may not act as manager of a European Economic Interest Grouping.

2. A Member State may, in the case of groupings registered at their registries pursuant to Article 6, provide that legal persons may be managers on condition that such legal persons designate one or more natural persons, whose particulars shall be the subject of the filing provisions of Article 7 (d) to represent them.

If a Member State exercises this option, it must provide that the representative or representatives shall be liable as if they were themselves managers of the groupings concerned.

The restrictions imposed in paragraph 1 shall also apply to those representatives.

3. The contract for the formation of a grouping or, failing that, a unanimous decision by the members shall determine the conditions for the appointment and removal of the manager or managers and shall lay down their powers.

Article 20.   1. Only the manager or, where there are two or more, each of the managers shall represent a grouping in respect of dealings with third parties.

Each of the managers shall bind the grouping as regards third parties when he acts on behalf of the grouping, even where his acts do not fall within the objects of the grouping, unless the grouping proves that the third party knew or could not, under the circumstances, have been unaware that the act fell outside the objects of the grouping; publication of the particulars referred to in Article 5 (c) shall not of itself be proof thereof.

No limitation on the powers of the manager or managers, whether deriving from the contract for the formation of the grouping or from a decision by the members, may be relied on as against third parties even if it is published.

2. The contract for the formation of the grouping may provide that the grouping shall be validly bound only by two or more managers acting jointly. Such a clause may be relied on as against third parties in accordance with the conditions referred to in Article 9 (1) only if it is published in accordance with Article 8.

Article 21.   1. The profits resulting from a grouping's activities shall be deemed to be the profits of the members and shall be apportioned among them in the proportions laid down in the contract for the formation of the grouping or, in the absence of any such provision, in equal shares.

2. The members of a grouping shall contribute to the payment of the amount by which expenditure exceeds income in the proportions laid down in the contract for the formation of the grouping or, in the absence of any such provision, in equal shares.

Article 22.   1. Any member of a grouping may assign his participation in the grouping, or a proportion thereof, either to another member or to a third party; the assignment shall not take effect without the unanimous authorization of the other members.

2. A member of a grouping may use his participation in the grouping as security only after the other members have given their unanimous authorization, unless otherwise laid down in the contract for the formation of the grouping. The holder of the security may not at any time become a member of the grouping by virtue of that security.

Article 23.   No grouping may invite investment by the public.

Article 24.   1. The members of a grouping shall have unlimited joint and several liability for its debts and other liabilities of whatever nature. National law shall determine the consequences of such liability.

2. Creditors may not proceed against a member for payment in respect of debts and other liabilities, in accordance with the conditions laid down in paragraph 1, before the liquidation of a grouping is concluded, unless they have first requested the grouping to pay and payment has not been made within an appropriate period.

Article 25.   Letters, order forms and similar documents must indicate legibly:

(a) the name of the grouping preceded or followed either by the words 'European Economic Interest Grouping' or by the initials 'EEIG', unless those words or initials already occur in the name;
(b) the location of the registry referred to in Article 6, in which the grouping is registered, together with the number of the grouping's entry at the registry;
(c) the grouping's official address;
(d) where applicable, that the managers must act jointly;
(e) where applicable, that the grouping is in liquidation, pursuant to Articles 15, 31, 32 or 36.

Every establishment of a grouping, when registered in accordance with Article 10, must give the above particulars, together with those relating to its own registration, on the documents referred to in the first paragraph of this Article uttered by it.

Article 26. 1. A decision to admit new members shall be taken unanimously by the members of the grouping.

2. Every new member shall be liable, in accordance with the conditions laid down in Article 24, for the grouping's debts and other liabilities, including those arising out of the grouping's activities before his admission.

He may, however, be exempted by a clause in the contract for the formation of the grouping or in the instrument of admission from the payment of debts and other liabilities which originated before his admission. Such a clause may be relied on as against third parties, under the conditions referred to in Article 9 (1), only if it is published in accordance with Article 8.

Article 27. 1. A member of a grouping may withdraw in accordance with the conditions laid down in the contract for the formation of a grouping or, in the absence of such conditions, with the unanimous agreement of the other members.

Any members of a grouping may, in addition, withdraw on just and proper grounds.

2. Any member of a grouping may be expelled for the reasons listed in the contract for the formation of the grouping and, in any case, if he seriously fails in his obligations or if he causes or threatens to cause serious disruption in the operation of the grouping.

Such expulsion may occur only by the decision of a court to which joint application has been made by a majority of the other members, unless otherwise provided by the contract for the formation of a grouping.

Article 28. 1. A member of a grouping shall cease to belong to it on death or when he no longer complies with the conditions laid down in Article 4 (1).

In addition, a Member State may provide, for the purposes of its liquidation, winding up, insolvency or cessation of payments laws, that a member shall cease to be a member of any grouping at the moment determined by those laws.

2. In the event of the death of a natural person who is a member of a grouping, no person may become a member in his place except under the conditions laid down in the contract for the formation of the grouping or, failing that, with the unanimous agreement of the remaining members.

Article 29. As soon as a member ceases to belong to a grouping, the manager or managers must inform the other members of that fact; they must also take the steps required as listed in Articles 7 and 8. In addition, any person concerned may take those steps.

Article 30. Except where the contract for the formation of a grouping provides otherwise and without prejudice to the rights acquired by a person under Articles 22 (1) or 28 (2), a grouping shall continue to exist for the remaining members after a member has ceased to belong to it, in accordance with the conditions laid down in the contract for the formation of the grouping or determined by unanimous decision of the members in question.

Article 31. 1. A grouping may be wound up by a decision of its members ordering its winding up. Such a decision shall be taken unanimously, unless otherwise laid down in the contract for the formation of the grouping.

2. A grouping must be wound up by a decision of its members:

(a) noting the expiry of the period fixed in the contract for the formation of the grouping or the existence of any other cause for winding up provided for in the contract, or

(b) noting the accomplishment of the grouping's purpose or the imposs-ibility of pursuing it further.

Where, three months after one of the situations referred to in the first subparagraph has occurred, a members' decision establishing the winding up of the grouping has not been taken, any member may petition the court to order winding up.

3. A grouping must also be wound up by a decision of its members or of the remaining members when the conditions laid down in Article 4 (2) are no longer fulfilled.

4. After a grouping has been wound up by decision of its members, the manager or managers must take the steps required as listed in Articles 7 and 8. In addition, any person concerned may take those steps.

Article 32. 1. On application by any person concerned or by a competent authority, in the event of the infringement of Articles 3, 12 or 31 (3), the court must order a grouping to be wound up, unless its affairs can be and are put in order before the court has delivered a substantive ruling.

2. On application by a member, the court may order a grouping to be wound up on just and proper grounds.

3. A Member State may provide that the court may, on application by a competent authority, order the winding up of a grouping which has its official address in the State to which that authority belongs, wherever the grouping acts in contravention of that State's public interest, if the law of that State provides for such a possibility in respect of registered companies or other legal bodies subject to it.

Article 33. When a member ceases to belong to a grouping for any reason other than the assignment of his rights in accordance with the conditions laid down in Article 22 (1), the value of his rights and obligations shall be determined taking into account the assets and liabilities of the grouping as they stand when he ceases to belong to it.

The value of the rights and obligations of a departing member may not be fixed in advance.

Article 34.   Without prejudice to Article 37 (1), any member who ceases to belong to a grouping shall remain answerable, in accordance with the conditions laid down in Article 24, for the debts and other liabilities arising out of the grouping's activities before he ceased to be a member.

Article 35.   1. The winding up of a grouping shall entail its liquidation.

2. The liquidation of a grouping and the conclusion of its liquidation shall be governed by national law.

3. A grouping shall retain its capacity, within the meaning of Article 1 (2), until its liquidation is concluded.

4. The liquidator or liquidators shall take the steps required as listed in Articles 7 and 8.

Article 36.   Groupings shall be subject to national laws governing insolvency and cessation of payments. The commencement of proceedings against a grouping on grounds of its insolvency or cessation of payments shall not by itself cause the commencement of such proceedings against its members.

Article 37.   1. A period of limitation of five years after the publication, pursuant to Article 8, of notice of a member's ceasing to belong to a grouping shall be substituted for any longer period which may be laid down by the relevant national law for actions against that member in connection with debts and other liabilities arising out of the grouping's activities before he ceased to be a member.

2. A period of limitation of five years after the publication, pursuant to Article 8, of notice of the conclusion of the liquidation of a grouping shall be substituted for any longer period which may be laid down by the relevant national law for actions against a member of the grouping in connection with debts and other liabilities arising out of the grouping's activities.

Article 38.   Where a grouping carries on any activity in a Member State in contravention of that State's public interest, a competent authority of that State may prohibit that activity. Review of that competent authority's decision by a judicial authority shall be possible.

Article 39.   1. The Member States shall designate the registry or registries responsible for effecting the registration referred to in Articles 6 and 10 and shall lay down the rules governing registration. They shall prescribe the conditions under which the documents referred to in Articles 7 and 10 shall be filed. They shall ensure that the documents and particulars referred to in Article 8 are published in the appropriate official gazette of the Member State in which the grouping has its official address, and may prescribe the manner of publication of the documents and particulars referred to in Article 8 (c).

The Member States shall also ensure that anyone may, at the appropriate registry pursuant to Article 6 or, where appropriate, Article 10, inspect the documents referred to in Article 7 and obtain, even by post, full or partial copies thereof.

The Member States may provide for the payment of fees in connection with the operations referred to in the preceding subparagraphs; those fees may not, however, exceed the administrative cost thereof.

2. The Member States shall ensure that the information to be published in the *Official Journal of the European Communities* pursuant to Article 11 is forwarded to the Office for Official Publications of the European Communities within one month of its publication in the official gazette referred to in paragraph 1.

3. The Member States shall provide for appropriate penalties in the event of failure to comply with the provisions of Articles 7, 8 and 10 on disclosure and in the event of failure to comply with Article 25.

Article 40.   The profits or losses resulting from the activities of a grouping shall be taxable only in the hands of its members.

Article 41.   1. The Member States shall take the measures required by virtue of Article 39 before 1 July 1989. They shall immediately communicate them to the Commission.

2. For information purposes, the Member States shall inform the Commission of the classes of natural persons, companies, firms and other legal bodies which they prohibit from participating in groupings pursuant to Article 4 (4). The Commission shall inform the other Member States.

Article 42.   1. Upon the adoption of this Regulation, a Contact Committee shall be set up under the auspices of the Commission. Its function shall be:

(a) to facilitate, without prejudice to Articles 169 and 170 of the Treaty, application of this Regulation through regular consultation dealing in particular with practical problems arising in connection with its application;

(b) to advise the Commission, if necessary, on additions or amendments to this Regulation.

2. The Contact Committee shall be composed of representatives of the

Member States and representatives of the Commission. The chairman shall be a representative of the Commission. The Commission shall provide the secretariat.

3. The Contract Committee shall be convened by its chairman either on his own initiative or at the request of one of its members.

Article 43.   This Regulation shall enter into force on the third day following its publication in the *Official Journal of the European Communities*.

It shall apply from 1 July 1989, with the exception of Articles 39, 41 and 42 which shall apply as from the entry into force of the Regulation.

This Regulation[1] shall be binding in its entirety and directly applicable in all Member States.

Done at Brussels, 25 July 1985.

For the Council, The President, J. Poos

---

[1] The text of the Regulation was published in OJ L 199, 31. 7. 1985.